THE ULTIMATE ENCYCLOPEDIA OF
CAGED AND
AVIARY BIRDS

THE ULTIMATE ENCYCLOPEDIA OF
CAGED AND AVIARY BIRDS

A practical family reference guide to keeping
pet birds, with expert advice on buying,
understanding, breeding and exhibiting birds

DAVID ALDERTON

southwater

This edition is published by Southwater, an imprint of Anness Publishing Ltd,
Hermes House, 88–89 Blackfriars Road, London SE1 8HA; tel. 020 7401 2077; fax 020 7633 9499

www.southwaterbooks.com; www.annesspublishing.com

Anness Publishing has a new picture agency outlet for images for publishing, promotions or advertising. Please visit our website www.practicalpictures.com for more information.

UK distributor: Book Trade Services; tel. 0116 2759086; fax 0116 2759090; uksales@booktradeservices.com; exportsales@booktradeservices.com

North American distributor: National Book Network; tel. 301 459 3366; fax 301 429 5746; www.nbnbooks.com

Australian distributor: Pan Macmillan Australia; tel. 1300 135 113; fax 1300 135 103; customer.service@macmillan.com.au

New Zealand distributor: David Bateman Ltd; tel. (09) 415 7664; fax (09) 415 8892

Publisher Joanna Lorenz
Project editor Sarah Ainley
Copy editor Marion Paull
Designer Michael Morey
Commissioned photography John Daniels
Illustrator Julian Baker
Editorial reader Hayley Kerr
Indexer Helen Snaith
Production controller Wendy Lawson

ETHICAL TRADING POLICY

Because of our ongoing ecological investment programme, you, as our customer, can have the pleasure and reassurance of knowing that a tree is being cultivated on your behalf to naturally replace the materials used to make the book you are holding. For further information about this scheme, go to www.annesspublishing.com/trees

PUBLISHER'S NOTE

Although the advice and information in this book are believed to be accurate and true at the time of going to press, neither the authors nor the publisher can accept any legal responsibility or liability for any errors or omissions that may have been made nor for any inaccuracies nor for any loss, harm or injury that comes about from following instructions or advice in this book.

CONTENTS

BIRD CARE AND MANAGEMENT

INTRODUCTION

◆ BELOW
The budgerigar is the most popular pet bird in the world today, thanks to its friendly nature, and the ease with which it can be kept in a home environment.

Birds have been popular as pets for at least 4,000 years, dating back to the time of the ancient Egyptians. Today, their appeal as companions spans the globe. The talking abilities of parrots, for instance, enchants owners living in stylish apartments in Paris, New York or London as much as tribespeople living in scattered village communities across the Amazon basin or in the rain forests of West Africa. When European settlers arrived in Australia in the 1700s they started to keep one of the smaller native parakeets as pets. Since then, these birds, better known as budgerigars, have become the most widely kept pet birds in the world.

It is not just their powers of mimicry, however, that have attracted people to keeping birds as companions; the song of the canary was responsible for the introduction of these rather plain-coloured, greenish finches to Europe in the late 1400s, from the Canary Islands off the west coast of Africa. Now, domestic canaries possess singing abilities that are vastly superior to those of

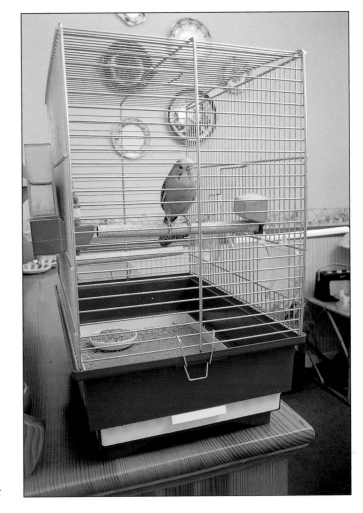

◆ ABOVE
A young budgerigar chick being hand-reared. Such birds will be very tame once they are weaned. They usually display no fear of people, and make ideal pets in the home.

their wild relatives. Canaries have also evolved into birds displaying a wide range of colours; many distinctive varieties have been developed, which are popular for exhibition purposes. The exotic appearance and coloration of softbills and finches underlies their popularity. They are a constant source of fascination in a suitable aviary, and the challenge of breeding such birds successfully appeals to many people. The same applies to pheasants and doves and these will thrive in a planted aviary.

Caring for birds has become more straightforward over recent years, thanks to a better understanding of their nutritional needs.

✦ BELOW
Budgerigars are now bred in a huge range of
colour varieties and are popular exhibition
birds. Here a group are being bred on a colony
basis in an aviary.

Special foods for all types of birds, ranging from humming-birds to flamingos, are produced commercially, with each one formulated to match particular needs. This, in turn, has been valuable in persuading pairs to breed successfully. Better general health means that if a bird does fall ill there is a greater chance of recovery. Advances in the field of equipment have helped to revolutionize the housing of birds, which contributes to their overall well-being.

Many people start out with a single pet bird and before long decide to construct an aviary. The exhibition side of the hobby often appeals to people once they have experience of bird breeding. Local clubs, catering for all types of birds, usually stage an annual show, and these provide an ideal way to meet fellow-enthusiasts in your area, even if you are not interested in exhibiting. National groups cater for particular types of birds, such as parrots or budgerigars, and the larger ones may operate through local branches. They usually produce an annual newsletter or magazine for their members, keeping them up-to-date with the latest information and details of shows. You can track down information about local or national clubs through the columns of the bird-keeping publications, your local library or via the Internet.

✦ LEFT
Parrots such as cockatoos are not only costly to purchase, but are difficult to accommodate in view of their destructive natures. They can also prove to be very noisy, as is the case with many large birds.

STARTING OUT

Once you have decided to keep a bird as a pet, it is vital to consider the options before committing yourself to a particular species, or you could choose one that is unsuitable for a variety of reasons – it may not settle in your home environment, or it may be noisy, leading to complaints from the neighbours. Having to find a new home for the bird soon after acquiring it is likely to be traumatic for all concerned, especially for a bird that is used to human company.

It can help to draw up a checklist. Consider such things as the bird's talking ability, how easy or demanding it is to look after, its lifespan, as well as its accommodation requirements, and whether it is particularly destructive.

Your budget is another important consideration. Suitable housing for any bird is likely to be more expensive than the bird itself. If you cannot afford both at the same time, never be tempted to buy the bird immediately and keep it confined in less than ideal surroundings. It may start to pluck its feathers as a consequence, and this can easily become an habitual problem. Wait until you can afford both together.

The price of birds does vary. A young, hand-reared parrot chick may cost almost twice as much as an older, untamed bird, but if you are seeking a pet, it really will pay dividends to select a young one that has been reared in the home. There is also a wide price variance among exhibition birds, because of their pedigrees, and it pays to research carefully, to be sure of obtaining the best value for money.

◆ OPPOSITE
It is worthwhile constructing an aviary in a part of your garden where it can be expanded if your interest in bird-keeping develops over time.

◆ LEFT
Finches prove to be attractive and lively aviary occupants, thriving in a planted setting. Many, such as the Bengalese or society finch seen here, will breed well in these surroundings.

◆ BELOW
An aviary can become a very attractive focal point in a garden, reflecting the changing seasons. Plants within the aviary provide vital breeding cover for the birds.

PLANNING AHEAD

Although birds are less demanding to look after than some pets, such as dogs, they still need to be cared for every day throughout the year. This is something to be considered right at the outset, before you finalize your choice of bird species.

It is usually not too difficult to find a friend or neighbour prepared to look after the bird while you are away, although it is not necessarily a good idea to leave the bird, especially a parrot, at home on its own for most of the time, particularly if you are going to be absent for longer than a day or two. It is likely to start to pine for company, having been used to constant contact with people. Parrots are highly social by nature, which is why they settle so well as companion birds, forming a strong bond with their owners. A change in their

routine, especially when it results in isolation and boredom, can be sufficient to trigger feather plucking. Once this problem develops, it can be very difficult to cure, even if the underlying stress is subsequently removed. Rather than arranging for someone to call in your absence, it is better if the bird is moved to their home, where it will have regular company. Try to avoid a friend who has a cat – there is always a chance that the bird will slip out of its quarters, while it is being fed or cleaned out, with disastrous consequences.

If you have a collection of birds, consider asking someone to stay while you are away, in order to look after them all. This is the least disruptive option. Professional house-sitters are available in some areas, if it's not convenient for friends

or relatives, but employing one of these will, of course, add to the cost of your trip.

In the case of aviary birds, you may be able to persuade a neighbour to feed and water seed-eating birds without too much trouble, but caring for softbills, with their more specific dietary needs, can present problems. One solution is to team up with another bird-keeper in the area, and arrange to look after each other's collections when either of you is away. A problem may arise if you both have to be away at the same time, but there may be someone else from the local bird club who will be prepared to help out. Forward planning is important; bear in mind when you book your holiday that at certain times of the year, such as Christmas, people are less likely to be able to help out.

◆ LEFT
A typical parrot cage, suitable for housing smaller members of this popular bird group in the home.

◆ ABOVE
Small finches are amongst the easiest birds to accommodate in an aviary, since they are neither noisy nor destructive by nature.

DOMESTIC CONSIDERATIONS

The bird's size is an important consideration, especially if you plan to keep it indoors, because of the size of the accommodation it will require. It is, for example, much easier to accommodate a Hahn's macaw (*Ara nobilis*), which measures barely 33 cm (13 in) long, than one of its larger relatives, such as the green-winged macaw (*A. chloroptera*), which is about 90 cm (36 in) in length. Even if the bird is going to spend most of its time out of its quarters, you still need to have a cage where it can be kept safely when you are away from home. Playstands take up space, and the bigger the bird, the bigger the playstand. Smaller species tend to be less noisy than their larger relatives, as well as being easier to restrain if you do not have any experience of handling birds.

Before you can let a newly homed bird out of its quarters, you will need to make a thorough check of the room from the point of view of the bird's safety. Choose one room in the house in which to release the bird, and prepare it carefully. The length of time that a bird spends out of its cage will depend on you; it is not recommended to leave the bird at liberty on its own. Although you will have dealt with the obvious dangers, there may be others, such as flaking lead paintwork, that are less obvious.

◆ RIGHT
Yellow-faced parrotlets are an ideal choice for a garden aviary, with pairs being quite likely to nest readily in such surroundings. They are also relatively hardy once established in their quarters outdoors.

◆ LEFT
Small birds, such as these doves and finches, are
at direct risk from rats or snakes in some parts
of the world. Aviaries must be planned and built
to exclude possible predators.

Look at your garden from a suitable
vantage point and try to visualize
how the aviary will look when it is
in position. There needs to be easy
access, preferably via a path. Avoid
choosing an area which offers no room
for expansion. Bird-keeping often
proves to be an infectious hobby, and
there can be considerable savings in
cost if you can adapt an existing aviary
set-up when expanding your
collection, rather than having to build
another from scratch.

In temperate areas, winter-time
care is an important consideration –
not all birds are sufficiently hardy
to winter outdoors. An indoor
birdroom which forms part of the
aviary provides snug, winter-time
accommodation. Alternatively,
assemble an indoor aviary in a spare
room and move the birds into the
house. If you have a couple of pairs
of finches, however, housing them
in a spacious flight cage will be a
simpler option.

AVIARY CONSIDERATIONS

If you are planning an aviary you will
need to work out how large an area
you are prepared to devote to it, and
where it should be positioned in the
garden. It should be quite close to the
house, particularly if you are intending
to keep finches or softbills, so that if
you want to extend your domestic
electricity supply to provide additional
lighting and heating, it can be done
fairly easily and cheaply. However, it is
important to site the aviary so that it
will not upset the neighbours, who
may not appreciate the sound of bird
song outside their bedroom windows
at the crack of dawn.

It helps to choose a level site that is
not overhung by trees. These may
provide shade during the summer, but
leaves are likely to accumulate on the
roof in the autumn, possibly blocking
the guttering, and any branches that
break off are likely to damage the
structure, as well as scaring the
occupants of the aviary.

The greatest danger posed by
overhanging trees, however, comes
from wild birds roosting in their
branches. Droppings are likely to fall
down through the mesh and these can
introduce infections into the aviary.
Squirrels, too, can be a hazard,
clambering over the aviary from the
trees above. They may damage the
structure with their teeth, allowing
the birds to escape as a consequence.

◆ LEFT
This aviary, housing
Indian ringnecks,
is screened on the
roof with translucent
plastic sheeting.
This helps to
protect the aviary
occupants from the
droppings of wild
birds, which could
transmit disease.

✦ LEFT
A birdroom is very
useful, especially
if you are interested
in breeding
exhibition stock,
as these birds need
to be housed in
individual pairs for
breeding. It may be
possible to convert
an existing garden
building, such as
a shed, into
a birdroom.

You may be able to adapt an existing garden building, a disused garden shed for example, to make an aviary or birdroom. This can reduce the costs of setting up, but make sure that the existing structure is sound.

Once the birds have settled in and started nesting, it is difficult to carry out major repairs. Brick or blockwork structures are preferable because they are durable. They are ideal for parrot housing, in particular.

CLIMATIC CONSIDERATIONS

In various parts of the world, specific factors have to be borne in mind when planning an aviary.

● In hot climates, it may be preferable to have an open-fronted shelter (which can also reduce building costs). Birds can be housed outdoors but there must be adequate protection for them during tropical downpours, with the floor of the aviary being designed so that water will drain away quickly. If a bird becomes waterlogged and falls to the floor, it could drown.

● Wooden structures are vulnerable to attacks by termites, so additional investment in brick or blockwork designs is advisable in areas where they proliferate.

● Aviaries must be secured against possible hurricane damage in areas where they occur.

● Snakes will readily enter aviaries, taking chicks or even adult birds, which will be particularly vulnerable in nest boxes. Make sure the size of the mesh takes this into account.

● In colder climates, invest not just in heating but in removable transparent plastic screening which fits around the sides of the aviary to protect the occupants from the worst of the wind chill. It is not a good idea to expose birds to very cold conditions, because aside from the obvious risk of frostbite, there can be insidious damage, particularly to the kidneys, which ultimately could serve to shorten their lives.

✦ ABOVE
Even smaller members of the parrot family, such as this Hahn's macaw, are likely to be destructive. They are relatively hardy once acclimatized, especially if provided with a nest box for roosting purposes.

ACCOMMODATION

The choice of bird housing is large, and it is worthwhile finding a local store specializing in birds, or even a bird farm, where a good selection of flights and cages will be on view. Space is especially important and indoor cages should be as large as possible. A flight cage is a better option than a traditional cage, even if the bird is going to spend lengthy periods out of its quarters with you.

Aviaries are sold ready for home assembly. Most are of rectangular design, comprising a mesh-covered flight and a smaller shelter area, where the birds are fed and to which they can retreat in bad weather. They come in sectional form, so you can construct a structure of virtually any size. You can, of course, build your own aviary, although this will be more expensive. If you want something a little more unusual, there are elaborate options available, ranging from hi-tech octagonal designs to precise copies of ornate Victorian architecture.

If you intend to establish an exhibition stud, or have decided to keep the more delicate finches and softbills, a birdroom is a good idea. It will offer more space for breeding cages and for indoor flights, where birds can be housed in winter.

♦ OPPOSITE

Think carefully about where to site your aviary. Choose a sheltered, well-screened locality, which will help to protect the birds from cold winds.

♦ LEFT

A birdroom will provide an indoor area for housing less hardy birds during the winter. Attaching the birdroom to the aviary will make the set-up very convenient to use.

INDOOR QUARTERS

A wide selection of cage designs is now available for pet birds in the home. This means you are more likely to find a cage to blend in with your interior decor, but it also means you could be sold a cage that is more ornate than functional, and does not follow recommended guidelines.

Worse still, spending a lot of money is no guarantee that the cage will be suitable. It always helps to visit one of the larger pet superstores or a specialist bird farm, where a good selection of cages will be on view, and you will be able to ask advice from trained staff.

CHOOSING A FLIGHT CAGE

Always select a large flight cage. By providing your pet bird with plenty of space for exercise, you will help it to remain fit; obesity is a health risk and it can shorten a bird's life. In the home birds use relatively little energy to maintain their body temperature, and this, combined with lack of opportunity to exercise, means that they will put on weight rapidly. This, in turn, means that they will have progressive difficulty in flying, partly due to their excess weight, but also because their flight muscles will have become weakened through lack of use.

◆ ABOVE
This type of cage is used for either a pet budgerigar or canary. Budgerigars and other parrots prefer cages with horizontal bars, which makes it easier for them to climb around their quarters.

◆ LEFT
A small parrot cage, suitable for a Senegal parrot, for example. The bird should be let out of the cage each day for a period of exercise.

◆ RIGHT
The size of flight cages means they can be difficult to move around. Castors on the legs will be a great help.

because they are easier to move. This helps with cleaning and if you want to transfer the parrot from one room to another. Wheeling the cage is more convenient and less disturbing for the bird than carrying it, especially if the cage is large and heavy.

The metal surfaces of bird cages are usually coated with a tough, easy-wipe covering. This makes them easy to clean, especially as there are special wipes available from good suppliers, intended for use on bird cages. This covering prolongs the life of the cage, preventing it from rusting.

In the case of mynah birds, because of their messy feeding habits, you should opt for a box-type flight cage, rather than one with open-mesh sides. This will help to keep the environment around the cage cleaner.

It is a good idea to start looking for suitable accommodation well in advance of acquiring your pet, simply because you may not immediately be able to obtain the unit you want. It might be that the pet store has a suitable model, but that the colour is not ideal for your home, which will necessitate a different cage being ordered specially for you. When looking for bird housing, visit larger pet stores and bird farms in your area, where you are likely to see a better selection on display; remember, too, that a large price tag is no guarantee of a comfortable home for your pet.

It is no coincidence that birds housed in spacious surroundings are far less vulnerable to feather plucking than those housed in cages. If kept closely confined, parrots in particular will often suffer badly from boredom, and are likely to react in this way.

There are a number of spacious and stylish cage designs available. Those mounted on castors are preferable,

✦ RIGHT
Not all cages are designed with much thought for the needs of the occupants. This model provides very little space, and cannot be recommended for any bird.

✦ LEFT
Remember to close the cage door securely when a bird is returned to its cage after a period of exercise, to prevent escape. In the case of parrots, you may also need to reinforce the door catch with a padlock.

◆ LEFT
Provide wooden rather than plastic perches for
all birds. Parrots, such as this grey, gnaw their
perches, which will need to be replaced over
time, but the activity will keep its bill in trim.

PERCHES

The almost universal inclusion of plastic perches in flight cages is a serious flaw. Although in theory these perches are easy to keep clean, it is possible for their hollow interiors to become home to the red mite parasite. They are especially unsuitable for members of the parrot family. Parrots naturally keep their bills in trim by gnawing at branches, and the plastic perches will not stand up to it.

Some birds appear to find their ridged design uncomfortable after a period of time, probably because, being of an even diameter, they offer no variety in perching grip. The birds then resort to spending more time clinging on to the sides of their quarters. You must therefore be prepared to replace plastic perches at the outset.

Dowel perches are sometimes supplied with cages but these, too, have the drawback of being of a constant diameter. They do not appear to cause the birds as much discomfort as plastic perches, however, and they can be scrubbed off easily. Larger parrots are quite capable of gnawing them through, though, which means they will have to be replaced often.

Natural branches, cut from non-poisonous trees such as apple, are the best choice as perches, but do not use wood that may have been sprayed recently. Parrots especially will gnaw the bark and may swallow some of the slivers, in which case they could poison themselves. Sycamore is a good choice because it is relatively hard and grows straight, so that it is quite easy to cut perches to the requisite length. Elder is softer than sycamore and provides an outlet for parrots at their most destructive, although its gnarled bark makes it harder to clean than sycamore. In all cases, it is a good idea to wash off branches before placing them in the bird's quarters, just in case they may have been spoiled by wild birds previously.

When cutting branches to fit in a flight cage, allow for an overlap at the ends in order to hold the branches firmly in place. If you use wire to fix the perch, make sure that this is located safely outside the cage. Do not use string because this could choke a bird if it swallows any of the fibres, and there is also a risk of the bird becoming entangled.

The width of the perch is important. The diameter should be sufficiently broad to allow the bird to sit comfortably, without its front claws coming into direct contact with its rear toes. If not, the bird may encounter difficulties in perching easily, and if its sharp claws puncture the undersurface of the rear toes, there is a risk, especially in mynah birds, that an infection could develop. If budgerigars are kept in cages with perches of constant diameter, pressure sores will develop, and these are likely to become infected, creating the condition often described as bumblefoot. Even if the perching facilities are improved at this stage, treatment of the condition is likely to be difficult, because of its deep-seated nature, with the situation being made worse if the bird is obese because of lack of exercise.

WOOD FOR PERCHES

Use these:
Apple
Sycamore
Elder

Avoid these:
Laburnum
Lilac
Yew

DOOR FASTENINGS

A point of weakness in parrot cages is the door fastening. A simple hook will present little by way of a challenge to these intelligent birds, allowing them to escape into the room in your absence, with potentially serious consequences. Aside from the risk to furniture, a parrot may turn its attention to live electrical flex and electrocute itself as a result. It is always a good idea to reinforce the door fastening by means of a combination padlock, which the parrot will have much greater difficulty in opening.

In most cases, you will be able to replenish the bird's food and water from outside its quarters, but check that the pots cannot be dislodged by a bored parrot in search of a challenge. If you are in doubt, use a padlock for them as well. Once a parrot has mastered the knack of opening a door of any kind, it is likely to continue to do so, even if it leaves itself without food and water as a result.

REMOVABLE FLOORING

The other important thing to assess when looking at a flight cage is the ease with which it can be cleaned. Some cages are supplied with mesh grids above the floor area in order to stop the lining, such as sheets of newspaper, being disturbed and gnawed up by the parrot. In reality, however, droppings collect on the mesh, and so this has to be removed and scrubbed off. It can also represent a danger to the bird because it might end up with its foot stuck as it tries to walk over the floor area. It is therefore a good idea to remove a grid of this type from the outset. The tray itself should be heavy-duty. Check for dangerous gaps, particularly at the corners where the metal has been folded up at the sides to make a lip. It is quite possible for a bird to become trapped there and to slice its toe on the sharp edges of the metal. Finches and canaries are less vulnerable than parrots and mynah birds because their cages usually have plastic trays, but beware as there could be a large enough gap for them to escape through when the tray is removed for cleaning purposes.

✦ ABOVE LEFT
A large door opening provides good access to the interior of the cage, and this will make it easier to tame your bird.

✦ ABOVE RIGHT
Most parrot cages are provided with plastic containers, which can be used, as here, for food and water. A drinking bottle can also be used.

✦ LEFT
Ease of cleanliness is an important consideration in cage design. The lining tray of this flight cage can be easily removed for washing.

GARDEN AVIARIES

The design of a garden aviary will be influenced by the type of birds you wish to keep, and this in turn will have an impact on the cost of the aviary structure. Finches, for example, are relatively easy to accommodate as they are not destructive by nature, but they will need snug winter housing, and it would be beneficial to incorporate a birdroom into their aviary design. At the other extreme, large parrots can be very destructive and will need to be housed in steel rather than wooden-framed structures, with block-built shelters.

CHOOSING AN AVIARY

Scan the advertisement pages of the bird-keeping publications for details of aviary manufacturers and send for the catalogues. Be careful to compare like with like. Some firms offer simply the basic aviary, and charge extra for weatherproofing the timber, whereas in other cases, this is included in the total cost.

READY-MADE DESIGNS

Aviary manufacturers generally offer a range of their own designs as well as sectional units – mesh-clad flight panels, doors and similar units – from which you can construct a modular aviary to your own design. Before you buy, check the timber framework. Sometimes this is too thin and the mesh is not always securely attached to it. The framework should be made of wood which is at least 4 cm (1½ in) square, and proper netting staples should be used to attach the mesh. Ordinary staples will work loose over a period of time, creating gaps through which small birds may escape without difficulty. The situation may be exacerbated in a planted aviary by foliage growing up the mesh – its weight is likely to pull the wire off the framework if it is not firmly fixed in place. Netting staples should be driven in every 2.5–5 cm (1–2 in) around the frame to keep the mesh secure; regular checks on the mesh are essential.

It is quite easy to work out the number of panels you will need for an aviary, although it is worthwhile having your figures checked by the manufacturer before finalizing your order. Any discrepancies highlighted at this stage can be resolved easily, rather than when the structure is being assembled, by which time it will be too late.

Access to the structure will be influenced to a large extent by the layout of your garden. Try to disguise the entry point as far as possible, rather than placing it at the front of the flight, where it will be unattractive and make it harder to see the birds. A basic aviary design comprises a flight measuring 2.7 m (9 ft) long by 90 cm (3 ft) wide, attached to a shelter which is 90 cm (3 ft) square. For this design a single access point, at the back or on one side of the shelter, will be adequate. Entry to the flight, which is necessary for cleaning purposes and to catch the birds, is through a connecting door opening outwards from the shelter into this part of the aviary.

It is worthwhile incorporating a safety porch into the aviary design, to eliminate the risk of any birds escaping when you go in or out of the outer door into the flight. The safety porch allows you to enter the enclosed area and shut the door behind you before opening the aviary door. As a result, if a bird does happen to slip past you, it will remain within the confines of the safety porch, from where it can easily be returned to the aviary. A typical

✦ OPPOSITE LEFT
Not all aviaries have to be rectangular in shape.
This is an octagonal structure. Designs of this
type are available commercially from a number
of aviary suppliers.

✦ BELOW
A view from inside a service corridor, extending
along a block of metal-framed flights. This
design avoids the need for a safety porch and
makes it easier to attend to the birds' needs.

safety porch, measuring 90 cm (3 ft) square, is constructed from wood and mesh panels, like the flight itself. Allow sufficient space, when designing the aviary, for the safety porch to open outwards. The door into the aviary itself should be hinged so that it swings into the flight. This makes access easier, especially when carrying cleaning tools, food pots or the like. The safety porch can be concealed, in the fullness of time, by training evergreen climbing plants up the wire frame.

MESH

The type of mesh used to cover the aviary panels can have a significant effect on the cost of the finished structure. The cost rises significantly as the strands become thicker. The thickness of the strands is very important – 19 gauge (19G) mesh is quite suitable for smaller birds, including finches, canaries, cockatiels and budgerigars; thicker 16G is needed

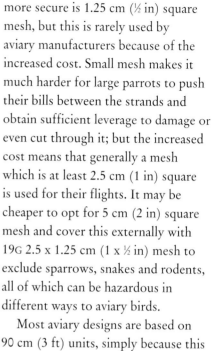

for most parrots, including the Senegal (*Poicephalus senegalus*), and 14G or even 12G may be needed for the larger cockatoos and macaws.

The separation distance of the strands is also a vital consideration to prevent escapes and safeguard the birds' well-being. Most aviaries are constructed using 2.5 x 1.25 cm (1 x ½ in) mesh, which is small enough to

exclude all but very young mice. Even more secure is 1.25 cm (½ in) square mesh, but this is rarely used by aviary manufacturers because of the increased cost. Small mesh makes it much harder for large parrots to push their bills between the strands and obtain sufficient leverage to damage or even cut through it; but the increased cost means that generally a mesh which is at least 2.5 cm (1 in) square is used for their flights. It may be cheaper to opt for 5 cm (2 in) square mesh and cover this externally with 19G 2.5 x 1.25 cm (1 x ½ in) mesh to exclude sparrows, snakes and rodents, all of which can be hazardous in different ways to aviary birds.

Most aviary designs are based on 90 cm (3 ft) units, simply because this is the most commonly used width of mesh rolls. Although wider rolls are available, the mesh may tend to sag on the framework of the flight, and this will detract substantially from the finished appearance of the aviary.

A view from inside an aviary showing a safety porch in use. The purpose of the porch is to stop birds escaping when you enter the aviary by means of a double-doored entry system.

Doors must be hinged in such a way that they give easy access to the interior of the aviary. Once the structure is erected, it is difficult to change the direction in which the doors open.

Over a period of time, and especially outdoors, hinges may start to rust and seize up. It is important to oil them at regular intervals to prevent this from happening.

MAKING YOUR OWN AVIARY

In temperate areas, the best time to start building an aviary is in the spring, once the risk of frost has passed. You will be able to release the birds into their new home soon afterwards. Pairs may even breed that year, if they are already acclimatized to aviary life.

If you are building your own flight, it is best to use tanalized timber, i.e. timber that has been treated against rotting and has a long life expectancy. This is usually safe to use with livestock but, as always, check with your supplier if in doubt.

If, however, you are treating the timber yourself, ensure that the preservative you use will cause the birds no harm if they gnaw at it. The treated timber must be thoroughly dry before being assembled into frames and, as it is likely to require more than one coat, the whole process may take two or three weeks. Arrange to have the sections of timber cut to the

✦ ABOVE
It is worth examining ready-made display aviaries on site before deciding to build your own. This gives you the opportunity to consider various designs and to compare total costs.

✦ LEFT
Aviaries with boarding around the base are recommended for ground birds such as pheasants and quails, protecting them from dogs and cats, which could disturb them in the flight.

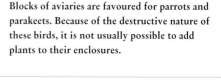

◆ BELOW
If you have space available, an aviary can be incorporated alongside existing features in the garden, such as this stone archway, with the shelter being built out from the existing wall.

◆ BOTTOM
Blocks of aviaries are favoured for parrots and parakeets. Because of the destructive nature of these birds, it is not usually possible to add plants to their enclosures.

appropriate lengths at the outset, to save time and effort. It is better to screw and preferably joint the timber for the framework, rather than nailing it together. The resulting frames are less likely to twist, which may in turn loosen the netting staples holding the mesh in place. Remember to treat any cut ends with a wood preservative before assembly, because it is in such areas that the timber is most likely to start rotting.

An aviary is an expensive investment, but if well built at the outset and carefully maintained, a timber structure of this type should last for well over 20 years. Buying the cheapest materials can prove to be false economy – rolls of aviary mesh may look very similar, but the cheaper unbranded rolls are unlikely to prove as durable in the long term, succumbing much more rapidly to rust. This is harmful for parrots of all types, because they climb over the mesh and ingest particles which are likely to cause irritation in their crops or lower down in the digestive tract.

When it comes to attaching the wire mesh to the frames, start by placing the frames on a level surface. It is a good idea to wear a pair of gardening gloves when handling the mesh. Be careful about cutting the band around the roll because it is likely to spring open at this point, and could catch your face. Fix the cut end in place, level with the top edge of the flight frame, and unwind the roll, taking care to keep it level and running parallel with the sides of the frame. It helps to have someone assisting you with this task, so that you can tap netting staples in while the mesh is kept taut on the frame. If it runs across at a slight angle, or is allowed to hang loose, this will detract from the appearance of the aviary once it is finally assembled. At this preliminary stage you can make slight adjustments to tighten it as necessary, once it is tacked in position.

You will need wire cutters to cut off the mesh from the roll. Take care to trim it so that loose ends, on which the birds could injure themselves, are cut right back to the nearest horizontal strand at the top and bottom of each panel. Finally, go round and put in all the necessary netting staples. Hardwood battening, fixed over the edges of the mesh, will keep the netting staples buried. Some birds are likely to whittle away at this, however, so check it regularly and be prepared to replace it every so often, once the aviary is occupied.

PREPARING THE SITE FOR AN AVIARY

◆ BELOW
Just as in a garden it takes time for plants to develop, the same applies in a planted aviary, and results are likely to be seen more quickly in a warm climate.

Before the aviary is ready to assemble on site, mark out the area on the ground where the structure is to be located, using canes as a guide. Clear the site as far as possible, carefully removing any turf that you may want to use in the aviary for landscaping purposes. This can be cut out with a sharp spade, rolled up and stored in a shady spot until required. It is worth clearing an additional area of turf from around the perimeter, to be replaced later, because the grass here will inevitably be damaged during the construction process.

The next stage is to mark out the dimensions of the aviary accurately, so that you can prepare the footings on which the structure will rest. Secure foundations are not only important as an anchorage point; they also prevent rodents, particularly rats, from tunnelling into the birds' quarters. Proper foundations prolong the life of a wooden structure because the timber is not in direct contact with the ground, which can cause wood to rot prematurely.

You will need to dig a trench around the perimeter of the aviary base to a depth of approximately 45 cm (18 in), using shuttering to support the sides. Pour a thick layer of concrete into the bottom of the trench and allow it to set hard. This is the foundation for the blockwork walls. As the blocks are laid, check that they are level, using a spirit level. Above ground, you may prefer to use bricks, which are more attractive than blockwork. These should be laid in the traditional way so that they overlap from row to row, to give greater strength to the finished structure. The wall should extend approximately

30 cm (12 in) above the level of the ground. Ideally, this work should be carried out when the weather is fine and it is unlikely to be frosty at night, although there are products that can be added to the mix to prevent it deteriorating in the event of frost. During hot weather, covering the walls with damp sacking will prevent the mortar drying too fast and cracking as a result.

Decide on the floor covering at this stage, while the area is fully accessible. There are several options, depending partly on the number and type of birds you intend to house in the aviary. Grass is often very appealing, but unfortunately impractical. Drainage is a major problem and often the grass is replaced by moss. Where grass does thrive, it soon becomes overgrown and looks untidy; trying to cut it back during the breeding season is not to be recommended, because this disturbs the birds. Maintaining an adequate level of hygiene can also be a problem, particularly if the aviary is home to a relatively large number of birds.

The simplest solution is to opt for a solid concrete base. This will add to both the cost and work involved in building the aviary, but in the long term it will make it much easier to keep the birds' surroundings clean. Rain will help to wash away dirt from the floor out of the aviary, and it can be disinfected regularly. You will need to incorporate a few small drainage holes for this purpose at the opposite end from the shelter. These openings must not be large enough to allow mice or snakes to gain access to the aviary by this route. It is also important to check them periodically to ensure they are not blocked; if they are, the aviary is likely to start flooding quite rapidly when it rains hard.

For a concrete base, dig out the floor to a depth of approximately 30 cm (12 in), pack the area with hardcore and lay a 3:1 mix of ballast and cement on top. Finally, lay a smooth coat of mortar mixed with sharp sand (very fine sand) on top, to a depth of 15 cm (6 in). In the shelter, thick plastic sheeting should be laid between these two layers to act as a damp-proof course. It may be advisable to employ a bricklayer or plasterer to apply this final layer for you, in order to create a surface which slopes evenly down to the drainage points, with no areas where water will pool on the floor. Rapid drainage can help to prevent the development of unsightly green algae on the base as well, which could be dangerous as it may cause you to slip when you are moving around in the flight. This top layer can be applied only when the weather is sure to be fine; otherwise, it may be washed away before it sets.

A solid concrete base is especially valuable when you are housing a number of birds together because diseases can spread easily via soil contamination, and it is very difficult to eliminate harmful organisms once they have become established.

Parasitic worm eggs may survive in soil for more than two years, presenting a constant risk to birds foraging on the ground throughout this period.

Concrete presents problems if you decide to move house. The sectional design of aviaries means they can usually be dismantled and moved without any great difficulty, but this leaves the base, and prospective buyers may be put off by a large slab of concrete in the garden. One alternative, that provides the benefits of concrete without its permanence, is to use paving slabs for the floor. Make sure that they are slightly sloped for drainage. It is easy to move them along with the aviary, should you ever need to do so.

Another option, especially suitable for aviaries occupied by individual pairs of parakeets, is to spread a layer of coarse gravel about 25 cm (10 in) thick on the floor of the aviary. Paving slabs can be set into the gravel beneath the perches, where the vast majority of droppings will accumulate. These can be easily scraped off with a small shovel, and the slabs can be thoroughly disinfected.

As an added precaution against rodents entering an aviary with a gravel base, cover the floor area with mesh, attaching this to the blockwork before tipping the gravel on top and setting the paving slabs in place.

By providing a good depth of gravel, not only will rain wash any dirt down between the stones, but there should be no risk of the birds having access to stale water before it drains away into the ground. A small drainage hole leading out of the flight at low level may be helpful as a further precaution.

✦ RIGHT
Where there are blocks of aviaries, it is important to be able to clean them easily. A concrete base, which can be hosed down from the outside, with the dirty water draining away along a gully, is often recommended.

27

ASSEMBLING THE AVIARY

This task requires two people. It helps to have all the sections identified with chalk, so that you can see how they fit together, and to arrange them on site accordingly. It is important to remember that in all cases, the wire-mesh face of the panel forms part of the interior of the flight. In the case of more destructive species, such as parakeets, this helps to protect the wooden framework from their bills.

Do not be tempted to fit the aviary doors at a preliminary stage – these should not be hung until the structure is in place; otherwise, they will be an obstruction. You will need bolts of the appropriate length to hold the wooden panels together, while frame-fixers can be used to anchor the frames down on to the base itself.

Start by fixing the end and one neighbouring side in place. The frames will be easier to support while you are working on them by being at right angles in this way. Stand them on a bed of concrete on top of the supporting wall for more anchorage. Do not forget to insert washers before the nuts, and oil them as well. This will make it easier to dismantle the aviary, should you need to move it. Oil the nuts every four to six months to prevent them from rusting and fusing on to the bolts. Thread the bolts through their fixing holes and tighten them in place.

Add the other side, and then the front of the shelter, which should be set on a course of bricks at the appropriate height. Fix on the sides of the shelter before finally adding the back. Fix the roof sections in place, on top of the assembled panels. Ensure that the roof of the flight is securely fixed to the sides.

ASSEMBLING THE AVIARY

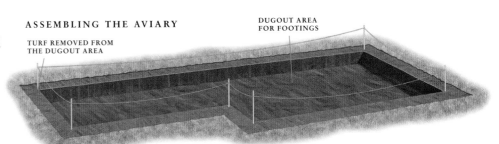

TURF REMOVED FROM THE DUGOUT AREA

DUGOUT AREA FOR FOOTINGS

1 Preparing the site and footings to support the aviary is important, both to ensure the stability of the aviary, and also to exclude rodents. You may need to use shuttering to hold back the soil when you are digging out the base. Keep turf from the dug out area to be refitted later around the outside.

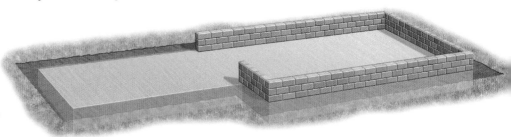

2 Blocks can be laid below ground level, but brickwork will create a more attractive appearance above the soil. It is vital to ensure the course of bricks overlaps, because it is this that will make the structure secure. It may be necessary to recruit the help of a professional bricklayer at this stage.

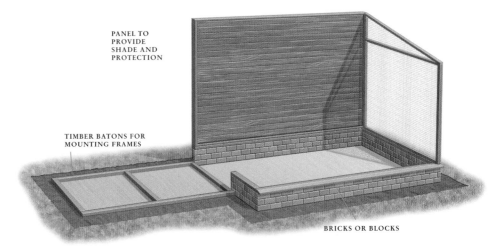

PANEL TO PROVIDE SHADE AND PROTECTION

TIMBER BATONS FOR MOUNTING FRAMES

BRICKS OR BLOCKS

3 The actual design of aviaries can differ significantly. The back panel in this case helps to provide additional protection for small non-destructive birds, such as finches and the smaller softbills. Note the space provided here for the safety porch.

The roof of the shelter can be built to form an apex, but it will be much simpler to have a roof section which slopes down away from the flight. Cover it with two layers of a good-quality roofing felt. Tuck these firmly down at the sides, to lessen the risk of the felt being torn off in strong winds.

The interior needs to be well lit in order to attract the birds into this part of the aviary, so it should have an opaque glass window. Avoid clear glass

4 The sections of the aviary should be bolted together. Do not fit the doors in place until everything is assembled on the base, because it will be harder to manipulate the panels. Because of the size of the structure, assembling the aviary is a task for two people.

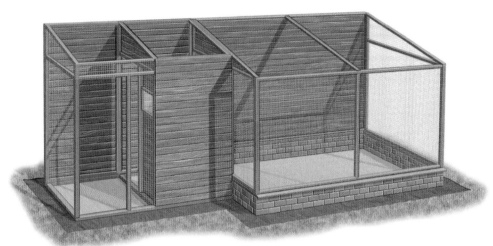

5 The safety porch should blend in as far as possible, rather than detracting from the aviary's appearance. If the translucent plastic sheeting applied over the mesh on the roof is linked with guttering, rain water can be channelled off to a water-butt.

– the birds will not see it and may attempt to fly through what they see as an opening, injuring or even killing themselves. If for some reason clear glass is unavoidable, this must be adequately screened with mesh.

Fit the door of the shelter once everything else is in place. Select robust hinges. It will save you time and money in the long run to spend a little more at this stage. It is a nuisance to be faced with a door that sticks because the hinges have started to rust within a few months of setting up the aviary. Keep the hardware well oiled, however much you spend. This applies equally to the door lock, which should, if possible, be an integral part of the structure so as to offer more security. The number of thefts of aviary birds has increased over recent years, and every effort should be made to deter casual thieves from gaining access to the aviary, especially as once stolen, birds are rarely recovered.

6 *(right)* Security is an important feature of aviary design. Fitting a combination lock to the outside door will mean you do not need to worry about carrying a set of keys each time you visit the birds. A bolt should be fitted on the inside of both doors, so that you can close them securely as you enter the aviary.

FINISHING OFF

Even if you buy a complete aviary, you will probably need to invest in some corrugated plastic sheeting and guttering. The sheeting should be fixed on the flight roof nearest to the shelter, using the special fitments available for this purpose. It will provide protection for the birds when they are in the flight, and should be extended down the sides. Use a wooden framework to slope the plastic sheeting away from the shelter, and fix guttering at the lower edge to prevent rainwater from pouring into the flight itself. Guttering will also be needed at the lowest edge of the shelter roof. The down pipe can be connected to a water butt, to provide water for the garden.

Perches in the aviary should always be arranged across the flight, but do not clutter the area, so the birds can benefit from the flying space. Have two main perches at either end of the flight, one located under cover. Make

✦ ABOVE
Devise your planting scheme at the outset. Include plants which will give the birds cover for nesting purposes, and will attract insects.

✦ BELOW
Climbing plants and hanging baskets can be used outside the aviary, but ensure these will not damage the structure in any way.

sure that this one does not block the connecting door leading from the shelter to the flight. Allow sufficient space for the birds to move freely on the perches, with no risk of rubbing their tails on the mesh at the far end.

It is not a good idea to force the perches up against the wire mesh because after a while, with the constant friction caused by the birds moving on and off the perch, the mesh will be weakened, holes will develop in it and the perch is likely to collapse. It is much better to arrange the perches so that they can be supported by the wooden uprights in the flight.

Another possibility is to set perches in a container. A crown of branches is especially good for this purpose. For larger parrots, which need relatively strong perches to carry their weight, it may be better to fix these on a length of timber approximately 5 cm (2 in) square, which can be set into a pre-formed hole in the aviary floor. It is easy to replace such perches when they are destroyed, by knocking off

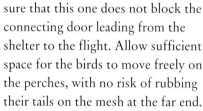

the branch from the wooden support and fixing a new one in place.

Many birds, particularly finches and softbills, benefit from being kept in an enclosure with growing plants. These not only provide cover, which can be vital for nesting purposes, but also attract insects, which will help to supplement the birds' diet. Suitable shrubs, such as conifers, can be introduced to the flight in tubs, while ground cover can be provided by means of annuals, such as nasturtiums (*Tropaeolum majus*).

It is important to landscape the aviary into the garden once building work is complete. You may decide to have a flowerbed around the base of the aviary for example, and you can soften the outlines of the shelter by growing a climbing plant up the sides. Replant some of the turf, and set a row of paving stones around the perimeter of the aviary to give easy access to the safety porch off an existing path.

✦ ABOVE
If building a pond in your aviary, make sure there is a shallow area at one end: smaller birds in the aviary can easily fall in and drown.

✦ BELOW
Even alongside bare aviaries, flower beds can be included to create colour and a changing focus of interest through the seasons.

BIRDROOMS

✦ BELOW
A birdroom in the form of a garden shed. Wire frames must be placed over windows to prevent birds escaping or injuring themselves on glass.

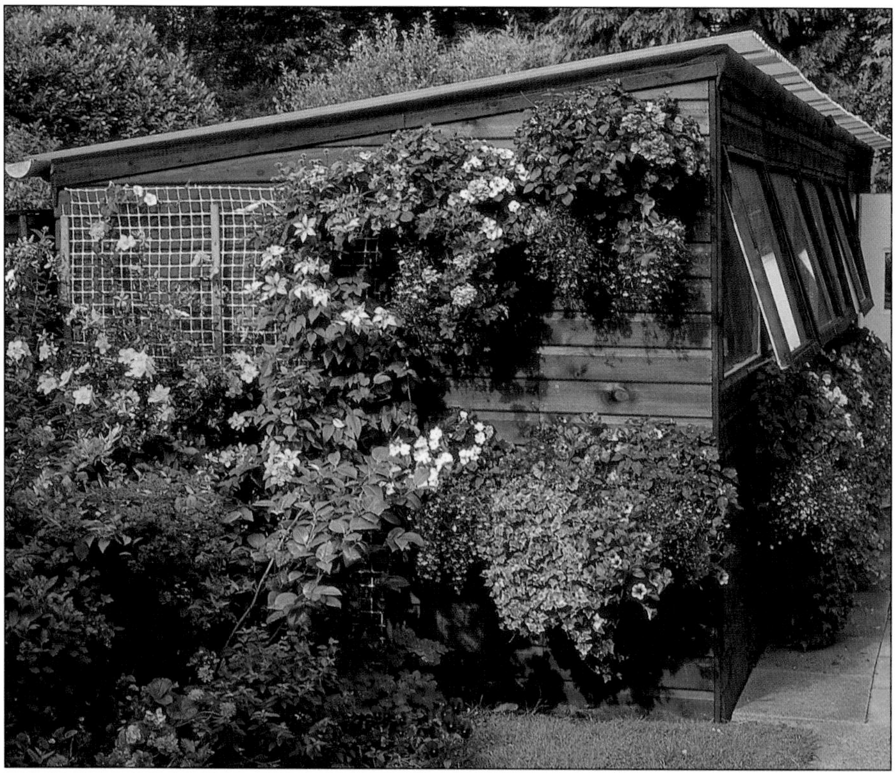

Although the basic aviary design will be adequate in many cases, it can be helpful to have a birdroom as well, particularly if you are interested in keeping the more delicate species, including various finches and softbills, which require warm indoor housing in winter, or are keen to exhibit your birds. The additional space provided by a birdroom will be invaluable in either case.

As its name suggests, a birdroom is an indoor area where birds are housed. If at all possible, purchase an integrated birdroom and aviary at the outset. Often, the birdroom structure will connect with the aviary flight and will include the shelter; this is the most convenient set-up. You could adapt a large existing garden shed to use as a birdroom, although this may mean having two separate buildings, and you will be constantly moving back and forth between them, sometimes carrying birds.

✦ BELOW
In a large set-up, birdrooms provide space for indoor flights, breeding cages and food storage.

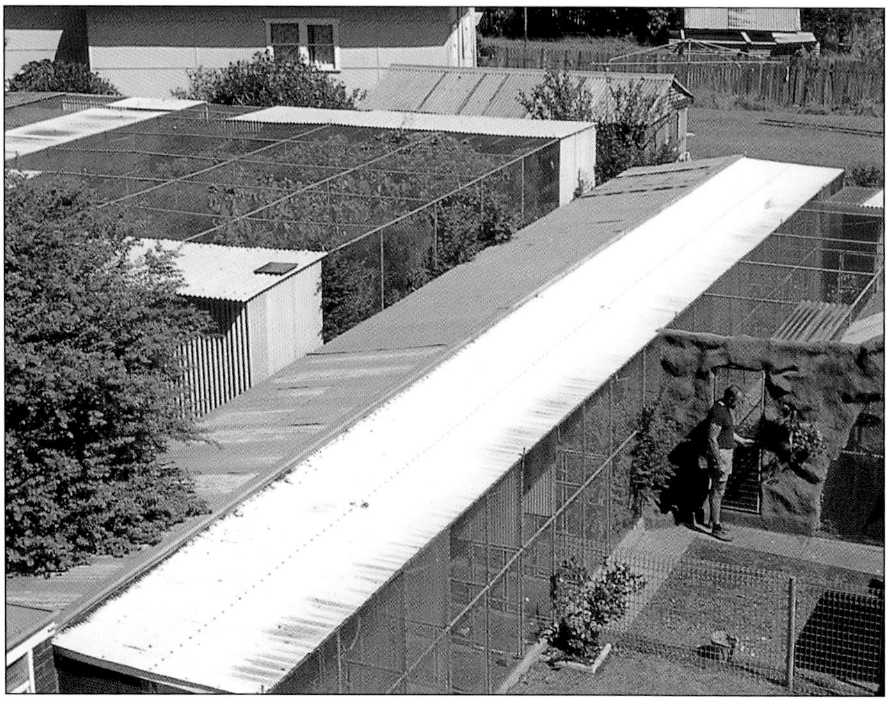

In an integrated set-up, the aviary shelter forms part of the birdroom, usually occupying the far end of the structure. This allows for breeding or stock cages to be positioned down one side, while there may be an indoor flight opposite. There is also space for the storage of foodstuffs and other equipment, such as nest boxes and extra food and drink containers.

During the winter in temperate areas, the interior can be heated by means of a thermostatically controlled tubular heater. Heating costs can be drastically reduced by fitting draught excluders around the doors and windows, as well as fitting insulation material into the walls of the birdroom. This can be placed behind plywood or even hardboard, but beware of rodents; they can establish themselves rapidly in such warm and comfortable surroundings.

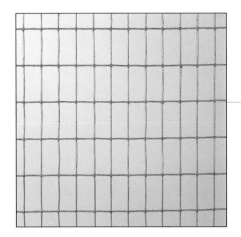

The strength of wire mesh depends partly on its gauge size. This is 19 gauge (19G), the thinnest mesh used in aviary construction.

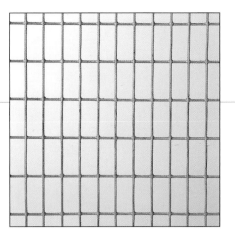

Although the strand dimensions are the same 2.5 x 1.25 cm (1 x ½ in) this sample of mesh is 16G, which is heavier than 19G.

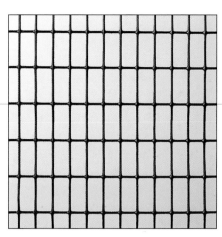

Plastic coated mesh is suitable for finches and softbills but not for parrots, which may nibble off the protective coating.

Artificial lighting can also be fitted in a birdroom, extending the feeding period when days are at their darkest. It is possible to operate birdroom lighting automatically, using either a time switch or a light sensor. Incorporating a dimming control in the circuitry allows birds to find their way back to the perches if they are feeding when the lights go off, rather than plunging them into sudden darkness. Restrict their light exposure to no more than about 12 hours in total each day or you could start interfering with the breeding cycle.

Some birds, particularly finches and some parrots, can generate large amounts of feather dust, and this in turn may cause allergic reactions, particularly in people susceptible to asthma. Although good hygiene will minimize the problem, incorporating an ionizer into the birdroom can reduce the particles in the atmosphere. A constant stream of billions of electrons is released from the tip of the ionizer, and when these collide with a dust particle, the particle falls down on to an earthed surface from where it can be wiped away with a damp kitchen towel. Another advantage of having an ionizer in a birdroom is that it destroys potentially harmful microbes, such as the virus responsible for French moult.

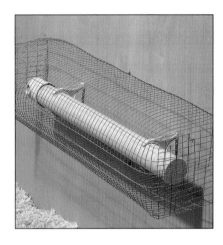

A tubular convector heater should be shielded in a metal cage to prevent birds gnawing the electrical connections or burning themselves.

An ionizer will improve the environment within a birdroom by removing dust and germs from the air.

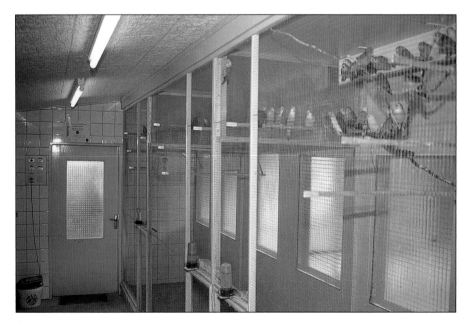

Additional lighting can be very valuable in a birdroom, particularly in temperate areas, allowing the birds' feeding period to be extended on dull days. Fluorescent strip lights give off a more natural light, although they cannot be operated with a conventional dimmer switch.

HOUSING CHOICES

A number of different housing options are available, when it comes to accommodating birds in outdoor quarters, but you may need to adapt a standard aviary to meet the needs of the birds which you want to keep. This might entail cutting a pop-hole at ground level, through the door connecting the flight and shelter, to give easy access to quails living in the aviary. Alternatively, it could be a matter of running wire strands on vertical uprights around the edge of the entire roof of the aviary, with a view to stopping cats from climbing up here and disturbing the birds. If you are having the aviary built for you, most manufacturers will be happy to incorporate such personal refinements during the construction process, at a cost which needs to be agreed in advance. You can then simply concentrate on the finishing touches – fitting out the aviary with perches and plants to meet the birds' needs.

✦ TOP
A concrete base is easily cleaned and disinfected at intervals as required, preventing a build-up of parasites such as intestinal worms in the birds' environment.

✦ ABOVE LEFT
Food such as seed husks will often end up scattered by the birds outside indoor quarters, so it helps to ensure that the surrounding area can be cleaned easily. Castors will allow the cage to be moved for cleaning purposes.

✦ ABOVE RIGHT
When a group of birds such as budgerigars are housed together, the perches often become dirty. These should be removable, if possible, so they can be scrubbed clean on a regular basis.

✦ LEFT
Good ventilation in birdrooms is important to prevent a build-up of stale air, which could be harmful. Separate housing to accommodate new birds for the first few weeks will help safeguard the health of established bird stock.

HOUSING CHOICES

Finches: these relatively small birds are generally kept in planted aviaries, either in a colony or as part of a mixed collection. In temperate areas, they require heated wintertime accommodation, with extra lighting to extend the feeding time.

Softbills: size is often quite a good indicator of their relative hardiness. The more delicate species will be most at home in a snug conservatory-type aviary, which is well protected, but others are quite hardy, with the larger species thriving in large aviaries. Ease of cleaning is an important design consideration.

Parakeets: while some parakeets, such as the budgerigar, can be kept in a colony, the majority need to be accommodated in individual pairs. Their aviaries can be arranged in blocks, provided the sides of adjoining flights are double-wired.

Larger parrots: if timber is used in the construction of the flights for these birds, it must be well protected from their powerful bills. The mesh, too, must be suitably robust. A brick-built shelter offers a more durable option than a wooden structure, with a metal framework being used for the aviary panels. These can be obtained from specialist aviary manufacturers.

Pheasants and quails: pheasants in particular require spacious flights, and are often housed in the company of larger softbills, such as touracos. They spend much of their time on the floor of their flight, so a well-drained base is essential. There must be vegetation to provide them with cover, preferably with areas of grass, and gravel should be available, spread around the perimeter of the flight.

✦ TOP RIGHT
Some birds, such as quails and pheasants, appreciate more seclusion in their quarters than others, like Australian parakeets. Adapt housing to the birds' needs wherever possible.

✦ ABOVE RIGHT
Secure door fastenings are very important on aviaries, especially those situated at a distance from the house. A lock built into the door will help to deter potential vandals and thieves.

✦ BELOW
A block of raised aviaries intended for parrots and parakeets. The birds are fed at the back of the structure, and the raised floor area will usually have a mesh base.

✦ ABOVE
The aviary framework can be securely attached to an aviary wall, and this will create a snug environment, especially for smaller birds. Making birds more comfortable in their home will help them to settle down quickly.

35

FOODS AND THEIR USES

The nutritional needs of pet birds are better understood now than in the past, and it is easier than ever to feed them well. Seed mixes are available from pet stores, along with an increasing range of complete diets, which provide not just the essential carbohydrates, fats and proteins, but also the vitamins and minerals which are equally important to a bird's well-being. Unfortunately, however, not all birds take to complete diets straight away. Much depends on the bird's background – hand-reared parrots are more likely to sample unfamiliar foods than birds that have been fed on seed for most of their lives.

Softbills and nectar-feeders have the most specialized feeding habits. You may need to buy some foods by mail-order, and the preparation is more time-consuming than for seed-eaters.

Better nutrition results in better breeding, particularly in the case of parrots. It is not a coincidence that those birds adapted to feed and breed on fairly meagre rations, such as the budgerigar and other Australian species, were the first to reproduce readily in captivity. Today, however, almost any parrot can be expected to breed in suitable surroundings, if provided with a varied and nutritious diet.

♦ OPPOSITE
Cockatiels rank among the easiest birds
to feed, as they will subsist mainly on seed,
although a wide selection of greenstuff
should also be provided.

♦ LEFT
Fruit plays an important part in the diet
of many birds, particularly softbills and
parrots. The way in which the food is
prepared depends on the feeding habits
of the individual species.

FEEDING SEED-EATERS

◆ BELOW
This budgerigar will feed happily on a
proprietary seed mix, but fresh foods should
also feature in his regular diet.

Parrots and finches are generally
classed as seed-eaters to distinguish
them from the softbills, which are not
fed significant amounts of seed. The
seeds used as bird food can be broadly
divided into two categories, based on
their nutritional values. There are the
oil seeds, characterized by relatively
high fat content, and the cereals, the
main chemical constituent of which
is carbohydrate.

OIL SEEDS

These form the basis of seed mixtures
for parrots. The major ingredient is
usually the widely available striped
sunflower seed, with its blackish
and white stripes. Other forms of
sunflower seed may also be included;
black sunflower has a smaller, plumper
seed than the striped, as does white
sunflower. White sunflower seed is
sometimes confused with another
ingredient of some parrot mixes,
safflower seed, although this is
plumper and more angular. In
nutritional terms, white sunflower is
generally the best option for bird food
because it has a lower oil content, but
the yield from these seedheads is
lower than from the striped form,
and so the price is slightly higher.

Peanuts are another typical oil seed
included in most parrot mixes. They
can be purchased still in their flaky
shells as groundnuts, but buying them
in this state means that they are
correspondingly expensive because
the parrots discard the casing. For
the same reason, it is usually not
worth choosing the larger grades of
sunflower seed – in most cases, the
kernel within is no larger than in small
seeds, so you are paying for wastage.
Peanuts can be dangerous, because it

is very difficult to spot contamination.
The harmful *Aspergillus* mould can be
detected only by testing, and for this
reason it is important to buy peanuts
from reputable suppliers who can
guarantee the quality of their seed.
Unfortunately, the effects of the
toxins produced by this fungus are

FOOD FOR SEED-EATERS

Oil seeds:	Cereals:
Blue maw	Canary seed
Hemp	Groats
Linseed	Maize (corn)
Niger seed	Millet
Peanuts	Paddy rice
Perilla seed	
Pine nuts	
Pumpkin seed	
Rape seed	
Safflower seed	
Sunflower seed	
Teasel seed	

not immediately apparent, and they
can result in long-term liver damage.

Not all the seeds included in parrot
mixes are grown commercially. Some
are still gathered from the wild,
notably pine nuts, which are collected
in the vast coniferous forests of the
former Soviet Union and China.
The larger nuts are suitable for most
parrots, and the small nuts are valuable
for larger finches as well. Always
check the nuts carefully for signs of
any obvious fungal contamination,
which can give rise to a bluish growth
on chipped nuts. These could be
harmful to the birds.

Smaller oil seeds feature
prominently in seed mixtures for
canaries. Red rape is an important
ingredient, although other types of
rape seed are also used. Black rape is
particularly valued as soaked seed,
while German rubsen rape is favoured

by keepers of roller canaries because it is believed to enhance the birds' singing abilities.

Hemp is probably the most popular seed with canaries themselves, and they will frequently scatter the contents of their food container, seeking it out. A round, darkish seed, hemp is also included in parrot seed mixes but it should be used sparingly, and not just because of its high oil content. It can actually alter the appearance of some birds, giving rise to the phenomenon described as "acquired melanism". This causes lighter-coloured areas of the plumage, such as the red chest of a bullfinch (*Pyrrhula pyrrhula*), to turn black. The effect is not permanent, but it will last until the next moult when the plumage is replaced, assuming that the bird's diet is corrected before then.

A variety of other oil seeds are used as bird food, often in larger amounts

◆ LEFT
Many bird-keepers buy seed mixes, which contain a variety of different seeds, rather than preparing their own mixes. This is a typical parrot seed mix. As a rule, the more expensive mixes will usually have a wider range of ingredients.

at certain times of the year. Niger, for example, with its unmistakable elongated blackish shape, is considered valuable to protect against egg-binding, and is fed primarily before the start of the canary breeding season. Teasel seed is expensive but

highly valued by breeders as a rearing food for canaries and similar species, such as serins. Once the chicks are ready to be weaned, blue maw is often sprinkled on top of their softfood to encourage them to start eating seed on their own, its small size being ideal for this purpose.

New seeds are regularly added to the list of those used as bird food. In recent years, perilla has become favoured as a tonic seed, and is used when birds are moulting or recuperating from illness. Pumpkin seeds are now widely used for parrots, providing a valuable source of the antioxidant Vitamin E.

Linseed

Pine nuts

Pumpkin seeds

Safflower seeds

Sunflower seeds

✦ BOTTOM
It is possible to provide food in open pots, which will fix on to the cage front. There is likely to be more wastage, however, as the bird will scatter seed on the floor.

✦ BELOW
Seed hoppers come in various designs, suitable for different birds, such as these Norwich canaries. All provide a reservoir of seed, which is kept free from the birds' droppings.

CEREALS

The term "canary seed" can be confusing, because it can refer to either a mixture or an individual seed, often called a "straight" in the trade, to distinguish it from a mix. Plain canary seed is widely grown as bird food in a range of countries, including Australia, Canada and Morocco, with smaller amounts being cultivated commercially in other countries, including England. It is a relatively small, light-brownish seed with a dark covering to the kernel inside, and is oval in shape with pointed ends. Aside from featuring significantly in canary seed mixes, it is also an important ingredient of blends of budgerigar seed and is included, to a lesser extent, in the diets of finches.

Millet is the other major cereal seed used in bird food for a wide range of species. A number of distinctive forms of millets are available, often sold on the basis of their colour, such as red, yellow and pearl white millets. The most popular variety tends to be panicum, which is sold in seedhead form as millet sprays. Millet is a valuable rearing food, often being provided in a soaked form when there are chicks in the nest. The larger, harder millets such as pearl white are most suitable for budgerigars, cockatiels and parakeets, rather than small finches, which may encounter difficulties in cracking the seeds.

Groats, which are the dehulled form of oats, are sometimes added to seed mixtures, as well as being used by budgerigar breeders to feed breeding stock. Groats can be fattening, however, particularly for birds housed in breeding cages, and the amount offered should be restricted accordingly.

While most parrot mixtures contain little in the way of cereal seeds, they may incorporate kibbled maize (corn), i.e. broken maize. Whole maize is a very hard seed once it has been dried, and only the largest parrots have bills strong enough to crack it. Flaked maize, which looks something like cornflakes, is included in some mixes.

Some mixtures include paddy rice. This is a relatively flat, yellowish seed that may be eaten by small parrots and large finches such as Java sparrows, which are also known as rice birds (*Padda oryzivora*).

Pheasants and quails may be fed on cereals of various types; special mixes are available for them from larger pet stores and bird seed suppliers; these will ensure they receive the correct nutritional balance. Pellets sometimes feature in their diets.

PREPARING SEED

Over recent years, there has been a growing appreciation of the fact that in the wild, virtually no birds feed predominantly on dry seed, and that birds can gain considerable benefits from being fed either soaked or sprouted seeds. Many of the pulses, such as mung beans, which are popular for human consumption are now often used as bird food, especially for parrots, along with more conventional seeds such as millets and canary seed.

Start by washing the required quantity of seed in a sieve under running water to remove any dust that may have accumulated during storage. Then tip the rinsed seed into a heatproof container, cover with hot water, and leave to stand overnight. Such treatment triggers the germination process, causing the protein levels in the seed to rise, and increasing the level of Vitamin B. The seed also changes in texture when saturated, becoming softer and more digestible. Soaked seed is especially valued during the breeding period, when there are chicks in the nest. It can also prove to be a lifesaver for sick

Self-sown canary seed

or weak birds, especially small finches; they may not have the strength to crack the dry seed, but can often be persuaded to sample a soaked millet spray, which will significantly improve their chances of recovery.

After being left to stand, soaked seed must always be washed again, very thoroughly, before being fed to the birds. It will now be perishable, so that any seed left uneaten at the end of the day must be removed and disposed of before it becomes contaminated with moulds. This is especially likely during hot weather.

The same applies in the case of sprouted seed, which is prepared in the same way as for human consumption, washing off the sprouts thoroughly in fresh water before offering them to the birds. You will soon be able to gauge the amount of seed required by your birds, to avoid unnecessary wastage.

Chick-peas

Oats

Japanese millet

Mung beans

Hemp

Panicum millet

BUYING SEEDS

Where you obtain seed will depend on the type and number of birds you are keeping. If you have a pet budgerigar, the simplest solution is to buy a packeted seed mix from a local pet store. If you have a large collection of birds, it may be more convenient to find a mail-order supplier who will arrange delivery direct to your door. Most pet stores can offer mixtures to suit different types of birds, but they may not be able to offer you straights such as teasel or perilla. These will have to be obtained through a more specialist bird feed supplier. Look through the advertisements in the bird-keeping publications.

From a pet store, buy seed that is bagged or packeted rather than loose, especially if birds are kept in the store. The viruses responsible for French moult and psittacine beak and feather disease (PBFD) can be spread easily via feather dust, and may also contaminate any nearby seed supplies.

There is also a risk from rodents. Any seed which is soiled with their droppings or urine is a potential health hazard to all birds and must be discarded. Storing seed in metal bins helps to exclude rodents from gaining access to it. Unfortunately, buying seed from bins gives you no idea of its freshness. It may be that new seed is being tipped on top of old, rather than the bin being properly emptied before the new seed is added. An advantage of purchasing from one of the main seed suppliers is that they are likely to have a higher stock turnover than a pet store, and their supplies should be relatively fresh.

Bird seed will not deteriorate rapidly, provided that it is kept dry, but try to rotate stocks so that you have no more than about four months' supply on hand at any stage. This will also decrease the likelihood of contamination by fodder mites. These tiny creatures are barely visible to the naked eye, but they impart a characteristically sweet odour to the seed. Sniff a handful to check. Whether fodder mites harm the birds directly is unclear, but they will certainly not improve the nutritional value of the seed.

Most seed now is clean, containing little or no obvious traces of dust or harvesting debris, thanks to computer-controlled cleaning processes, but if you are offered dirty seed by a supplier, do not hesitate to reject it.

♦ LEFT
A range of foods will be eaten by parrots. Do not provide these birds primarily with dry seed. This is nutritionally unbalanced, lacking certain vital vitamins and minerals.

GRIT AND CUTTLEFISH

◆ LEFT AND BELOW
Cuttlefish bone and grit contribute to a seed-eater's mineral requirements. Cuttlefish bone is held in place in the aviary by special clips.

Seed-eating birds often consume grit – small pieces of stone that accumulate in the bird's gizzard. Grit helps the bird to grind up seeds by the muscular action of the gizzard walls, and it contributes valuable minerals. Two types of grit are sold to bird-keepers and they differ in their chemical properties. Oyster shell grit is soluble, and it breaks down in the acid medium of the gizzard, allowing the minerals to be absorbed by the body; mineralized grit is insoluble, remaining for a longer time in the gizzard. Grit should always be available to seed-eating species, although consumption may be variable. The grit container should be topped up regularly with fresh grit to ensure that the birds have a good supply of particles of a suitable size.

Cuttlefish bone is important as a source of minerals, especially calcium which is lacking in seed. Just prior to the breeding season, hens will often

Iodine nibble

spend much longer at the cuttlefish bone, nibbling away at it to build up their body calcium stores for the egg-laying period ahead. The soft powdery side should always be accessible to

them. For finches, it is a good idea to cut off some slivers with a sharp knife, making it easier for the birds to nibble at the surface.

An iodine nibble is recommended, especially for budgerigars. These parakeets seem to have a particular requirement for this trace element: any deficiency will slow the moulting process. If you have exhibition birds, it may be better to provide white iodine nibbles rather than the more traditional pink variety, which could stain the facial feathering just prior to a show.

Oyster shell

Kilpatricks salts

Limestone

Grit mix

Mineralized grit

Egg food

A BALANCED DIET

No bird should be expected to subsist entirely on a diet of dry seeds. Seeds are low in essential amino acids, which are the key components of protein, and also in vitamins and minerals, such as Vitamin A and calcium. Birds require a much wider range of foodstuffs to fulfil all their nutritional needs.

If your bird refuses to take a complete diet, you will have to rely on supplements to compensate for dietary shortcomings. These are available in both liquid and powdered forms. Liquid preparations should be added in the correct proportion to the birds' drinking water. They tend to be less comprehensive in terms of their ingredients than powdered supplements, and there is no guarantee that the birds will drink sufficient water to gain maximum benefit,

✦ L E F T
It is not unusual for seed-eaters to take a wider range of food than they might otherwise be offered. Do not be afraid to experiment within reason. Birds, like ourselves, have individual tastes.

particularly if the weather is wet, when they may prefer to drink raindrops off the mesh.

Powdered supplements should be sprinkled over greenstuff or fruit. They will not adhere well to dry seed, simply sinking to the bottom of the

food container. A variety of greenstuff is readily taken by many species ranging from parrots to pheasants. Most softbills prefer fruit, but touracos will consume large quantities of greenstuff as part of their regular diet. Aim to provide regular amounts

Parakeet mix

Parakeet mix and fruit

Pheasant mix

Pigeon and dove seed

Foreign finch seed mix

Aviary mix

◆ RIGHT
Greenstuff can be used to encourage a pet bird, such as this cockatiel, to feed from your hand. Always wash greenstuff and fruit thoroughly before offering it to birds.

GREENSTUFF AND FRUIT FOR SEED-EATERS

Use these:	Avoid these:
Chickweed	Avocado
Dandelion	Citrus fruits
Seeding	Bananas
grasses	
Spinach beet	
Brassicas	
Carrots	
Sweet apples	
Grapes	
Pomegranates	

of whatever is available, rather than large quantities occasionally, which can lead to digestive upsets if the birds gorge themselves.

Among wild plants, chickweed, dandelion and seeding grass are all likely to be eaten, but do not collect them from areas where they may have been sprayed with herbicides, such as roadside verges. In terms of cultivated vegetables, spinach beet can be grown easily and will provide a source of greenstuff even through the winter, as may brassicas such as broccoli.

Carrots, too, can be valuable, especially as they contain a precursor of Vitamin A. They should be peeled and cut into small pieces to prevent wastage; some larger parrots can be reluctant to descend to

the floor of their quarters if they drop their food, and they are less likely to drop the smaller chunks.

One fruit which should never be given to birds is avocado, because this may be poisonous for them. It is generally better to avoid citrus fruits because their acidic nature can lead to scouring. Bananas are not generally recommended because they can be messy and may stain the plumage around the bill. Any unripe fruit can be indigestible.

Pomegranate

Sweet apples are widely used, and grapes are a popular choice, although they contain relatively little in the way of nutrients.

In some cases, with mynah birds for example, you will need to dice the fruit into small pieces which the birds can swallow whole, whereas for other birds, including parrots, you can provide the fruit in chunks. A favourite fruit with parrots is pomegranates, which can be stored in a cool, dry place for a month or more, extending their availability after the end of the season. In tropical regions, a wider range of fruits is available, but try to select fruits which are firm and not especially juicy. The juice may stain the birds' plumage and this can attract insects such as wasps.

Apples

Grapes

Carrots

FEEDING NECTAR MIXES

Within the parrot family, the lories and lorikeets have adapted to feed naturally on nectar and pollen. Special tiny brushes on the tongue sweep the pollen granules into the mouth so they can be swallowed easily. Whereas pollen is a valuable source of protein, the carbohydrate content of the diet comes from the nectar itself, which consists of various sugars.

In the past, bird-keepers were forced to rely on home-made nectar mixtures using ingredients such as honey, which would often attract bees to the drinker. The birds were therefore in danger of being stung when they fed. Today, a good range of proprietary nectar mixtures is available, generally in powdered form. They simply need to be mixed with water. The mixtures are supplemented with vitamins and minerals and contain all the necessary ingredients to keep birds in the best of health.

There are several different types available for the various groups of nectivores. Besides those suitable for lories, lorikeets and hanging parrots, there are specific mixtures formulated for hummingbirds and other small nectivores, such as sugarbirds, sunbirds and white-eyes. Do not be tempted to change brands suddenly, particularly when acquiring a new bird. Instead, stick to its established diet, offering the new food in increasing amounts over a fortnight or so. This should avoid causing any digestive upsets, which may prove to be fatal in this group of birds. Nectar foods are not as widely available as seed – you will probably need to obtain them from a bird farm or specialist avian supplier.

✦ LEFT AND ABOVE
All nectar drinking equipment has a red spout, since studies have shown that this is the colour which is most likely to attract birds such as this hummingbird to feed. Tinted glass on the drinker will help to protect the vitamin value of the food.

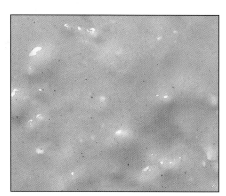

Lory mix nectar and fruit

Lory mix

FEEDING SOFTBILLS

A number of different brands of softbill foods are available. There are general softbill diets, and it is also possible to obtain more specialist foods, catering for either insectivorous or frugivorous species. In most cases, softbill food is sprinkled over fruit, to which it adheres well. Choose one of the low-iron brands; the birds that tend to be the most frugivorous in their feeding habits, such as tanagers, barbets and toucans, as well as mynahs, are especially vulnerable to iron storage disease. This condition, caused by a build-up of iron in the liver, is very hard to treat and usually proves fatal. These birds have a highly efficient iron absorption mechanism in their intestines, and lowering the level of iron in their diet is the best way of protecting them from the illness. Dried fruits should also be used in moderation for this reason.

Softbill pellets are available, including low-iron brands. Pellets are ideal for mynahs and touracos. The

Softbill mix

birds eat them rather like berries. You may need to soak the pellets in a cup of water beforehand in order to soften them and make them more palatable.

Food needs to be prepared fresh on a daily basis because it will soon start to deteriorate, particularly in hot weather, and this could endanger the birds' health. Do not be tempted to use ingredients which are past their recommended "use by" date; the vitamin content may have declined, and this can lead to a deficiency.

✦ LEFT AND RIGHT
Always prepare bird foods in clean surroundings, cutting up the fruit to meet the birds' individual needs.

LIVEFOODS

◆ BELOW
Livefoods need to figure prominently in the diets of some softbills. Here a blue-throated niltava has caught a mealworm, which will be swallowed whole in due course.

Many birds rely on livefood in their diet to a greater or lesser extent, particularly during the breeding season. Some softbills must be offered livefood on a regular basis, whereas the majority of parrots will not eat invertebrates at all. In the past, bird-keepers had either to forage for livefood themselves, or breed their own; today, the supply of livefoods has developed into a huge business worldwide. It is much safer to rely on those that are commercially available because you can be sure that they are free from the parasites that can afflict wild invertebrates, and spread to birds when they consume them.

The two most widely used forms of livefood are mealworms, which are the larval stage of the meal beetle (*Tenebrio molitor*), and crickets. You can buy them in a variety of sizes to suit all birds. These invertebrates do not have a good calcium:phosphorus ratio, so if birds eat them as the main part of their diet, they may develop calcium deficiency. In order to combat this, the technique known as "gut loading" has become popular. The mealworms and crickets are given special foods so that the bird, when it eats them, will benefit from the food still present in their gut.

There are also special nutritional "balancers" which serve to correct the deficiencies in livefoods, and are easy to use. The invertebrates are transferred to a plastic bag and powder is tipped over them before they are offered to the birds. Some of the powder will be swallowed by the bird when it catches the invertebrate in due course. In order to slow down crickets, and so make it easier for birds to catch them, you can put them in the fridge, in a suitable container, for half an hour or so before feeding time.

Micro-crickets can be offered to waxbills when they are rearing their chicks, as well as to softbills of similar size, while large crickets are suitable

Waxworm larvae

Mealworms

for birds such as laughing thrushes. Livefoods can be a useful aid if you are trying to tame birds in aviary surroundings. Before long, you are likely to find that a pair will come to recognize the livefood container, and may even be persuaded to feed from your hand.

Among other livefoods to choose from are waxworms, which are the larval waxmoths, and redworms, popular with larger softbills.

In most cases, breeding livefoods at home is unlikely to be worth the effort, partly because, as in the case of mealworms, the life cycle takes several months to complete. The mealworms turn into immobile pupae before hatching into blackish beetles and laying the eggs, which will ultimately hatch into more tiny mealworms.

However, two important types of livefoods, whiteworms and fruit flies, are available only in the form of starter cultures, which means that if you want to offer these to your birds, you will have to breed them yourself.

Whiteworms and similar tiny worms, such as microworms, need to be kept damp. Bury the starter culture with some bread, soaked in milk, just under the surface of peat, or a similar substrate, in a lidded plastic tub. The lid should have several small holes punched in it for ventilation. Top up the food supply as necessary. If left in a relatively warm spot, and not allowed to dry out, the worms can be harvested a month or so later. Simply spoon the substrate with the worm colony into a saucer of water and catch the worms with a fine tea-strainer.

Setting up several cultures in succession will guarantee a plentiful supply of these invertebrates throughout the breeding season.

Fruit flies are taken by hummingbirds and other smaller nectivores. Place a layer of the starter culture in the bottom of the special container supplied with it, where the flies can lay their eggs. Alternatively, a large glass jar covered with muslin (cheesecloth) and containing a banana skin should provide the appropriate climate to establish a culture, which needs to be warm. It may help to start out with the wingless strain of fruit flies, as they will be easier for the birds to catch. To feed the flies, simply cut a hole in the muslin; the flies will find their own way out, and the birds will catch them easily.

✦ BELOW
Mealworms will ultimately metamorphose into adult meal beetles, but keeping them relatively cool will slow this change. They first turn into pupae, becoming inactive at this stage.

COLOUR FOODS AND THE MOULT

It was back in the 1870s that an accidental discovery revolutionized the care of canary birds, when a breeder gave some cayenne pepper as a tonic to an ailing bird which was moulting. This canary not only survived, but the breeder was amazed to see how the colour of its new plumage was transformed into a much brighter shade than previously. In due course, this canary shone on the show bench, and breeders sought the secret of how the bird's plumage had become so magnificently coloured.

The secret soon leaked out, and before long, colour-feeding, as this practice is known, became widely-accepted for show purposes in the case of many canary breeds. During the early days, the emphasis was placed on natural ingredients which could exert the colour effect, but today, synthetic derivatives are much

✦ RIGHT
The effects of colour feeding are seen here in the richer tone of this canary's emerging feathers.

✦ BELOW
Colour food for birds is available either in the form of a softfood, or as a liquid.

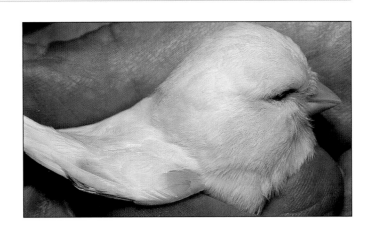

✦ RIGHT
An unflighted canary. The description "unflighted" refers to the pale flight and tail feathers in this young bird.

more commonly used. These are available either in the form of liquids, which need to be added to the bird's drinking water, or alternatively, as colour food added to softfood.

The timing of colour feeding is vital if it is to be successful, because the colouring agent will only be taken up into the feathers when these are growing. It means that the colour food must be provided just prior to and throughout the moult, in order to obtain even plumage coloration which is vital for exhibition purposes. If the colouring process starts too late, then the first feathers to be replaced will be a lighter colour than the others, and a mottled effect will be the finished result.

It may be both easier and more beneficial to use a colouring softfood rather than a liquid, firstly because it avoids the need to mix the preparation with the bird's drinking water. It is harder to predict how much birds will drink, because this depends on their environment and their diet. They will obviously drink correspondingly more when the weather is warm for example, but less when they are being given fruit and greenstuff, as these contain relatively high percentages of water. The amount of the colouring agent consumed will vary from day to day on this basis.

Using a softfood is therefore a more reliable means of colour feeding, and it also boosts the protein intake of the birds' diet, at a time when the demands for protein are increased, as their new plumage grows. The softfood needs to be fed in basically the same way as eggfood. Virtually all brands available in this form can be offered straight from the packet, rather than having to be mixed with water, but always check the instructions in advance.

This also applies when using a liquid colour food. Although overdosing with a product of this type is not likely to be deadly, it will result

✦ LEFT
Intensive red-brown coloured canary. Colour
food improves the coloration of such canaries,
providing more contrast in the plumage, as
well as emphasizing their reddish coloration.

they shouldn't be; this has as much
to do with the amount of time and
money the owner is prepared to spend
managing their bird's feeding plan as
anything else.

Among foreign birds, the familiar
pink coloration of captive flamingos
is maintained by well-managed colour
feeding, while among aviary species,
male weavers such as the orange
bishop may benefit from being
colour fed, as may sunbirds,
which have areas of bright
red plumage. Much will
depend on the birds'
normal diet however,
with any fall-off
in the depth of
feather coloration
occurring progressively over several
moults, rather than suddenly
over just a few weeks.

Although cayenne pepper
is no longer used as a natural
colouring agent, the addition
of fresh carrots in some form
to the diet of foreign birds
will help to maintain their
coloration, without the use
of commercial synthetic
preparations. Carrots
contain a carotenoid
colouring agent which is
incorporated into the feathers.
Small amounts of carrot juice
given to the birds can have the same
effect as a serving of grated
or diced carrot.

YOUNG CANARIES
When canaries of those breeds which
are colour-fed leave the nest, their
plumage will be noticeably paler than
that of adult birds. They can take their
first colour feeds at the time when

they begin their first moult. The
colour food at this early stage of the
bird's life will deepen the feathering of
the body plumage only, rather than
that of the flight or tail feathers. This
provides a means of aging young
canaries, as it is not until the bird's
first full moult that the bigger flight
and tail feathers are replaced. Until
this stage, the young canaries are
described as unflighted, or sometimes
as non-flighted, and they must
be exhibited accordingly in the
appropriate classes at bird shows.
Once the early feathers have been
shed, the birds can be described as
flighted, which indicates that they are
in full possession of coloured flight
and tail feathers.

✦ LEFT
Colour feeding can be very
important for exhibition birds,
helping to ensure that they
catch the judge's eye, but it is
not permitted under the show
rules in every case.

in the birds' droppings turning red
in the short-term, and will cause
emerging feathers to have an
unwanted burnished appearance.
There is nothing that can be done
under these circumstances, and
unfortunately, this means that the
bird's exhibition potential will be
spoilt until these feathers are shed
again at the next moult.

COLOUR-FED BIRDS
Colour feeding is most commonly
practised in a number of the canary
breeds being kept for exhibition
purposes – notably the Norwich,
Yorkshire fancy, and lizard canaries,
as well as new colour variants, such
as the red factor. Mules, too, may
be colour-fed, in order to emphasise
the existing red coloration in their
plumage. Birds that are kept as
companions, rather than as exhibition
stock, are not often colour fed,
although there is no real reason why

CARING FOR
A PET BIRD

Looking after a pet bird is not difficult, but it helps to develop a set routine, which your bird will come to recognize. If you uncover its quarters in the morning and greet it with the words "good morning", you will find that the bird soon responds to you in a similar fashion.

Pet birds generally need to be fed once a day, preferably first thing in the morning, particularly if you are supplying fresh food of any kind. Birds are less likely to eat fruit or vegetables when they are just going to roost, so fresh food offered then will effectively be wasted. It will have to be removed in the morning if the leaves have wilted and before it can turn mouldy.

✦ OPPOSITE
Parrots will become bored if left on their own for long periods, so it may be better to start out with two at the outset, to keep each other company. A pair of Goffin's cockatoos is shown here.

✦ LEFT
Smaller parrots, such as this peach-faced lovebird, are often easier to manage in the home than in an aviary. This particular African species is now being bred in a wide range of colours.

POSITIONING THE CAGE

The location of the bird's quarters in the room is important, especially for a new arrival, to give it a sense of security and to help it settle in its new surroundings. It helps if the cage is kept at eye level, preferably in the corner of the room or along a wall, rather than in the centre. Never place the bird directly in front of the window. Not only may this attract potential bird thieves, but it could prove fatal for your pet in hot weather. The bird could succumb to heat stroke, unable to escape from the sun. Although many parrots do come from the warmer parts of the world, they rest in the trees, seeking cover during the day when the sun is at its hottest.

You may have a suitable piece of furniture on which to put the cage; alternatively, you could invest in a special cage stand. Be sure that this is secure, particularly if you have young children who may try to reach the bird by attempting to climb up the stand, pulling it over with potentially dire consequences for all involved. Larger flight cages, even those that do not extend down to the ground, are usually equipped with castors, which means they are free-standing, and can be moved around when necessary.

Covering the cage is a good idea if you stay up late in the evenings. It is not recommended to expose birds to more than 12 hours of light each day because this may affect their moulting

cycle, causing them to suffer what is sometimes described as a "soft moult" – they drop feathers all the time rather than having distinct moulting periods like birds in outdoor aviaries. Covers designed for the purpose may be hard to find, but you can use a sheet or blanket; never use a woollen cover, as the bird may become caught up by its claws, and be injured.

Parrot cages for the home usually comprise of a wire top mounted on a solid base. These birds enjoy climbing around their quarters, so it is a good idea to place a screen behind the cage if it is located close to a wall, in order to protect the wallpaper from bird droppings and scattered pieces of fruit, which might otherwise stick there.

◆ LEFT
It is a good idea to cover your bird's cage if you stay up late, because even in the tropics, birds are exposed to a maximum of 12 hours of daylight, and a longer period could trigger persistent moulting.

MAKING THE ROOM SAFE

✦ BELOW
Be sure the room is safe, with all doors and windows closed, and other pets, such as cats, excluded before you allow your bird out of its quarters. Establish a routine to prevent mishaps.

✦ BELOW
The length of time a bird spends out in the room depends on you. Never be tempted to leave a bird out on its own. There could be other less obvious dangers, such as flaking paintwork.

It is very important to allow your bird out of its quarters regularly, to prevent it from becoming bored and to allow it to exercise. Birds generally follow a routine once they are used to being out of their quarters, and there are toys that you can offer so that it does not wreak havoc in the room.

You will need to prepare the room with your bird's safety in mind. First and foremost, ensure curtains can be

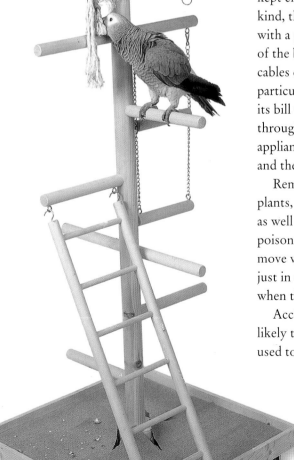

✦ LEFT
A typical playstand for a parrot, mounted on castors so that it can be wheeled from room to room. An array of toys will keep the bird occupied.

drawn over the windows to prevent the bird from attempting to fly through the glass; otherwise a fatal brain haemorrhage or a broken neck could be the result.

Other pets, especially cats, must be excluded from the room, and the door kept closed. If you have a fire of any kind, this must be properly shielded with a guard, so that there is no risk of the bird burning itself. Electrical cables can be equally hazardous, particularly if you have a large parrot – its bill will be strong enough to cut through the flex. Check that electrical appliances not in use are switched off, and their plugs are disconnected.

Remove any potentially dangerous plants, such as cacti with sharp spines, as well as those which are likely to be poisonous. It is also a good idea to move valuable or treasured ornaments, just in case they are knocked over when the bird flies around the room.

Accidents of this type are most likely to occur when the bird is not used to being at liberty in the room,

and so flies around without having anywhere to land comfortably. It may flop down clumsily as a result. For budgerigars, provide perches in prominent locations, where the bird can rest easily. For larger parrots, there are perch systems, which are intended to rest on top of cages, as well as free-standing exercise gyms. Once the novelty of coming out of its quarters subsides, a parrot will soon be content to spend much of its time playing and resting on equipment of this type.

When you let your bird out for the first time, allow it to come out on its own, rather than removing it from its quarters – there is more chance of it returning of its own accord. At first, though, be prepared to catch it to put it back in; for this it will help if the bird is hand-tame. Follow the same routine each day; the bird will soon get to know when it is time to return to its quarters and is likely to do so of its own accord. If you find that your bird is flying around wildly and is difficult to catch, draw the curtains, equip yourself with a torch and wait for the bird to settle in a convenient place. Switch out the light and, using the torch, move cautiously towards the bird. You should be able to catch it easily in the dark.

KEEPING CLEAN

✦ BELOW
In the case of a pet budgerigar, special sandsheets are available in a range of sizes to line the floor of the cage. This covering will need to be changed at least twice a week.

How often you clean the cage depends to some extent on the type of bird you are keeping. Mynahs in particular are very messy and must be cleaned out every day. For parrots, on the other hand, cleaning every two or three days is adequate, with a weekly scrubbing of their food and water containers. Cages which have a coating on their bars are easy to wipe clean, if some fruit becomes smeared on them for example, although it is still a good idea to dismantle the cage and wash it thoroughly every few months. Special disinfectants are available for use on avian equipment; these are quite safe if the instructions are followed. In some designs of budgerigar cage, the top and base units may separate for cleaning purposes. Always double check when reassembling them that they are properly joined together. Otherwise, if you pick the cage up by the hook on its roof, the bottom may fall away, allowing the bird to escape into the room.

Perches must be kept clean, and will need replacing from time to time – frequently in the case of parrots, which will whittle them away with their powerful bills.

CAGE FLOOR COVERINGS

Sandsheets are traditional for use with budgerigars and canaries. Different sizes are available so that it is not necessary to overlap the sheets, which are relatively expensive. By way of economy, some owners tip the seed husks into a rubbish bag and scrape off the droppings, two or three times, replacing the sandsheet once a week. Hen budgerigars usually start to shred their sandsheets when they approach breeding condition. This is normal

behaviour and no cause for concern.

Another option, less expensive than sandsheets, is loose bird sand, which is often blended with a little oyster shell grit. As the bird flies, its wing movements may disturb the sand, so a suitably thick layer is required in order to prevent some areas of the tray from being left uncovered, which will ultimately make it harder to clean. There are some other drawbacks to using sand, not least of which is that it is heavy to carry, which in turn may make it difficult to dispose of, particularly if you live in an apartment. Also, it can be scattered outside the confines of the bird's quarters quite easily, and it is not advisable to use it if a hen bird shows signs of becoming broody. When spending time on the floor of its cage, some of the sand may

work its way into the bird's vent, causing serious irritation.

A major drawback of using bird sand in cages housing mynahs or parrots is that any fruit which falls on to the floor will be contaminated with particles of sand. This is why it is important to use only specially prepared bird sand, rather than cheaper alternatives available from builders' outlets, which may not be clean. It may be better to use one of the other commercially available floor coverings for parrots, provided absorbency is good. The floor covering for mynah birds should be absorbent. A thick layer of newspaper can be used for them because, unlike parrots, mynahs are unlikely to shred the paper. Mynah birds will need their floor covering changed every day.

✦ BELOW
A stainless steel pot, suitable for feeding smaller birds such as finches. Although easy to clean, it is relatively light and could be tipped over easily by bigger birds perching on the rim.

✦ BELOW
Feeding pots are available in a variety of sizes, with plastic containers on the left and a ceramic bowl on the right. These should always be positioned so they are not beneath perches.

CONTAINER CARE

Food and water pots should be cleaned every day. The food pots should be washed out with a detergent, rinsed thoroughly and dried with a paper towel, before being refilled. This will ensure that there is no stale food which could harm your bird's health, nor will its quarters start to develop an unpleasant odour.

Unlike parrots, mynah birds need to be provided with an open water pot, rather than a drinking bottle, because of their pointed bills. Wash this container like the food pot: wipe with a paper towel to ensure the interior is clean, before rinsing and refilling it. Most mynah cages are of a box-type design, open just at the front to prevent droppings

✦ BELOW
Offering food from your hand can build a strong bond between pet and owner, as shown in the case of this young cock budgerigar. Note that if your pet bird's appetite unexpectedly declines, this could be a sign of impending illness.

being scattered around the room. Cages of this type are usually equipped with pots that fit securely in place in the cage front so they cannot be dislodged.

These members of the starling family are very keen bathers, and should be provided with a clean bowl of water for this purpose. In the absence of one of these, they are likely to resort to bathing in their water pot, which can become contaminated as a result. Choose a heavy earthenware container of the type sold for dogs, so that there is no risk of the bowl being tipped over, spilling the water all over the floor of the cage.

Taming a pet bird

If you start out with a young budgerigar or hand-reared parrot, the likelihood is that it will already be hand-tame. Any bird will need a few days to adjust to its new surroundings, and it may take even longer for it to become used to you, especially in the case of a parrot that has been reared from the egg by one person.

Although individual birds differ in their training responses, you will inevitably need to be patient with your new pet. Regular short training sessions, three or four times every day, are likely to be far more useful than the occasional marathon, especially as birds have a relatively short attention span and are likely to be bored by the proceedings after five minutes or so. You may be able to speed up winning your pet's confidence by offering a piece of fruit, for example, in your other hand. This means that not only will the bird have to step on to your hand in order to reach the tidbit, it will have to stay there to eat it.

Start the taming regime by offering tidbits and encouraging the bird to step on to your hand. Place your hand parallel with the perch, and gently lift the bird's toes up, so that it transfers its grip forward to your hand. Keep your hand level, so that the parrot has no difficulty in keeping its grip. For a budgerigar, use the index finger of one hand rather than your whole hand, to ensure that the bird can maintain a firm grip – otherwise, it will step off your hand. For larger parrots, bear in mind that, particularly as youngsters, their claws tend to be much sharper than those of adult birds, and so it is a good idea to wear a pair of thin leather gloves during the training process, to avoid painful scratches. In due course, after several weeks of perching properly, the sharp tips will be worn down. If you are scratched, wash the wound thoroughly and apply an antiseptic cream.

Once the bird is sufficiently confident to step on to your hand, the next stage is to take it out of its quarters in the same way. At first, you may find that it hops off at the last minute, particularly if the door opening is not very large. Try to persuade it to step across from one hand to the other, positioned just outside the cage. Before long the bird will realize that it can step out through the opening, or it may clamber round on the mesh. If possible, avoid the situation where you have to restrain the bird in order to take it out through the door. Most birds resent being held, and this will interfere with the training process. On release, your pet is likely to try to fly off, rather than continuing to perch on your hand.

In the room, it is useful to perch-train your pet. This entails using a relatively short length of perch, placed up near the bird, on to which it will step readily, should it be out of reach of your hand. You can carry the bird back to its quarters on this perch, if it can't be tempted on to your hand.

In many cases, parrots like to rest on their owner's shoulder, but be certain to remove any earrings beforehand or your parrot may try to remove them itself. It might even nibble at your ear, with painful consequences. It may be worthwhile investing in, or even making, a protective pad to fit over your

1 Once you have encouraged a bird out of its quarters, the next stage is to persuade it on to your hand. A bird will respond more readily if a piece of fruit is offered as a reward.

2 Keep your hand at perch level and place a finger in front of the bird's toes. Hold out the tidbit to tempt the bird on to your hand. Wear protective gloves if the bird's claws are very sharp.

3 Feed the bird the tidbit treat when it has stepped on to your hand, in order to build his trust in you. If the bird is a new recruit, end the training session now, before it becomes bored.

shoulder, so there will be no risk of the bird damaging your clothing directly with its claws, or soiling it when perching there.

TEACHING A BIRD TO TALK

You can start teaching your bird to talk almost as soon as you acquire it. Some young hand-reared parrots may already be starting to speak, although there are individual differences. Young grey parrots have the potential to develop into the most effective mimics – both speaking with clarity and also whistling tunes – but according to studies in this field, they may make no attempt to mimic human speech until they are at least six months old.

As well as its own abilities, the bird's teacher has a direct effect on its talking skill. Birds generally find it easier to pick up words from women or children because of their higher pitch. Again, several short sessions through the day are likely to give the best results, with no distractions in the form of other people or noise. You should have your bird's entire concentration. Repeat the chosen word or phrase slowly and clearly, giving the bird an opportunity to respond before progressing.

You may find that the first words are uttered when you are out of the room, almost as if the bird is practising its speech by itself. Do not rush the bird by trying to expand its vocabulary rapidly; this will only confuse it. Instead, gradually add new words while not neglecting the old ones, which may otherwise be forgotten. An essential piece of information to teach your bird at an early stage is your telephone number; then if it does escape, whoever finds it will be able to contact you.

Mynah birds are excellent mimics, and can learn to repeat the ring of the telephone and the doorbell with unerring accuracy. Keep these birds out of earshot of these sounds, if possible, to ensure you are able to distinguish between them.

BATHING

Birds housed indoors must have the opportunity to bathe regularly, in order to keep their plumage in good condition. This is naturally achieved by means of a waterproofing oil released from the preen gland, a slightly swollen area, which is normally hidden under the feathering at the base of the tail. The readiness of birds to bathe in a pot of water differs according to the species and the individual. Mynahs will do so readily almost every day. While some budgerigars will regularly use a plastic bath attached around the entrance to their cage, others may be more reluctant to do so, in which case they will need to be sprayed twice a week.

Buy a plant sprayer, clean it out, fill with tepid water and set the nozzle to spray a fine mist. Remove food containers from the bird's quarters before spraying. The best time to do it is just before cleaning out the cage because the water will also help to damp down feather dust lying on the tray. Do not point the nozzle directly at the bird; aim slightly above its head, so that the droplets fall down like rain.

On the first few occasions, the bird may be nervous, squawking and moving around its quarters, but this will soon pass and before long it will be waiting to be sprayed. This will be followed by an intense session of preening, after which the feathers will look immaculate. Regular spraying should help to prevent a parrot from plucking its feathers, which can be a particular problem in the case of household pet birds.

✦ LEFT
Some parrots make better talkers than others but much will also depend on the teaching plan; hand-reared parrots are often encouraged from an early age to mimic speech.

CARING FOR AVIARY BIRDS

In the aviary, new birds are likely to be nervous for the first few weeks, until they have settled down. This applies especially to Australian parakeets, as well as pigeons and doves, which will fly around wildly at first if disturbed unexpectedly. It is therefore a good idea to be sure everything is in place, even the water drinkers, before releasing the birds into their new home.

Confine them to the aviary shelter at first, where they will find their food and water without difficulty and have time to settle. If they have access to the flight, they may fly straight out and stay there, resolutely refusing to return under cover. You will have no option but to catch them up and return them to the shelter, which will be upsetting for them.

When the time comes to allow the birds out into the flight, choose a day when the weather is likely to be fine and settled for a period. If the birds, especially softbills, are out in a downpour, they may become waterlogged and unable to fly. They will have to be allowed to dry off indoors, before being returned to the aviary. This is one reason why it is important to spray birds that are being temporarily housed indoors, so that the natural waterproofing on their plumage is not lost.

◆ OPPOSITE
Cleanliness is especially important in a
colony aviary, such as this, where a number
of birds are housed. Establish a regular
cleaning routine and keep to it.

◆ LEFT
When catching a bird for any reason, close
your hand lightly around its body, so as
not to cause undue distress, or any damage
to its plumage.

EVERYDAY CARE

Everyone develops their own system for looking after their own birds, but it is important that you find time each day to look at them carefully. This is the best way to recognize when a bird is off-colour, before any more obvious signs of illness develop.

Birds are very adept at masking signs of injury until they are seriously ill. A bird is usually less active in the early stages of ill-health, perhaps flying from a perch momentarily later than a group of others. If you notice an individual bird looking at you from one angle, for example, this may be an indication that its other eye is infected or swollen, impairing its vision. Something like this is easy to miss if you are hurrying to feed and water your stock in the morning before heading off to work.

The risk of illness arising is most likely in the first few months of setting up the aviary, when the birds are adjusting to their surroundings and often to different food as well. Once new birds are settled, and providing they are housed in clean surroundings and are well-fed, you are unlikely to encounter significant health problems. This is especially true if the birds are housed in pairs rather than in a colony.

FEEDING CONTAINERS

Always provide food and water in the aviary shelter rather than in the flight – seed in particular is less likely to attract the attention of rodents, and the food will remain dry, which is important because damp seed can rapidly turn mouldy. Mould represents a serious threat to birds' health.

If you have a hopper for budgerigars, this will keep their seed free from any droppings, with the husks falling down into the tray beneath, which helps to keep the floor clean. For other birds, different types of feeding containers are necessary. Hook-on plastic food containers can be used for various species, including finches and softbills, but they are less suitable for parrots because parrots may dislodge them, scattering the contents on the floor. The plastic is also unlikely to be robust enough to

◆ LEFT
These metal containers are sufficiently robust for use with large parrots, which are likely to destroy plastic pots of a similar size.

◆ FAR LEFT
Some birds, such as quails, feed on the floor, and will often eat seed spilt by birds perching above them. Even so, they should always be provided with their own supplies of food and water.

◆ LEFT
Flowers have been provided to supply nectar and pollen to these Goldie's lorikeets.

CARING FOR NECTAR FEEDERS

Hygiene is especially important for nectar feeders. Their drinkers must be washed out at least once a day. It helps to have two sets, so that one can be left soaking in a disinfectant solution while the other is in use. Use a jug to measure out the correct volume of nectar, and stir this in water thoroughly so that it dissolves completely. Do not mix more than you need for a single feed; discard any excess. During hot weather, you may have to prepare two feeds a day.

withstand the bills of the larger species. With containers of this type, it is important to position them near a perch, so the birds have easy access.

It may be possible to attach food containers to the mesh used for covering the window. For softbills, the mesh must be on a removable framework so you can wash the window behind, which will inevitably become soiled with scattered food. Another alternative is to knock two netting staples into the wood of the shelter itself, through which you can drop the supports for the container. Make sure that these are held firmly in place because if the container tilts forwards, there will be more wastage.

For parrots, choose heavy-duty metal, hook-on containers, attaching them to the side of the aviary. Some designs come equipped with a pot that screws on to a supporting bracket, enabling them to be placed close to a perch. Alternatively, heavy-duty earthenware pots can be used, although they will have to be supported on a feeding tray, rather like a bird table. The top must be easy to wipe clean, with no nooks or crannies.

This option is also a possibility for softbills, but bear in mind that a single feeding station may be inadequate, especially at the approach of the breeding season. The cock bird may be chasing the hen to the extent that she

cannot eat at the main feeding site without being persecuted, so that a second site will be required. Occasionally, this occurs with parrots too, particularly the Eclectus (*Eclectus roratus*). These hens can prove to be very assertive over cock birds.

Food must be provided on the aviary's floor for those species that are primarily ground-dwelling, including pheasants and quails. Quails can be very wasteful in their feeding habits, scattering seed widely, so a special feeder is needed to counteract this. Hopper-type feeders can be used for pheasants, but make sure that the flow of food does not become obstructed at any stage.

✦ TOP
Hummingbirds are unique in that they can hover in front of their food source. For other nectivores, place the nectar supply next to a perch for easy access.

✦ LEFT
Always ensure that the aviary floor area is kept clean, particularly where food supplies are located. Otherwise, birds may pick up enteric infections.

◆ LEFT AND BELOW
Ensuring birds have an
uncontaminated supply of fresh
drinking water is very important.
Use a water fountain for this purpose.

◆ LEFT AND BELOW
Drinkers should always be
positioned out of direct sunlight.
Otherwise, they will be prone to
a rapid spread of algal growth.

WATER CONTAINERS

Drinkers should be located inside the shelter, partly because they are less likely to freeze during spells of cold weather. Tubular drinkers can be used for finches, budgerigars and birds of similar size. These are supplied with special clips to hold them in place on the mesh. There are also bottle drinkers, intended for parrots, that have a ball reservoir to stop the flow when the drinker is not in use. These drinkers must not be filled to maximum capacity in cold weather,

because as water freezes it expands, and the drinker may split. Allow the drinkers to thaw out gently in a clean bucket of warm water. When refilling the bottle types, ensure that the water can flow freely through the spout – often there is a hidden plug of ice between the two ball valves. You can check this quite easily by holding up the nozzle and seeing if the ball in the spout slips back into the spout.

Although these drinkers provide clean water, they are easily detached from the mesh by a mischievous

◆ ABOVE LEFT
Birds must always have easy access to fresh
drinking water. A typical drinker, which is ideal
for breeding cages, attached to the outside of
the cage.

◆ FAR LEFT
This type of drinker needs to be securely
suspended by the metal loop from the mesh
or a perch in the aviary.

◆ LEFT
A plastic water fountain can be placed on the
aviary floor, and is recommended for quails,
which spend their time at ground level. It can
also be used for pigeons and doves.

1 Birds in a birdroom are not affected by the noise of a vacuum cleaner. This type of equipment is very useful at preventing the build-up of dust in the bird's environment.

2 One of the advantages of having a solid floor in the birdroom is that it can be cleaned and disinfected easily. This is especially important in this part of the aviary, where the birds are fed.

parrot; some parrots can even manage to puncture the plastic of the bottle. It is advisable, therefore, to invest in a protective guard so the birds are not left without water at any stage. This can be critical, particularly if there are young chicks in the nest, because they are susceptible to dehydration.

Large plastic drinkers are suitable for pheasants and quails; place these on the floor of the shelter, taking care that they are not overhung by perches, or the water could be soiled from above. The birds should be provided with fresh water every day. Bacteria that pose a serious threat to the birds' health can multiply rapidly in stale or dirty water.

When it comes to washing out water containers, these should be scrubbed out with a bottle brush of the appropriate size, partly to prevent the development of green algal growth up the sides. It is especially important to wash out the drinkers if a food supplement has been added to the drinking water. Use a detergent and disinfectant before rinsing out the container thoroughly and refilling it with fresh water.

AVIARY MAINTENANCE

Once the aviary is occupied, the shelter will need to be cleaned every week. If you use newspaper on the floor, simply fold up the old sheets and discard them. Replace them with fresh sheets and, if necessary, stick down the overlying sections using adhesive tape, so that they will not be disturbed by the birds flying around.

Around the perimeter of the aviary, keep the grass cut reasonably short. Long grass provides vital camouflage for rodents, especially rats. Rats represent a real hazard, because not only can they spread serious diseases such as pseudotuberculosis, but they may also harm the birds directly, particularly if they are breeding. Sound footings and underlying the floor of the entire aviary with mesh are the best defences. Any tunnelling activity in the floor is indicative of rats, although you are unlikely to see them. The safest option is to transfer the birds elsewhere while you deal with the rodents, but if this is not feasible, invest in a live trap, which should be set overnight after an initial period of simply being baited. Once

you are sure that the rat or rats are entering it, the trap can be primed. Break-back traps should never be used in the presence of birds, nor should any poisons.

It is vital to act as soon as you see any signs of rodents, because otherwise you could soon be overrun with them, such is their reproductive potential. While rats tend to burrow in, mice will slip in through any gaps, sometimes even squeezing beneath an ill-fitting door. Mice may start breeding in aviary surroundings almost immediately after gaining access, often invading the space behind the shelter lining. Hardboard is no match for their sharp teeth. The only solution is to remove the lining and flush out the rodents directly. You will know if mice are present by their droppings in the vicinity of the food pots and the strong odour of their urine, which pervades a closed space. A live trap will catch a number at a single setting, without any risk to the birds, which will not need to be removed. These traps are highly effective in most cases, and unlike rats, mice do not appear to become suspicious of traps.

CATCHING AND HANDLING AVIARY BIRDS

It is inevitable that at some point you will have to catch birds in the aviary. This can be stressful, for both you and the birds, and must be carried out with care to prevent injuries.

Do not try to catch any birds when the weather is hot, but wait until the relative cool of the morning. Take down perches that will restrict your ability to move around the aviary. It is easier to catch a bird in the shelter, so go into the flight and encourage the birds to fly back into the shelter; you can confine them there by closing the birds' entry hatch. Some birds are easier to catch than others because they are slower in flight. Some, such as parrots, can inflict a painful bite, so it is a good idea to wear protective gloves.

Bird nets are available in different sizes. If you decide to use a net, which can be helpful with smaller birds such as finches, it is important that the rim is well padded. Even so, this is no guarantee that you will not injure the bird as you catch it. The net should be a good depth, so that once a bird has

✦ BELOW
Lift a bird very carefully out of the net. Most birds anchor their claws into the material, and these will need to be freed first.

been caught, you can grip the material at the top, below the rim, to stop it flying out again. Use the net when a bird is on the ground or on the mesh; it is difficult to catch a bird in flight.

Have a ventilated wooden box with a secure lid within reach, so you can put the bird into it quickly. If put in a cage at this point, the bird is likely to fly around wildly and may damage its plumage or injure itself. You may not even have to pick the bird out of the net. Invert the net gently above the open carrying box. If you need to free the bird, use your left hand (assuming you are right-handed). With your right hand, hold the rim of the net, tilting it

◆ BELOW
Pheasants can be restrained by carefully holding them at the top of their legs, but you must take care to ensure they do not struggle and injure themselves as a result.

◆ RIGHT
Parrots can inflict a painful bite, and although young birds may be handled with the help of a towel, as here, older individuals will be more safely restrained if you are wearing gloves.

over to prevent the bird from flying out. Place your left hand inside and feel your way down to the bird's head. Put your first and second fingers gently around the sides of its neck, and wrap your other fingers around its body. With its wings now secured in your palm, the bird will cease to struggle and you can lift it out. This movement will cause the bird to tighten its grip on the net, using its claws, so once the bird is restrained, lay the net on the ground and use your hand to prise the claws free.

Always aim to catch even smaller birds individually, rather than two or three together. This will make it easier, and will reduce the risk of injury.

LOST BIRDS

Escapes can happen at any time, but if you have a safety porch attached to your aviary, the likelihood of any birds slipping past you and out of the aviary is very remote. If a bird does fly into the safety porch as you enter the aviary, it can be encouraged to fly back into the aviary without difficulty. Problems are more likely to arise as the result of damage to the aviary. Storms and high winds are a particular problem, so if you live in an area prone to severe weather, it is important to ensure the aviary is carefully sited and solidly anchored to its foundations. Vandals too can cause the escape of birds, which is why the external

door to an aviary should always be padlocked, as a basic security measure.

If you do lose a bird, the first thing will be to keep watch in the vicinity of the aviary to see if it returns of its own accord. This is very likely with species which possess good homing instincts, such as doves; other species – parakeets, for example – will often fly off wildly, and may end up some distance away from home.

Unless the bird is exhausted, trying to catch it with a net will require considerable guile: move very slowly so as not to frighten it. If there is no sighting of your escapee, contact neighbours, local bird clubs and animal welfare organizations, in case someone has seen or already caught your bird.

The length of time that an escapee can survive depends on the species and the individual bird. It also depends on the time of year, since in late summer, food will be more readily available and the weather will be warmer than in the wintertime.

BUYING BIRDS

The choice of where to buy a bird will depend on the species you are seeking and where you live. It is preferable to find a local source of supply, but in some cases, you may have to travel some distance. Bird-keeping publications are a useful source of information. If you are interested in establishing an exhibition stud, it is worth reading the show reports regularly, and attending as many shows as possible, to familiarize yourself with the type of birds that are catching the judges' eyes, and the breeders who are winning consistently.

In other cases, with parrots for example, you may be able to find a breeder via one of the many parrot-keeping organizations which now exist. Again, look in the bird-keeping press or try a search on the Internet, as many specialist organizations now have their own websites. Many such clubs organize sales days, where a number of different bird species will be available to buy. In comparison, most pet stores only stock a limited range of birds. They may be able to source a particular bird for you, but if there is a bird farm in your area, you will not only find a wider range of birds on offer, but you will also be able to pick up expert tips on their care.

MAKING YOUR CHOICE

Never rush into a decision – if you feel unhappy for any reason, it is better not to buy the bird. If you are seeking a hand-reared parrot, you may need to be patient. There is usually a good supply of hand-reared grey parrots available throughout the year, but the breeding season of other species, such as Amazons, tends to be much more restricted. As a consequence, young Amazon parrots are likely to be on offer in the greatest numbers at one time of the year only, the early autumn in northern temperate latitudes.

Should you be looking for aviary stock, bear in mind that if you purchase birds from the late summer onwards, there will be no possibility of them becoming acclimatized before the onset of winter if they have not been outside or have been recently

✦ ABOVE
Sale days organized by bird societies are a good way of obtaining new stock, and will provide an opportunity to discuss bird care with breeders.

✦ BELOW
Do not feel rushed into making a purchase. You must allow time to look at the birds properly, to ensure as far as possible that they are healthy.

Special travelling boxes are available for birds.
Cardboard boxes, such as this, are suitable for
smaller birds, but use the more robust plywood
structures for strong-billed parrots.

✦ LEFT
Take the opportunity
to ask the breeder
any questions you
may have regarding
both the life history
of the bird, and the
type of food they
have been receiving.

imported, and so you must be
prepared to keep them indoors until
the spring.

The price of birds can vary
dramatically, even in the case of the
same species. Expect to pay more for
established stock, and also for true
pairs, rather than unsexed individuals,
in the case of those species where it is
not possible to distinguish between
the sexes visually. A premium price is
usually attached to proven pairs of
the larger parrots; here, compatibility
between members of a pair is an
important aspect in terms of achieving
breeding success. Simply having two
birds of the opposite gender is no
guarantee that they will form a pair,
bond, and mate successfully, no
matter how long you wait for them.

✦ BELOW
Find out if the birds have been kept indoors.
It is inadvisable to allow them into an outdoor
aviary until all risk of frost has passed.

With birds where compatibility is
not a problem, such as budgerigars,
pricing may be influenced by the bird's
coloration. Blue series individuals, such
as cobalts and violets, as well as bright
coloured lutinos, sell for more than
a green or grey bird. With exhibition
stock, however, the price depends not
on the bird's colour, but on its pedigree
and the success-rate of the breeder
concerned. Birds from a breeder who
wins consistently at high levels will
cost more than birds from a novice.

WHAT TO LOOK FOR

When faced with an aviary full of birds for sale, it is a considerable help to have a clear idea of what you are looking for. As a general indication, the bird should be lively and flying readily, and its plumage should look in good condition, although in the case of a young hand-reared chick, its feathers may not be as sleek as those of an older bird. Do not be tempted to buy a chick before it is capable of feeding on its own; the weaning phase can be traumatic, and the risk of problems arising is increased if the chick has recently been rehomed.

◆ ABOVE
A mature cock budgerigar. It is usually possible to distinguish between young fledglings and adult birds, but it is not easy to age adult birds, unless they have been banded with a closed ring.

◆ LEFT
There is usually nothing seriously wrong if a bird is feeding properly, but a closer check will still be needed.

◆ BELOW LEFT
It is possible to age African grey parrots by the coloration of their irises. In young birds, these are dark.

◆ BELOW RIGHT
This is the typical yellow iris coloration of an adult African grey. Adult birds do not make good pets, unless they are tame and talking, but they should settle well in aviary surroundings.

Check the bird's eyes, which should be bright, with no signs of swelling. Diamond doves are the notable exception here; swelling of the peri-orbital skin around the eyes is associated with cock birds of the species when in breeding condition.

Check the feet for signs of swelling or difficulty in perching. If you plan to exhibit your bird, it is vital to ensure that it possesses a full complement of claws. Look at the balls of the feet for any obvious inflammation.

A closer examination will be needed once the bird has been caught. Look carefully to ensure the nostrils are of even size, and are not blocked. Any enlargement of the nostrils may be indicative of a long-standing infection that could flare up again. This is often a problem with grey parrots.

The bill itself should be free from any damage, and not overgrown. Budgerigars sometimes suffer from undershot bills, where the upper part of the bill does not curve down over

+ BELOW
Heavily scaled legs, especially in the case of
finches, canaries and softbills, are often a sign
of old age. They may also be indicative of the
parasitic illness known as scaly leg.

+ BELOW
Always check the claws, particularly if you are
hoping to show the bird. Damaged or missing
claws will ruin any competition chances,
although overgrown claws are easily remedied.

the lower part, but curls back within it. This problem can often be traced back to poor nest hygiene, resulting in nest dirt hardening and distorting the growth of the bill, although it may also be an inherited condition. In either instance, there is nothing that can be done to correct the deformity, other than trimming back the lower bill. Without the constraint of an overlapping upper bill, this will grow more readily than is usual and will have to be trimmed back regularly for the rest of the bird's life.

Another problem that can affect the bills of budgerigars is scaly face. This is caused by a mite and will spread readily if untreated, causing permanent distortion of the bill. In the initial stages, scaly face shows up as tiny snail-like tracks running across the upper bill. The more characteristic coral-like encrustations develop later.

The overall condition of the bird is most reliably assessed from examining the breastbone, which lies in the midline of the body, just below the neck. This should be well covered with muscle; distinct hollows either side are a cause for concern, indicating that the bird is underweight. This could mean that it has not been eating properly, or

it could be suffering from intestinal roundworms, or a more serious chronic illness, such as an internal tumour. Buying birds in such condition is therefore a decided risk, particularly if there is staining of the feathering around the vent, which indicates a digestive disturbance.

It is impossible to age birds reliably once they have moulted into adult plumage. In the case of finches and softbills, the legs may provide a clue – heavy scaling tends to indicate an older individual, although it would be more helpful to compare a group of the same species.

+ LEFT
Healthy birds,
such as this cock
fawn zebra finch,
are alert and lively,
with sleek plumage.

SETTLING IN A NEW ARRIVAL

✦ BELOW
A colony of peach-faced lovebirds. These small parrots can be very aggressive and it is important not to introduce a new individual to an established group.

Moving a bird to a new environment, particularly if there is a long journey involved, is likely to be stressful. Reducing the stress should mean that birds will settle down with minimal problems. Preparation is important. Have everything organized before the bird arrives so that you can simply transfer it to its new quarters.

Hand-reared birds are perhaps more vulnerable than most to digestive upsets, which means it is especially important to maintain them on their usual diet. Make any changes gradually after a couple of weeks or so. The same applies to softbills and all nectar-feeding birds because they are particularly prone to potentially fatal digestive upsets if their diet is suddenly changed.

You can minimize the likelihood of illness in the critical early days after acquiring a new bird by the use of an electrolyte and probiotic products. An electrolyte will help to restore the body's fluid balance, following a period when the bird may not have been eating and drinking normally. Probiotic food contains beneficial bacteria, like those in live yogurt, which will colonize the gut and stabilize its acidity, assisting the digestive process and making it much harder for potentially harmful microbes to gain access to the body via this route.

If you already have other birds, it is important to keep new arrivals away from them, to be sure that they do not

✦ LEFT
Australian parakeets have a justifiable reputation for being very nervous when first moved to new surroundings. It may be a good idea to let them settle in an aviary shelter at first. Crimson rosellas, also known as Pennant's parakeets, are shown here.

✦ BELOW
A parrot which has been in another home
will take time to adjust to new domestic
surroundings, particularly an older bird, such
as this grey. Breeding pairs may also be shy.

introduce any disease to your
collection. Releasing a newly arrived
bird straight into an existing collection
also increases the stress on that bird
because it may be bullied by the
others. This, in turn, will increase the
risk of it falling ill. Wait at least three
weeks before adding a new bird to an
existing collection, during which time
you can have various tests carried out
to establish the bird's state of health.

Faecal samples provide a simple
means of determining whether the
bird is suffering from intestinal
roundworms, which can be a particular
problem in Australian parakeets,
while tapeworms may be present in
ground-dwelling species which hunt
invertebrates. The tests for these
are not expensive and can save you
introducing the parasites into the
aviary, where they will be much harder,
if not impossible, to eliminate. You
would have to de-worm the birds
regularly and often in order to ensure
they remained healthy.

When you do decide to transfer
new birds to existing accommodation,

✦ LEFT
Try to avoid
introducing new
birds to an aviary
during the breeding
season, because
the likelihood of
fighting breaking
out is dramatically
increased, as in the
case of these two
royal starlings.

moving them into an outside aviary
for the first time, then it is a good idea
to keep them confined in the shelter
for the first few days. They will then
return here to feed without fear in the
future, and, hopefully, will roost here
as well, particularly if the perches are
positioned at a slightly higher level
than in the flight.

When it comes to breeding, it can
take some parrots several years to
settle down to nesting, while Australian
parakeets are likely to breed the
following year. Certain birds may even
nest soon after a move; this is most
likely with domesticated finches.

ADDING TO AN EXISTING COLLECTION

Adding birds to an existing collection, rather than introducing a pair to an aviary on their own, can be a difficult process at any time of the year, and is especially problematic during the breeding season. It is usually better to wait until this period has passed, because otherwise the newcomer may be severely harassed – a hen in particular may be bullied by a would-be partner in its enthusiasm to breed. Australian parakeets, pheasants, quails, pigeons and doves rank among the worst offenders in this respect.

At other times, the intrusion of another bird or pair into an existing flock should be monitored carefully for signs of aggression from any of the established birds. It could be that introducing a bird of similar coloration, albeit of a different species, may lead to displays of aggression. Blue-capped waxbills (*Uraeginthus cyanocephala*), for example, will often react aggressively towards red-cheeked cordon bleus (*U. bengalus*) for this reason.

✦ ABOVE
Pigeons and doves, in spite of being seen as symbols of peace, are actually aggressive by nature, particularly when a new individual is added to an existing group.

✦ LEFT
The diamond dove is usually tolerant of the company of others of its kind. Compatibility is best achieved if the birds are all transferred to their aviary at the same time, prior to breeding.

◆ RIGHT
Most parakeets, such as this rosa form of Bourke's parakeet, need to be housed in individual pairs for breeding purposes. Young birds should be removed as soon as they are independent; otherwise, they may be attacked.

conflict, particularly if the flight is planted, with plenty of retreats available. Offer a choice of feeding locations to prevent the cock bird monopolizing one area and preventing the hen from being able to feed.

Within an established colony, it is equally hazardous to introduce a male newcomer if the breeding season is underway. You will need to wait until the end of this period, when the birds are less territorial and other changes are being made to the flock. Again, when you do introduce the newcomer, make sure there is plenty of vegetation, and a choice of feeding stations to ensure that all birds have access to food.

Aggression is least likely to occur with finches, and most common with parrots, where the flock structure is rigorously upheld against intruders. Adding a different species, such as a pair of diamond doves, to an aviary of finches is unlikely to result in conflict. Again, it is important not to do this when the birds are nesting, because the change in environment could cause a nervous pair to abandon their nest.

The best time to add new bird stock to the aviary is after the end of the breeding period, when established birds will be moulting. The greatest selection of stock is available for sale at this time, as breeders reduce their bird collections at the end of the breeding period.

Dealers, too, may have sales, but beware of buying recently imported birds at this time of year; it will be too late to acclimatize them to an outside aviary, and they will need to be housed in heated winter-time quarters until the following spring. If you intend to overwinter your existing birds under these conditions, you can introduce the newcomers during this period, if you are certain that they are healthy. This will give the group time to settle down before being released into their breeding quarters in the spring.

AVOIDING CONFLICTS

In the case of birds which are likely to be aggressive, it is better to remove the established individual from the aviary first for a few days, assuming that alternative accommodation is available. This is especially important if you are intending to introduce a hen to the aviary, as she is likely to be harried relentlessly by the cock, especially if acquired during the breeding season.

Taking out the cock bird, and replacing both cock and hen at the same time, will reduce the risk of

◆ ABOVE
Red-cheeked cordon bleus do not agree well with others of their own kind, but they are generally compatible with other waxbills, and with small, non-aggressive softbills and doves.

KEEPING BIRDS HEALTHY

Birds are most likely to fall ill soon after being moved to a new home, as they may encounter unfamiliar microbes or may not have been eating properly for several days. Once established in their quarters, however, and after moulting there for the first time, the risk of illness is greatly reduced.

Illness may also arise in a collection where a number of birds are being kept in the same aviary, budgerigars for example, rather than being housed on their own or in a pair, as in the case of a pair of parakeets.

Good hygiene plays a vital role in preventing the spread of infection in an aviary where a number of birds are present. This is not just a matter of keeping the aviary floor clean, but also of ensuring that food containers are washed at least twice a week, and of using sealed drinkers and hoppers to reduce the likelihood of their contents becoming contaminated with droppings. Regular measures to control parasites, such as spraying to eliminate any risk of red mite becoming established, are also vital; it is very difficult to spot any signs until these almost invisible creatures are well established in the aviary environment.

DETECTING ILLNESSES

Birds must be watched very closely for signs of illness. The bird's condition deteriorates rapidly if sickness goes undetected. If it loses its appetite to the point that it is no longer eating, medication has very little opportunity to work successfully. Thankfully, products have been introduced over recent years which provide all the bird's nutritional needs. They can keep a sick or injured individual alive for weeks, greatly enhancing the likelihood of a successful recovery. Advice on using products of this type should be obtained from your avian veterinarian.

The number of veterinarians with experience in this field has grown in the last decade, along with increased interest in the birds. It should not be difficult to find someone in your area with the requisite expertise. An avian

veterinarian will treat illness affecting your stock, and can also help when it comes to sexing birds, and offering preventive health care advice, which can be especially valuable if you have a large collection of birds.

Once established in their quarters, birds are generally very healthy. You are most likely to face health problems in your stock when a number of birds are housed together, rather than as individual pairs on their own.

✦ ABOVE
A green-rumped parrotlet showing abnormally coloured areas of plumage as a result of poor diet.

✦ ABOVE
This parrot suffers from an old injury to its toe, which is causing the nail to grow at an angle. Regular trimming of this nail is essential.

✦ RIGHT
Dirty cages can be hazardous for birds. Both disease and parasites, such as red mite, can spread rapidly in such surroundings.

COPING WITH A SICK BIRD

When confronted with a sick bird, the first thing to do is to remove it from the aviary and transfer it to a warm environment. There are special hospital cages available for this purpose, suitable for smaller birds. For larger species, you will need to invest in an infra-red heat lamp, equipped with a variable heat controller. This should be suspended over the bird's isolation quarters, preferably so there is a temperature gradient across the cage, with one end being warmer than the other. As the bird recovers, it will seek out the cooler area. A reflector around the bulb helps to direct the lamp's rays effectively, while an adjustable controller enables you to lower its heat output, a necessary step in re-acclimatizing the bird.

One of the difficulties of avian medicine is that symptoms are remarkably similar for several illnesses; unravelling the cause can be very difficult, which is a problem when treatment has to be started immediately. In many cases, however, the illness is likely to be caused by a bacterial infection, which will respond well to antibiotic treatment. These drugs are available only on veterinary prescription in the UK, but are easily obtainable elsewhere, in the USA for example, where antibiotic remedies may be sold in pet stores.

When using antibiotics, follow the instructions implicitly and do not stop a course of treatment before the recommended period because, although the bird may appear to have recovered, its condition could deteriorate again. If the surviving bacteria develop a resistance to the antibiotic, further treatment is likely to be unsuccessful.

The most common means of administering antibiotics to birds is via their drinking water, but this is not a particularly reliable method, because you cannot be sure how much a sick individual will drink – it may not consume enough of the medication for the drug to be effective. Avoid offering foods which contain a large percentage of water, such as fruit or greenstuff, so as to encourage the bird to drink the treated water. Place the water alongside the perch if the bird is resting there, rather than on the floor, so that it is within easy reach.

In some cases, especially with larger species, your veterinarian may prefer to give the bird an injection. This can speed its recovery quite dramatically,

with subsequent treatment given via the bird's food or drinking water.

It is important not to rush the bird's recovery, once its condition starts to improve. It will almost certainly have lost weight, as reflected by the increased prominence of its breastbone. Do not put the bird back in its aviary until such time as its condition has been restored to normal, or it could suffer a relapse. The weather is important, too – the bird must be gradually re-acclimatized to room temperature and then life outdoors. This may mean that a bird that has been ill will have to remain indoors over the winter, until it can be safely re-acclimatized to outdoor life again in the spring.

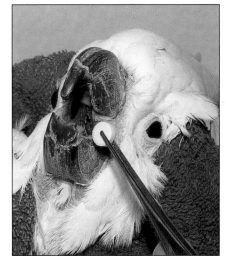

EYE PROBLEMS

Swelling and inflammation of the eyes can strike any bird, and although the signs are reasonably clear, it is important to remember that they can be indicative of either a localized or a more serious disorder, such as chlamydiosis. Much depends on the bird's demeanour. If just one eye is affected, it is more likely to be the result of a scratch, particularly if the bird appears to be lively and alert and is eating normally. Should both eyes be affected, however, and the bird becomes progressively more depressed, the likelihood is that it is suffering from a more serious illness.

In localized cases, treatment using special ophthalmic ointment or drops

should be adequate to resolve the condition rapidly. Be prepared to apply the treatment at least four times daily. Reapplication is necessary because

inflammation causes the eye to water, and this will wash out the medication.

It may be easier to apply drops rather than ointment, but you must ensure that the drops are not lost by the bird blinking at the wrong moment. With ointment, smear it out of the tube along the eye, and be sure that it reaches its target. Hold the bird for a few minutes afterwards so that the ointment can dissolve in the tear fluid, or the bird may wipe it off on to a convenient perch as soon as it is returned to its quarters. Recovery in most cases of this type is rapid, and the inflammation soon subsides, but do not cease treatment prematurely.

Try to identify the cause of the problem if you have several birds in one aviary affected by eye ailments. It might be, for example, that the perches are dirty, and by rubbing their heads on the sides of the perches, the birds are acquiring an infection. The problem may also be linked with the diet: a shortage of Vitamin A can trigger eye problems. Cataracts will develop on occasion in birds with red eyes, and will also occur in elderly parrots. Other eye problems are relatively rare in pet or aviary birds.

1 A white-breasted kingfisher afflicted by an eye ailment. Seek experienced veterinary advice to obtain the correct diagnosis at the outset.

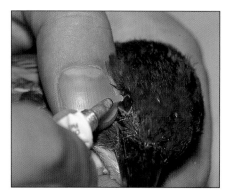

2 Apply treatment carefully to prevent the medication missing its target, in the case of drops, or being wiped off immediately.

3 Holding the patient for a few moments after the treatment will allow the medication to start dissolving into the eye fluid.

4 Provided that the bird can see well out of one eye, and the problem is localized, then it should continue to eat normally.

VIRUSES

Bacterial illnesses can be controlled by means of antibiotics, but this group of drugs is ineffective against viruses. The most serious viral illnesses encountered in aviary birds affect the plumage of parrots. French moult was first recorded in the huge breeding establishments set up in the late 1800s, and can be devastating in its effects. It afflicts young budgerigars at the age of four weeks or so, and results in the loss of flight and tail feathers. Some birds are affected much more severely than others, to the extent that they cannot fly.

There is nothing that can be done by way of treatment. Chicks suffering from French moult should be homed as pets, rather than kept for breeding purposes. In a number of cases, they will regrow their missing feathers, but they may retain tell-tale signs, such as traces of dried blood in the feather shaft, close to the skin.

Good hygiene is important in preventing the spread of this illness. Do not clean nest boxes with the same brush because this can transmit the virus, and wash concaves (wooden blocks hollowed out at one end, used in budgerigars' next boxes) in disinfectant. The virus spreads easily through feather dust.

The other serious viral ailment encountered in aviculture is psittacine beak and feather disease (PBFD). This was first recognized in cockatoos, but it has now spread to many types of parrot. Affected birds show loss of feathering, with the tissue of their bills becoming soft and overgrown. The claws, too, are affected in a similar way. The depressive effect of this virus on the immune system means that the bird will succumb to other infections as its condition deteriorates over the course of several months.

Although there is no treatment available as yet, there is a diagnostic test which enables sufferers from PBFD to be identified early. The condition in its early stages can be confused with feather plucking. Affected birds must be kept strictly on their own because they represent a serious threat to the health of others. The PBFD virus also spreads easily through feather dust.

INJURIES

✦ BELOW
The bill of this Indian ring-necked parakeet has been badly damaged. In some cases, artificial bills are fitted, enabling the bird to eat properly.

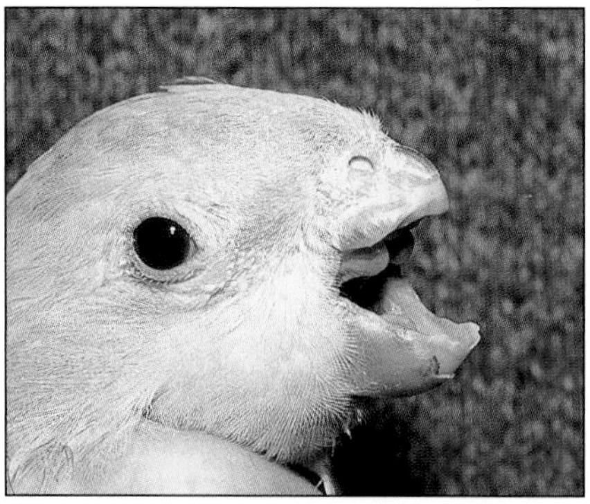

Unfortunately, there is always a possibility that injuries will arise, both within the confines of the home and in aviary surroundings outdoors, and you need to take adequate precautions to minimize the risks. You also need to be aware of what to do and who to contact when an injury does occur. The outcome may otherwise prove fatal, or could leave the bird permanently handicapped.

One of the most common injuries occurs when a bird flies into an obstruction, such as a pane of glass in the home, or even the mesh of the aviary flight, in the case of young Australian parakeets, which are especially nervous when they first leave the nest.

With this type of injury, the affected individual is likely to end up stunned and disorientated on the floor. There may be no immediate sign of the collision on the bird's body, but if you look closely at the area of the cere, above the bill, you may notice a slight sign of impact here, particularly if the bird collided with mesh. It is impossible to treat this condition but, if transferred to quiet, darkened surroundings, the bird should recover uneventfully on its own. Occasionally, however, the skull may have been fractured and there could be an underlying brain haemorrhage. In almost all cases this will prove fatal.

Where birds are being housed in adjoining flights, it is vital that both sides of the panel separating them are clad with mesh, as this should create a barrier which prevents neighbouring pairs from coming into contact with each other. Even so, you should check the panel at regular intervals, because the mesh can sag, allowing the birds direct contact. This in turn can lead to badly bitten toes. If necessary, you can slide wooden spacers in between the mesh to keep the panel sheets apart. The treatment of fighting injuries in birds depends greatly on their severity. Stemming blood flow has to be the first priority, after which the bird should be left in a quiet and darkened area to recover from the shock. An electrolyte solution can also be helpful in such cases.

Fighting between neighbouring birds can also result in bill injuries. This may have serious consequences for the bird's appearance, and it emphasizes the need to check the double-wiring in the flight at regular intervals. Bill injuries can also arise as the result of displays of aggression between birds sharing an aviary – notably cockatoos, where cocks can launch into sudden, vicious attacks on their would-be mates on occasions.

With an injury of this type, handling must again be kept to a minimum because it may exacerbate the effects of shock. You may need to do no more than stem the blood flow by pressing on the damaged part of the bill, particularly the central area in the case of the upper beak.

The advice of a specialist avian vet should be sought, to ascertain the best

TRIMMING THE CLAWS OF A NORWICH CANARY

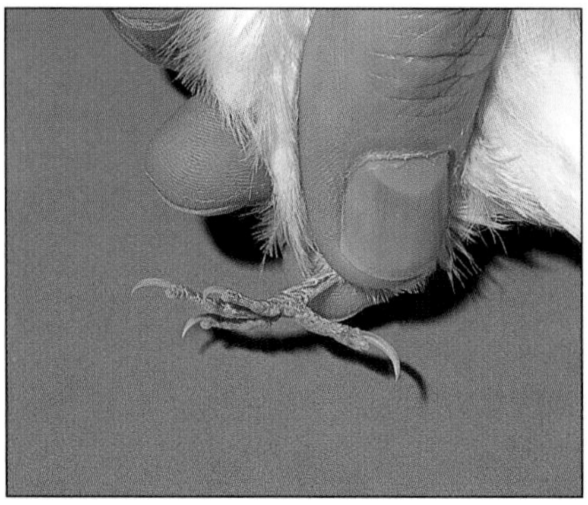

1 Overgrown claws are hazardous. Birds can become caught up in their quarters, or breeding pairs may drag chicks out of the nest.

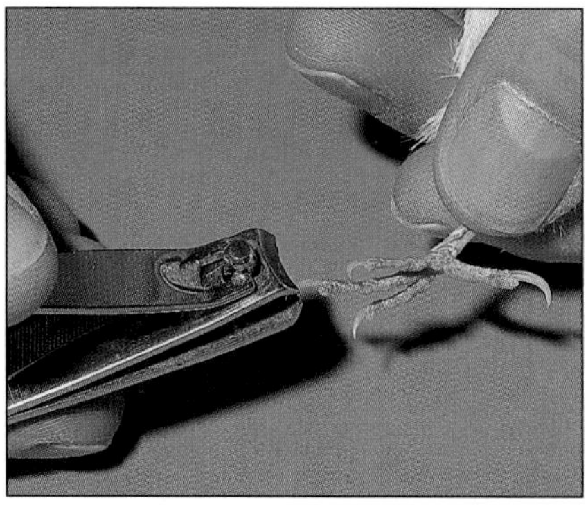

2 Use special nail clippers. Trimming is carried out at the start of the breeding season, when the birds are moved to breeding cages.

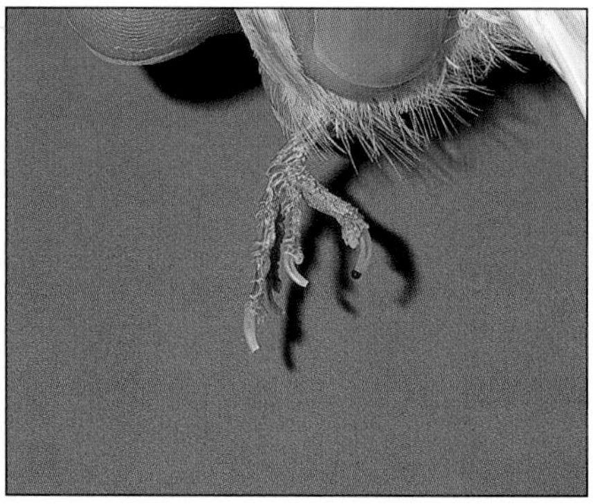

3 Carry out clipping in a good light, so as not to cut the nails too short and cause them to bleed. Take particular care with dark nails.

way of treating the injury in the longer term. Initially, however, a diet of softfood is likely to be needed, so that the bird can continue feeding. The injury will be painful, and the bird is unlikely to be able to crack either seeds or a complete diet.

So long as the bird can be kept alive through this critical early phase after injury, and depending on how badly the bill has been damaged, it is possible that the tissue will regrow. This is usually a slow process, and the bill is unlikely to reach its full length again. Even so, the regrowth should be adequate to allow the bird to eat hard foods again in due course. Some reshaping of the bill may be needed to improve the bird's appearance once the bill starts to regrow. Reshaping of the bill should be undertaken by an avian vet.

Modern veterinary materials mean that in certain cases where the bill has been badly injured, it may be possible for a false bill to be fitted, even on a temporary basis. The false bill should function almost as effectively as the original. This type of surgery is highly skilled however, and may not be advisable in all cases.

Fractures of the limbs are quite unusual in aviary birds, but should be suspected in cases where a bird suddenly appears to have difficulty in perching or flying. Treatment may involve immobilizing the injured area; the degree of function which returns after treatment depends in part on the site of the fracture. An X-ray assessment will usually give the best insight into the extent of the damage.

In cases where fighting has occurred and the bird has suffered a loss of feathers and skin trauma,

REPAIRING A LOVEBIRD CHICK'S LEG

1 Pictured are the legs of a lovebird chick, which have become splayed in the nest. If they are not treated, the bird will be unable to perch properly.

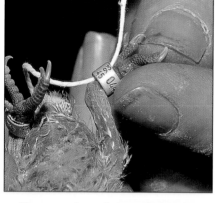

2 There are various techniques which can be used, and an experienced avian vet will be able to give you the best advice on what to do.

3 By effectively shackling the legs together, the weakened legs are strengthened. They will now carry the bird's weight even when it is mature.

4 Care must be taken not to constrict the blood flow to either limb. Check that the string is not so tight that it cuts into the bird's flesh.

healing should occur naturally without too many problems. Birds rarely develop abscesses, unlike mammals, although bruising, which causes the skin to turn a deep shade of purple, is often associated with this type of injury. Bruising will usually fade after a few days. Lost feathers will be replaced almost immediately, emerging as spikes at first before unfurling.

Provided that the injury is superficial, healing should leave no lasting damage. Even so, do not reintroduce the bird to its mate as soon as it appears to have recovered because it is likely to be attacked

again. Instead, introduce the pair on neutral territory. In the case of parrots, once one bird has turned on its partner, do not reintroduce them; fighting can occur again, and this time the outcome could be fatal. With other birds, such as pigeons and doves, it may be possible to reintroduce pairs successfully before the end of the breeding season, but make changes to the aviary decor first. Providing more cover will help, because it could be that the hen did not feel sufficiently secure in her quarters to start nesting. This will also give the hen more protection from her mate.

PARASITES

The most common health problems encountered by bird-keepers come from parasitic ailments. For this reason it is extremely important to screen or treat newly acquired stock before adding them to an existing collection. Parasites multiply very rapidly in favourable conditions, while their small size and inconspicuous nature means their presence can be easily overlooked until they are posing a serious health risk. Young birds are generally most vulnerable. Parasites can be broadly sub-divided into two categories – external and internal.

EXTERNAL PARASITES

Mites and lice are the most commonly encountered external parasites in aviary stock. Red mites (*Dermanyssus gallinae*) are relatively common and have an unusual life cycle that makes them difficult to eliminate, particularly once they become established in birdroom surroundings. These mites spend only part of their time on the hosts, emerging under cover of darkness to suck the blood of the birds. Then they retreat to their hiding places – cracks in the corners of cages or other nooks and crannies. Red mites present a particular hazard during the breeding season because they live in nest boxes and nesting pans, sucking the blood of adult birds and chicks, which gives them their characteristic coloration.

They are capable of living for months without feeding, so they can survive from one breeding season to the next, with their numbers growing even more rapidly during the following year. Severe infestations can cause anaemia in the chicks, stunting their growth, and may even prove fatal. In addition, red mites are capable of transmitting microscopic blood parasites when they feed, which can also be very harmful.

The other mite of concern is the scaly-face mite (*Knemidocoptes*), which is most commonly seen in budgerigars, although some other birds, notably kakarikis, are vulnerable to it as well. It spreads readily from bird to bird by direct contact, and may also be picked up off the perches, as the bird wipes its bill in a bid to relieve the irritation. The earliest signs of scaly face are tiny snail-like tracks across the upper bill, with more obvious crusty swellings developing around the side of the bill, the cere and sometimes elsewhere on the body as well. In canaries, the legs are often invaded by these parasites, causing them to have an unhealthy, swollen and crusty appearance.

Treatment is straightforward, although it will be necessary to remove affected birds from the aviary until they have recovered. It is also a good idea to scrub off or replace the perches, to contain the spread of the mites. Traditional proprietary remedies to be applied to the affected areas are available from pet stores. Petroleum jelly can be equally effective, blocking off the breathing tubes of the mites. An application of ivermectin, in drop form, to the skin at the back of the neck from where it is absorbed into the body, can kill these mites very efficiently. Only one rather than

✦ LEFT
It is advisable to treat all new arrivals for parasites before allowing them into aviary surroundings. Here a cockatiel is being sprayed with a special aerosol to kill off any mites or lice.

TO PREVENT RED MITE INFESTATIONS

● Treat all new birds with a special red mite medication.

● Start out with new rather than secondhand equipment.

● Use special mite-killing preparations to wash out nest boxes and breeding cages.

● Discourage wild birds from landing on the aviary, because they are often infested with the parasites and can easily transmit them to aviary occupants.

♦ BELOW
Scaly face in a budgerigar. This disfiguring parasitic ailment must be treated as early as possible; otherwise the mites may spread around the eyes.

♦ BELOW
A sample of droppings can reveal much about a bird's overall state of health. This roundworm has been passed out with the droppings.

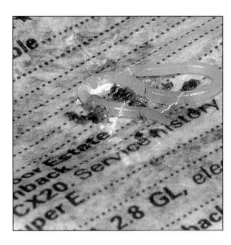

regular applications will be needed, but contact your veterinarian about this method of treatment. The correct dosage is critical for the bird's safety.

Lice, visible as thin dark streaks, often on the wings, represent far less of a problem than mites. They spend their whole life cycle on their host, and are spread by close contact in a nest or roosting site. Treatment as for red mite will kill these parasites. Untreated, they may result in tatty, frayed feathering. Affected individuals will be seen to preen themselves far more than usual.

INTERNAL PARASITES

Microscopic unicellular organisms called protozoa can cause serious ill-health in birds; pigeons, doves and budgerigars are especially vulnerable to the effects of *Trichomonas* protozoa. These multiply in the crop, causing it to swell with gas, and preventing the bird from eating properly. Affected budgerigars will spend longer than usual at their seed hopper or food pot, and appear to eat. On close inspection, you will see that the seed has not been swallowed, only dehusked; dark pieces of canary seed in the food pot are a tell-tale sign.

Treatment consists of emptying the crop gently, by holding the bird upside down and milking the gas out, massaging the crop in the direction of the head. Specific medication to treat trichomoniasis can be obtained from a veterinarian.

The infestation can spread quite widely through a colony before signs become apparent. Young chicks are vulnerable soon after fledging; they lose weight rapidly and fade away. It is a good idea to treat all the birds in an aviary when a case of trichomoniasis occurs because there are almost certainly others carrying the infection, and further outbreaks are likely.

Pheasants and quails are at risk from similar protozoa affecting the digestive tract, resulting

♦ RIGHT
The risk of parasitic illnesses occuring is much reduced in clean and hygienic aviary surroundings. This is one area of bird care where hard work really does pay off.

in severe and sometimes blood-stained diarrhoea. Examination of a fresh sample of droppings should serve to identify the actual cause of the infection, often called coccidosis after the name of the microbe concerned. Aside from treatment, thorough disinfection of the birds' surroundings will be needed to avoid reinfection.

Intestinal worms pose a serious health problem, and preventive treatment prior to releasing the birds into aviary surroundings is recommended. If the parasites become established in the environment, it will be almost impossible to eliminate them successfully.

Roundworms are like small white earthworms in appearance, as opposed to tapeworms, which have a flattened body shape. Both release thousands of eggs into the bird's quarters, but there is a key difference between them in terms of their subsequent development. After a few days, roundworm eggs will represent a hazard to birds that come into contact with them, whereas tapeworm eggs must be eaten by an invertebrate first.

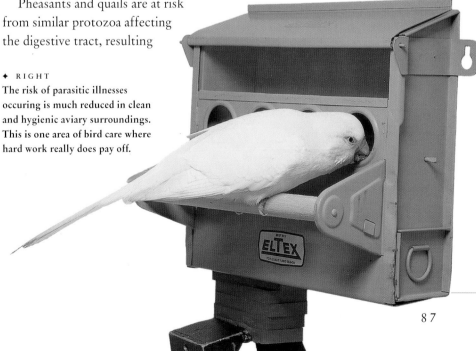

FEATHER PLUCKING

This disorder is a particular problem in the case of pet parrots. Unfortunately, there is no single cause; various factors may be involved, including boredom, an inadequate diet and lack of opportunity to bathe. This may be the most significant factor – the plumage becomes dry and will not lie flat, which may in turn encourage the parrot to remove its feathers as it becomes frustrated attempting to keep them in place.

Prevention is much easier than cure, particularly as once this problem arises, it can soon become habitual. There are deterrent sprays that you can use in an attempt to persuade the parrot to desist from this behaviour, but they are rarely successful. Changing the bird's environment can be just as effective. It is always worth using a spray to kill mites and lice, though, just in case parasites of this type are causing underlying irritation which has triggered the feather plucking. Seeking the advice of an experienced avian veterinarian may help to isolate the problem rapidly.

With finches and softbills, feather plucking is far less common, especially among established birds. If it does occur, it can be indicative of overcrowding, and once the birds are housed in spacious surroundings, the feathers will regrow without any further problem.

Feather-plucking is less common when parrots are housed in outdoor aviaries, although it may occur on occasion, and can often be linked with the hen's desire to go to nest. Hen Abyssinian lovebirds may pluck their feathers to use as a nest lining, but this is not a matter for concern – these feathers will soon regrow.

◆ LEFT
African grey parrots are especially vulnerable to plucking their feathers, typically on the breast and abdomen, as in this case. It can be very difficult to correct this behaviour.

Where feather-plucking is much more problematic is in the case of young chicks being plucked by their parents while they are still in the nest. This abnormal behaviour is most common in budgerigars and lutino cockatiels, as well as some lories and lorikeets. There is clear evidence that feather-plucking of this type is inherited, at least in some cases. Transferring the eggs of pairs known to pluck their offspring to those which do not is likely to result in the chicks being reared normally. Unfortunately, when these fostered birds are paired up as adults, the vice will re-emerge, and they will pluck their chicks.

It is sometimes possible to break this cycle, by using a special spray designed for the purpose, applying it when the chicks are at their most vulnerable, with their feathers emerging over the neck and shoulder area. Provided that you can deter the adult birds at this stage, there is a chance that the chicks will emerge from the nest with their feathering intact. Assuming this does prove successful, you will still need to treat future chicks in the same way.

When chicks emerge from the nest badly plucked, keep watch on them to ensure that they do not become chilled. The only other solution, aside from fostering, is to remove the chicks as their feathers start to emerge, and complete the rearing process by hand, to prevent feather-plucking occurring.

TUMOURS

These growths are not a common problem in most birds, with the notable exception of budgerigars, where they typically afflict about one in three. Tumours can be divided into two categories – benign (non-cancerous) and malignant. Benign tumours are usually fairly superficial. Pet budgerigars often suffer from fatty lumps of this type, known as lipomas, that appear on or near the breastbone. These can be removed surgically while they are still relatively small, although unfortunately they often recur and, as they become larger, interfere with the bird's ability to fly properly.

Internal tumours of the body organs are harder to detect. Weight loss and a change in cere coloration, in the case of the budgerigar, are typical signs, with the reproductive organs and kidneys being common sites for the growths. There is usually little that can be done.

The cause of such tumours is unclear, although it has been suggested that a virus could be implicated. Up to a third of budgerigars will develop a tumour at some stage in their lives, and although most strike middle-aged or elderly birds, such growths can develop in birds as young as 18 months, and are a common cause of death, especially in pet birds.

One type of tumour which is known to be caused by a virus is a papilloma. This is a particular problem in the larger parrots, especially in macaws and Amazons. Papillomas, with their distinctive wart-like appearance, are most obvious when they occur around the eyes, but they can also develop within the cloaca, which lies inside the vent; in such cases the tumour may have been sexually transmitted.

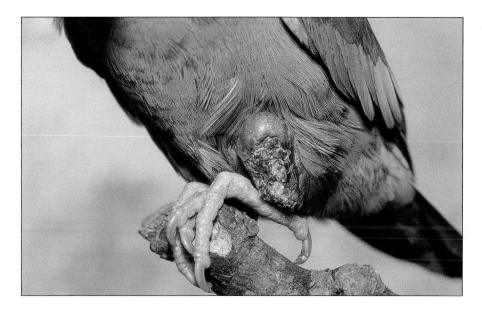

The first obvious indication of this condition, which is known as cloacal papillomatosis, is the emergence of the papilloma through the vent, or possibly unexplained blood loss on the floor of the parrot's quarters. Other symptoms may include constipation and blood-stained droppings, because of the delicate nature of cloacal papillomas, which bleed readily.

The link between papillomas on the head and in the vent is the result of the fact that pairs of parrots engage in vent preening prior to mating, so that the virus spreads between these parts of the body as a result. Surgery to cut out cloacal papillomas is not recommended, because of the risk of severe blood loss, so a technique known as cryosurgery is often used. The bird is anaesthetized and the tumour is frozen and killed with liquid nitrogen, ultimately sloughing off out of the vent. Another approach which has proved successful is for an avian vet to make a vaccine, which is given to the parrot. The vaccine stimulates the bird's immune system enough to kill the tumour.

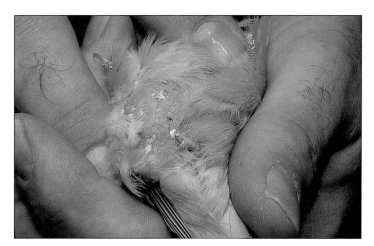

◆ LEFT
A budgerigar with a lipoma. These fatty tumours are quite common, especially in heavier-type pet birds. The tumour has a distinctive yellowish appearance.

THE SHOW SCENE

Details of bird shows can be found in the bird-keeping magazines and club newsletters. These may vary from small-scale local events to regional and national shows. Some cater for one particular type of bird, such as budgerigars, and some have classes for a variety of species. Even if you are not exhibiting, it is worth visiting a show. It will give you an insight into what is required to exhibit birds successfully, as well as enabling you to meet fellow fanciers and to learn more about the birds on view.

Judging standards differ according to the type of bird. As a general rule, condition is important – birds that are moulting will not do well at a show. For those species that have been selectively bred and have a number of colour varieties, such as the budgerigar or zebra finch, there are official judging standards. These specify what constitutes ideal appearance or "type" in exhibitor's parlance – coloration and markings among other things – with points awarded under different headings. The birds in a class are not being judged against each other, but against the ideal established for the variety concerned.

For those species without an official standard, including most finches and softbills, condition is the prime concern. Missing nails, for example, will mean lost points.

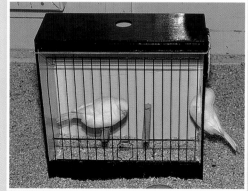

◆ OPPOSITE
Judging canaries at a show. These birds are assessed according to the breed standard, with the judge marking each bird against the ideal, rather than against the other entries in the class.

◆ LEFT
A considerable amount of time and commitment is necessary when it comes to successful showing. The birds must be properly trained for such events, and must be able to settle happily in their cages.

ENTERING A SHOW

✦ LEFT
There is a considerable difference between exhibition and pet-type budgerigars like this one, and you will need to buy show stock at the outset as the basis for an exhibition stud.

Much depends on the type of birds you are intending to exhibit. For those with judging standards, acquire stock from a reputable breeder. You are unlikely to find suitable birds in your local pet store. When setting out to establish an exhibition stud, quality is far more significant than quantity. It is always better to buy two pairs of good-quality birds than ten birds of a more mediocre quality. The cost of acquiring exhibition stock depends on not only the type of bird, but also the breeder's reputation – those who are doing well on the show bench are likely to charge correspondingly more for their birds. Budgerigars and certain canary varieties are among the most expensive, whereas top-quality examples of finches, such as Bengalese (society finches), are relatively inexpensive by way of comparison.

Join the relevant national society. Through this organization you will be able to enter your birds in the widest possible range of classes at a show. You will also receive a variety of publications giving details of the major show events.

Show cages are another essential purchase, especially for those varieties that are judged to specific standards. The idea is that the cages should all be the same so that judges are not distracted by the housing of the exhibit. It is vital to have the right type of show cage for the breed concerned. For instance, budgerigars are all exhibited in cages with white interiors and black exteriors. When several birds are exhibited together in "teams", the basic design is scaled up from that used for a single bird. Budgerigars and canaries are usually exhibited individually, whereas pairs of finches are more commonly shown. A good pair will always win over a single bird, simply because it is harder to stage a pair in top condition.

WHAT TO TAKE
Carrying case for bird cages
Water containers as necessary
Directions to the show venue
Paperwork for the show
Mobile phone in case of breakdown
Camera to photograph the winners
Carrying box in case you buy birds

✦ LEFT
Details of shows are normally advertised in the bird-keeping press. Larger events will typically attract thousands of entries.

✦ OPPOSITE BOTTOM RIGHT
Birds travel better in the dark, and because they are less prone to panic, there is less chance they will damage their plumage.

✦ OPPOSITE BOTTOM LEFT
A carrying box will be useful if you wish to buy any birds at the show.

TRIMMING THE MASK OF A BUDGERIGAR

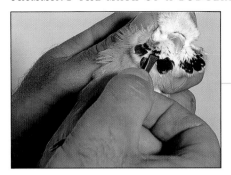

1 Exhibition budgerigars often have overlapping spots on their faces, when in fact there should only be three on each side.

2 Trimming the mask calls for patience and skill: mistakes can ruin the bird's exhibition potential. Work slowly around the bird's face.

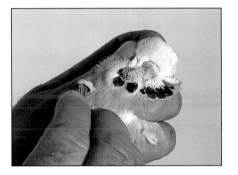

3 A pair of tweezers will allow you to pull out the overlapping feathers one at a time, making it easier to create the symmetrical pattern of spots.

4 Here is the finished result. The loss of the odd feather causes the budgerigar no discomfort. The feathers will regrow in time.

✦ ABOVE
A typical exhibition budgerigar with a trimmed mask. Take care not to damage other feathering when you catch and restrain the bird for the purpose of mask trimming.

No decor is allowed in the show cages, with the notable exception of softbill classes. The aim, in this case, is to devise a natural backdrop which complements the appearance of the bird or birds. Smaller softbills may be shown in pairs. A variety of materials, such as moss, bark and even exotic flowers, may be incorporated and,

although a good backdrop display will not win the class, it can make the difference when two entries are otherwise inseparable.

GOOD PREPARATION
Getting birds ready for a show is an art because they need to be in peak condition for the event. Should they

start to moult or even damage a feather, this will effectively ruin their chances. Regular spraying can help with the conditioning process. Special conditioners may be added to the spray to help develop a healthy gloss on the plumage.

There are no shortcuts to obtaining show success. If a bird is not in top condition, then it will not win, which is often why a winner at one show may end up being unplaced at another.

SHOWING

Having decided to enter a show, the first step is to write to the show secretary for the schedule, which will set out the different classes, and an entry form. Enclose a stamped, self-addressed envelope. Read the schedule very carefully alongside the entry form. If you make a mistake at this stage and enter your birds in the wrong class, they will be disqualified on the day and you will lose your entry fee. Return the completed entry form with payment as soon as possible, to be certain that it arrives before the closing date for entries.

A week prior to the show, check and clean the show cages. They should be in good condition for the show – restore any chipped paintwork, for example – because any damage may spoil your bird's chances of winning if it is up against a bird of equal merit in an immaculate cage.

Assess your bird's condition carefully as the time for the show approaches. Some budgerigars may need their mask trimmed, and you should do this a few days beforehand, taking great care not to damage the plumage when holding the bird.

✦ ABOVE
It is not simply a matter of catching your entries before the event. These Norwich fancy canaries are being trained with a show cage.

✦ BELOW LEFT
Watering of exhibits usually takes place after judging, so the birds cannot wet their plumage.

✦ BELOW RIGHT
Standard show cages mean that the judges are not distracted by the bird housing. The numbers on the cages identify the exhibits.

On the morning of the show, allow yourself plenty of time to reach the venue, particularly if you do not know the area. Remember to allow extra time for parking. Arriving early means that the birds will have time to settle down on the show bench before judging takes place, which is likely to improve their chances; agitated birds rarely look their best.

Stewards work alongside the judge, giving them an excellent opportunity to gain insight into the features which the judges are looking for in competitions.

◆ BELOW
Although official judging standards exist for many birds, other birds, such as this lineolated parakeet, are judged on the basis of their feather condition and steadiness.

Judging is carried out in most cases without an audience. If you want to see what is involved, volunteer to be a show steward. Those birds that are relatively tame and used to human contact will often show to best effect, simply because they will not retreat to the floor of the cage out of fear, when they are inspected by the judge at close quarters.

One of the more unusual aspects of showing birds is that a winning bird at one event may not even be placed at its next show. This is usually due to the bird's condition. So although purchasing other people's winning birds (usually at highly inflated prices) may seem like a good way to instant show success, in fact, consistent winners are those who pay attention

to detail, constantly seeking to improve the type of their birds by careful pairings. Whether or not your birds win, try not to lose sight of the fact that exhibiting is meant to be enjoyable, irrespective of the outcome. There is always the next event to look forward to, and there is every possibility that your birds could win a class there.

◆ RIGHT
Birds bred for their appearance or "type" are housed in plain cages, while many softbills are typically displayed for show purposes in decorated cages. The aim of the decor is to complement the bird's appearance.

SHOW PLANNING

The judging of birds can be a difficult task, and so much depends on the co-operation of the exhibits themselves. If a bird skulks on the floor of its show cage and refuses to co-operate with the judging process, it will be impossible to assess its potential and it will not score highly.

The best exhibitors are those who train their birds properly from an early age, so that the birds are used to being accommodated in show cages, with humans close to them. In the case of young budgerigars, this process may begin when the chicks are still in the nest; handling at this stage means that the birds will be finger-tame by the time they emerge from the nest.

Deciding which of the birds in your collection will be good enough to win at shows in the future can be very difficult. This is particularly true of youngsters, as their full potential may not be apparent until they are older. As a result, many exhibition breeders retain the majority of their young stock until they have moulted out,

✦ ABOVE
Although a trained show budgerigar will move from perch to perch, the use of a judging stick will help the judge gain a better overall impression.

✦ BELOW
Judges are only able to assess the birds for the short time they are put in front of them.

housing them in spacious flights where they can continue their development once independent. Regular training sessions at this stage will allow the birds to become used to their show cages.

Shows often hold classes for young birds, and these will allow you to test the show potential of your chicks, under the neutral eye of a judge. Even so, do not necessarily part with birds which fail to be placed at a handful of shows – it is also important to bear in mind their pedigree. Quality has a way of coming to the fore, and if for example, you have a hen bred from the best birds in your stud, who is not herself a top-ranked show bird, she could still make a contribution to the development of your stud. Champion exhibitors often breed their best birds not necessarily from their best show birds, but from closely-related individuals. Also, it can be especially

✦ RIGHT
A thorough understanding of the desirable characteristics of a particular bird variety are essential for the judge.

✦ BELOW
At larger shows, class winners are judged to find the best of breed, then breed winners are judged to find the best of group. The winners will compete for the best-in-show award.

difficult to acquire good quality hens, compared with cocks; you should always think carefully before disposing of a hen bird.

Once you have a bird which is doing well on the show bench, and is winning regularly, do not be tempted to enter it in as many events as possible. Birds need to rest after a show, and over-showing may adversely affect their breeding performance.

Lists of all shows – local, regional and national – are usually published around the start of the show season in the bird-keeping press, and it is a good idea to plan out well in advance which shows you want to attend, and even which birds you want to enter in particular events. Bear in mind that the birds you select at this stage may not be in top condition by the time of the show however, and that adjustments in your plans prior to some shows will be inevitable.

BREEDING BIRDS

The start of the breeding period is always exciting, as the birds start nesting. Some birds are easier to breed than others, partly because they can be sexed visually at the outset, although there are now reliable scientific methods of determining the gender of birds where both sexes are identical in appearance. It is important to make the necessary preparations for the breeding period well in advance, in terms of ensuring that the birds are paired up properly. It can actually be surprisingly difficult obtaining hen canaries, for example, right at the start of the nesting period, and following a move at this stage, they may also have little or no interest in breeding in strange surroundings.

You need to discover as much as possible about the breeding habits of the birds which you are keeping, to ensure that you offer them suitable nesting facilities. While parrots generally need a nestbox, softbills in particular vary quite widely in their nesting requirements. Some, such as starlings and mynahs, will use a nestbox, whereas others, such as sunbirds, will need suitable material and an environment where they can construct their own nest.

◆ OPPOSITE
The likelihood of successful breeding with finches and softbills, such as this green tanager, will be enhanced if the birds are housed in planted aviaries.

◆ LEFT
It is a rewarding time when chicks have hatched, but it is important not to disturb the adult birds, especially if breeding for the first time, as they may be nervous.

THE BREEDING SEASON

◆ BELOW
The age of sexual maturity differs between the species. These young Gouldian finches will be ready to breed within a year, but larger parrots can take more than five years to mature.

Today, successful breeding of many species has become commonplace, because of advances in incubator technology and the development of commercial hand-rearing diets. Parrots in particular are now being raised on a wider scale than ever before. Nevertheless, there are pitfalls along the path to success, and patience is necessary. It can take at least one year after a move – and perhaps four or five in the case of the larger parrots – for birds to settle down to breed.

At the outset, offer breeding birds a range of nesting options. Many parrots will refuse to breed in the open part of the flight, preferring the

◆ ABOVE
Birds such as this orange-winged Amazon cannot be sexed visually.

seclusion offered by the shelter. Finches and softbills, too, will show individual preferences when it comes to nesting. It may be possible to persuade them to use a nest box or a platform as a support for their nests, but often they prefer to construct their own nest in a bush. This can be risky because the structure might collapse, with eggs or even chicks being lost as a consequence.

Should you be interested in breeding colour varieties, you will need to house your birds in individual pairs, to ensure the parentage of the chicks. Breeding cages can be used for most of the smaller species but you will need a block of aviaries for larger birds, including parrots and parakeets.

Preparing well in advance for the breeding season will give you the greatest likelihood of success. In the case of breeding cages and nest boxes which have been used before, wash these out with a special safe avian

product to kill any parasites, especially red mites. Rinse out the cages and boxes and allow them to dry before reassembling. Inspect nest boxes provided for parrots for any signs of damage, carrying out any repairs as necessary. Check that the ladder in the interior has not become weakened by the birds gnawing at the sides of the box. Should this fall down at a later stage, making it hard to reach the bottom of the nesting cavity, it could result in the loss of eggs or chicks.

NEW BIRD STOCK

In most cases, it will not be until the following year that the birds will have settled down sufficiently in their new aviary to start breeding, but in the case of the more prolific species, such as budgerigars, cockatiels and zebra finches, for example, they will often start nesting quite soon after a move, particularly if this occurs in the early spring.

✦ BELOW
Parrots, including budgerigars, will generally
use a nest box for breeding purposes, or
sometimes a hollow log. They rarely build any
sort of nest within the box.

It can be helpful if the nest box is assembled with screws because you will then be able to replace one of the sides if this has been damaged by the birds' bills. If a hole develops here prior to egg-laying, the extra light entering through the gap may be sufficient to stop the hen from using the box; after egg-laying, there is a risk that eggs or chicks could be lost through the gap. Trying to carry out repairs when the box is occupied may cause the birds to abandon the nest.

A BALANCED DIET

Particular attention also needs to be paid to the birds' diet prior to the breeding season. A good diet can encourage breeding activity, and will help to ensure that the chicks receive the right nutritional balance to meet their growth requirements, and increase their chances of survival.

Soaked seed is valuable for seed-eaters, including parrots, at this time, and will raise the protein level of their diet if they are not fed a complete diet. Softening the seed improves its digestibility for young birds, and if the adults are used to this food, they will continue to eat it and in turn will feed it to their chicks. The same applies in the case of softfoods, such as egg food, which is widely used by canary breeders.

Calcium is of great importance to breeding birds, since it is the key component of eggshells. Because seed is deficient in calcium, seed-eating birds should have access to cuttlefish bone or a calcium block throughout the year. The drain on the hen's body may be too severe if calcium is only available during the breeding period.

Most softbills will obtain adequate calcium through their softfood, but highly insectivorous ones are also at risk of suffering a deficiency, because of the unbalanced calcium : phosphorus ratio in livefoods. A soluble calcium supplement is recommended, as is using a nutritional balancer with the livefood. This is important when there are chicks in the nest, otherwise the chicks could suffer from skeletal weakness, in the form of rickets.

✦ LEFT
Finches often prefer to build their own nests, concealing the site in vegetation. On occasions, however, they may adopt a wicker nesting basket or open-fronted nest box.

SEXING BIRDS

✦ BELOW
In many cases, cock birds are more colourful
than hens, but there are exceptions, as with
Ruppell's parrot, which is an African species.

The first stage in breeding birds successfully is to obtain a male and female. This is straightforward in some cases – budgerigars for example, where there is a clear visual means of separating the sexes. In other cases, however, it can be much more difficult. With finches such as nuns, breeders will often obtain a group of four or six individuals in the hope of ensuring that they have at least one pair.

How to determine the gender of birds when there is no visual distinction between the sexes is a long-standing problem. A popular method from the Victorian era is the pelvic bone test. Pelvic bones can be felt just above the vent and become more widely spaced in hens just prior to the laying period. Unfortunately, while this method is very effective at this stage, it cannot be applied reliably at other times of the year. By the time

the hen is in breeding condition, of course, other behavioural signs are apparent that enable the sexes to be distinguished. Cocks tend to sing more and display to their mates, while hens are likely to be searching for nesting material, and spending longer in their chosen nest site.

During the 1980s, bird-keepers concentrated on attempting to find ways of sexing large birds. This is particularly important in the case of parrots, where two birds may behave as a pair, feeding and preening each other, even though they are of the same sex. Surgical sexing, which entails inserting an instrument called an endoscope through the body wall to view the sex organs directly, was favoured at first. It is still useful, but because of the slight risk involved in using anaesthetic, it has tended to fall out of favour.

DNA sexing is now generally the preferred method, partly because it can be used on birds of any age, allowing chicks to be paired successfully, whereas endoscopic sexing requires the birds to be mature in order to give reliable results. A blood sample can be obtained by plucking a suitable feather, which is then dispatched to the laboratory by courier. There is no need to take the bird to a veterinary surgery for this procedure; it can be done at home.

Unfortunately, it is not just a matter of having a male and a female for breeding success, particularly in the case of the larger parrots. Compatibility is a vital factor. This is why proven pairs are more expensive than sexed pairs. By watching the birds closely, you may be able to see if they are compatible, interacting in a friendly way by perching close together and following each other around the aviary.

Even so, especially in the case of two parrots which have been housed together for a period of time, behaviour patterns can often be misleading. Behaviour is much more significant in the case of a group housed together, where there is a choice of partners available; here, matching up a pair can be a matter of trial and error. Mutual preening, feeding and even attempts at mating do not necessarily signify a true pair. If both birds spend long periods of time in the nest box, but no eggs are actually laid, then the likelihood is that the supposed pair is actually comprised of two cock birds. Conversely, if a relatively large number of eggs are laid, which prove to be infertile, then it is probable that you have two hens.

♦ RIGHT
The gender of many finches is only known from their behaviour. However, distinguishing the gender of the cut-throat is straightforward, as only the cock displays the red throat plumage.

The difficulty of distinguishing pairs in the case of finches is less significant, generally because they can be housed together and allowed to pair off on their own.

As the time for the nesting period approaches, so more obvious behavioural signs – such as the song of the cock bird – will enable you to separate the sexes more easily. If the birds can be caught with minimal disturbance, this is a good time to ring the singing cocks with celluloid rings, so that you will be able to identify them easily throughout the year ahead. However, do not attempt to enter the aviary to catch and ring birds if it is well into the season and there are other birds already breeding, as the disturbance might make them frightened, and you could unwittingly cause them to abandon the nests in their distress.

NESTING FACILITIES

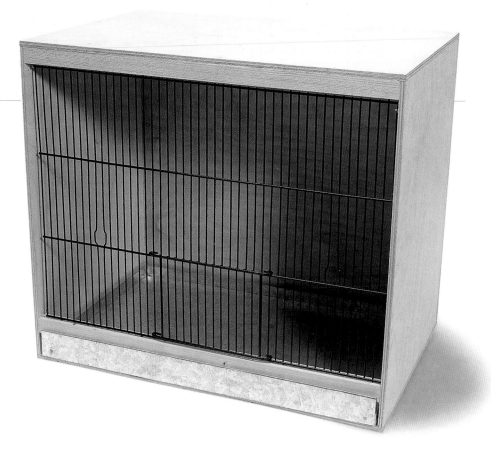

There is nothing to be lost by offering birds the opportunity to nest soon after a move. A choice of suitable nesting sites is obviously essential, and you will need to match these with the birds' individual nesting needs. With many finches, softbills and ground birds, such as quails, adequate cover in the aviary is very important to provide a sense of security. The vegetation may be used for nest-building by various species, but it is preferable to persuade them to adopt artificial nesting sites if possible. This reduces the risk of pigeons and doves losing eggs or chicks by having their rather flimsy nests collapsing under them. Position the sites so that the nests will not become flooded if there is a fierce summer storm.

A wide range of different types of nest are available, not just from pet stores but also from specialist mail-order suppliers, advertising in the bird-keeping magazines. For finches and softbills, open-fronted nest boxes of the appropriate size are useful, with a barrier at the front of the box to prevent the contents from falling out. Other popular alternatives for this group of birds are nesting baskets, of which there are various designs and shapes. These can be attached by means of wire loops, whereas the nest boxes should be screwed in place. It is vital to fix the nesting sites firmly in place, keeping them level as far as possible.

Canary nest pans, which may be used by other related species which build cup-shaped nests, such as serins, should be fixed in place with screws.

◆ ABOVE
A typical box-type breeding cage, with a sliding tray in place. In the case of finches, a wicker nesting basket can be suspended over the upper part of the cage front, whereas for canaries, the nesting pan will need to be screwed on to the back or sides.

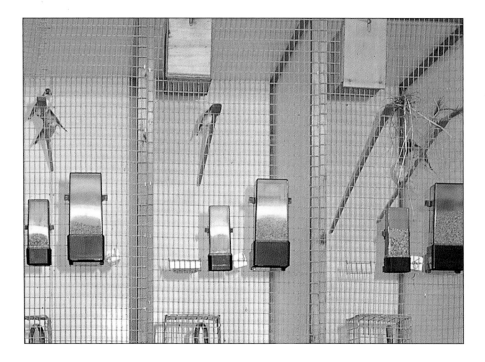

◆ LEFT
A well-designed birdroom housing breeding cages for finches. Accurate record-keeping is very important when breeding birds in this way, with details being recorded on each cage and then transferred to a stock register.

1 Trimming the feathering around the vents of cock and hen canaries is often recommended at the start of the breeding season.

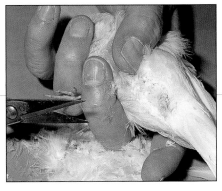

2 This procedure helps to ensure successful mating. However, it is safer to use round-nosed scissors, rather than pointed ones.

✦ ABOVE
A canary nestpan, lined with a layer of felt, holding four dummy eggs. These are used to substitute briefly for real eggs, which ensures that the chicks will be of similar age when they eventually hatch.

✦ ABOVE
Some finches are more likely to nest successfully in breeding cages than others. Most Australian finches are bred in this way, whereas waxbills are more commonly kept in aviaries for breeding purposes.

✦ RIGHT
A typical view of breeding cages stacked in a birdroom. These should be firmly supported on staging, as birds will generally not breed well if housed in cages on the floor.

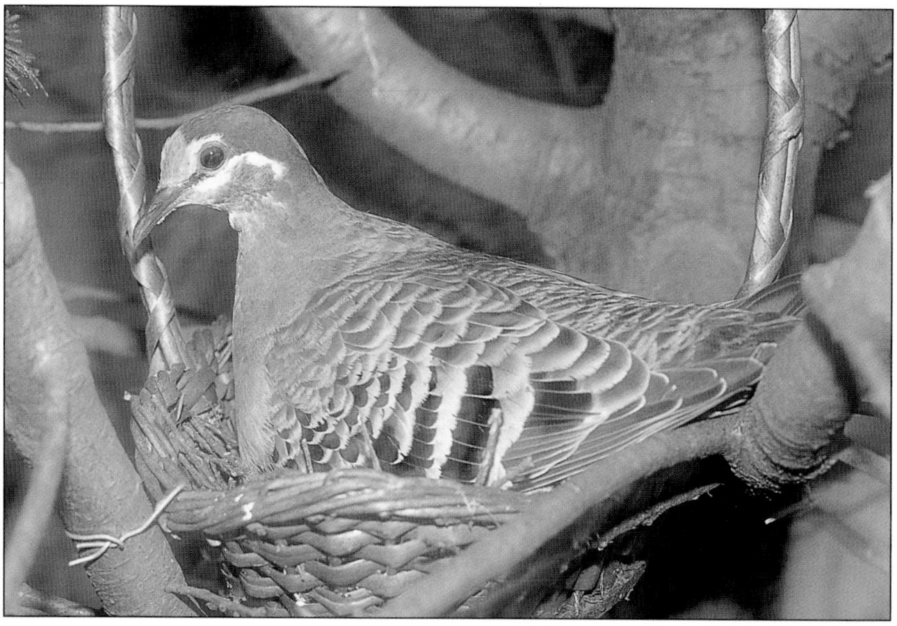

✦ RIGHT
Security is very important for nesting birds. The nest pan in this case is supported by branches in the aviary.

They are also likely to be occupied by smaller doves; their larger relatives should be offered bigger plywood trays as nesting receptacles.

Parrots require nesting boxes. Those produced for budgerigars have a wooden block, hollowed out at one end, known as a concave. The nest boxes are equipped with a sliding inspection hatch at one end, with a sheet of glass behind to ensure that eggs or chicks will not fall out when the box is opened. It is important that the concave fits snugly into the nest box so there is no risk of young chicks accidentally slipping down between the sides of the box and the concave and getting stuck there.

Nest boxes for other parrots tend to be of a significantly taller design, known as the grandfather-clock type. They are heavy, being made of thick ply or timber, partly to withstand the birds' bills; parrots become especially destructive as the time for breeding approaches. This means that the boxes have to be fixed securely, using brackets to distribute the weight. They should be positioned fairly close to the

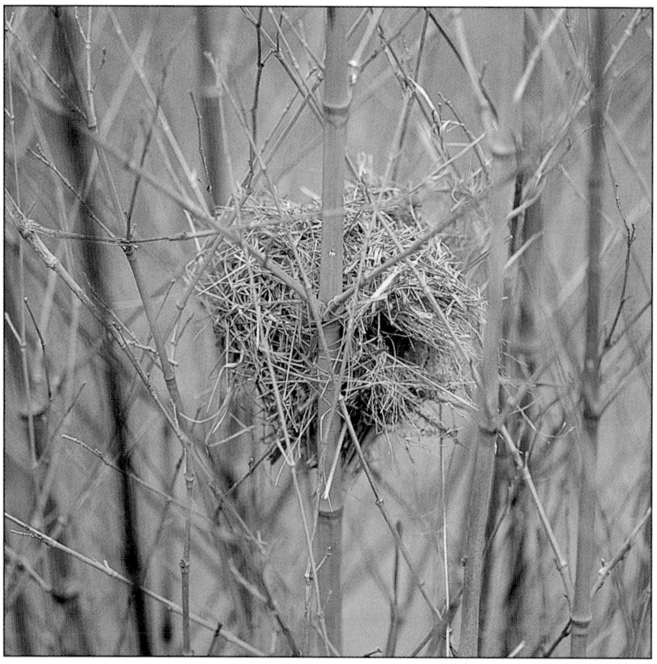

✦ LEFT
Some birds construct free-standing nests in vegetation. Bamboo, seen here, makes a good plant choice for an aviary for this reason.

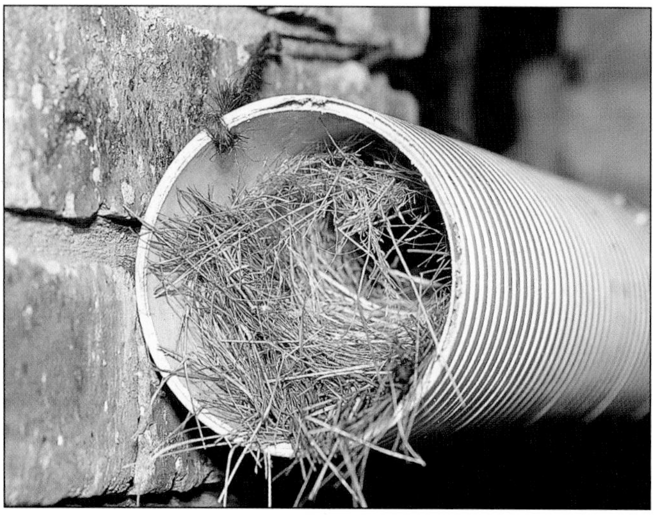

✦ BELOW LEFT
Unconventional perhaps, but birds may value the security provided by plastic tubing when selecting a nesting site in the aviary.

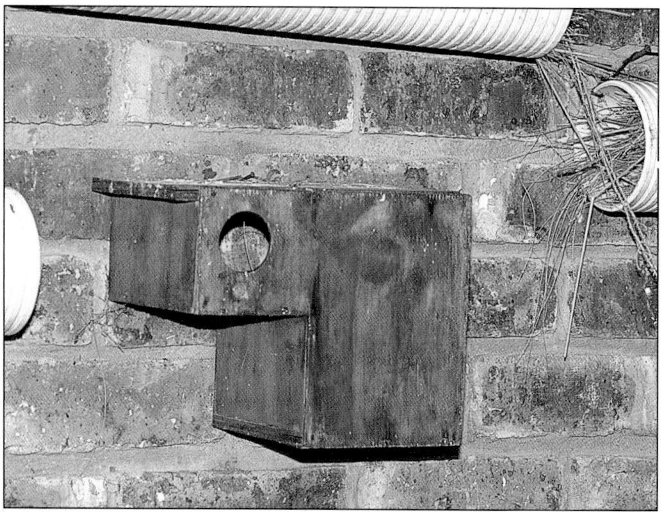

✦ BELOW RIGHT
Offer a variety of nesting sites, based on nesting habits, for the greatest chance of breeding success.

+ BELOW
A support, in the form of a basket-like structure, is recommended for pigeons and doves, which build loose nests that may otherwise collapse, with the loss of eggs and/or chicks.

top of the aviary, but allow enough space for the birds to rest on top of the box, and for you to lift the lid if necessary to reach inside. A sliding side-inspection panel that can be closed securely with a well-oiled bolt may be preferable.

The birds enter the box by means of a perch outside the nest hole with a mesh ladder extending down the inside. The perch must be fixed securely in place so there is no risk of it becoming dislodged, particularly by the gnawing activities of the adult pair,

+ ABOVE
Some birds, such as quails, need good ground cover for nesting purposes, with hens laying in a scrape in the ground, often under a bush.

+ BELOW
Encourage birds to use an accessible part of the aviary for nest-building. These fruit doves have chosen a spot that will make inspection difficult.

◆ LEFT
It is important to provide the birds with a
choice of nesting material for them to construct
an adequate nest. Some will build elaborate
structures, lining the interior with feathers.

the base of the pan. A special powder
to kill mites may be sprinkled on the
undersurface first. Loose nesting
material is used to build the nest
itself – twigs, coconut fibre (available
commercially) and dried moss. This
will also be used by other birds.
Pheasant and quail hens, however,
will simply lay in a hollow scrape
in the ground, often under a bush,
without using any additional nesting
materials whatsoever.

and blocking off the interior of the
box. Line the nest box with coarse
shavings, as sold for animal bedding.
For larger parrots, place short strips
of wooden battening on the floor of
the nest box, which the adult birds
can whittle away to form their own
nest lining.

A variety of materials can be
purchased for other groups of birds.
Canary nest pans are lined with
circular felt, sewn in through holes in

◆ RIGHT
Dense tussocks of grass
can be very useful in
providing a nest site for
birds which prefer to nest
on the ground.

◆ BELOW
Wicker finch nesting
baskets are available in a
variety of designs, and are
equipped with wire hooks
at the back, so they can be
suspended easily around
the aviary under cover.

The position of nesting sites can
be crucial when it comes to achieving
breeding success. While Australian
parakeets will breed in the flight under
cover, many parrots, especially those
of rainforest origins, will prefer to
use a nest box located in the relative
darkness of the shelter, although pairs
can prove to be highly individual in
this respect. It is important that the
nest will not become flooded when
it rains, however, and it should
preferably be positioned in a sheltered
corner of the flight, so that the eggs
and chicks will be protected from cold
winds. This is important in the case
of birds such as ring-necked parakeets,
which are likely to nest at an early
stage in the spring. Conversely, in hot

◆ BELOW
Offering a variety of nesting materials is the
best way of ensuring the birds can make an
adequate nest. Providing an iodine nibble will
help to supplement the hen's diet at this time.

◆ BELOW
Moss is a valuable nesting material, but this
should be purchased from bird suppliers or pet
stores rather than collected from the wild,
which in some countries is illegal.

climates, it is equally advisable to offer
protection from the heat in the form
of planted foliage.

In a colony aviary, try to provide
nesting sites around the aviary, to
avoid territorial disputes. Don't expect
to be kept up to date with progress:
in a planted flight you may not even
be aware of the fact that a pair have
gone to nest until you hear the chicks.

It is not a good idea to probe too
deeply in the vegetation at this time
of year, but simply keep a watch on
the birds from outside the aviary.

Birds are most likely to desert
their nest at the start of the incubation
period if they feel insecure. Do not
disturb them unless you have cause
to suspect that something is wrong.
A sudden fall-off in food consumption
is always a cause for concern, but bear
in mind that in an aviary housing
a number of birds, this may be less
obvious than with a single pair.

◆ ABOVE
Pigeons and doves
share incubation
duties. The cock
birds will occupy the
nest during the day,
with the hen taking
over at night.

◆ RIGHT
Some birds prefer a
deep, natural nesting
site. This Levaillant's
barbet has bored into
an old log to create
its nesting chamber.

SIGNS OF BREEDING ACTIVITY

A number of different signs indicate that breeding activity is likely. Cock birds may become more vocal; cock canaries sing loudly during this period. The cock bird will also be more attentive towards the hen, often chasing her around her quarters and sometimes pausing to try to feed her; this is especially true in the case of parrots. Hens will appear more alert, inspecting possible nesting sites and hunting for suitable nesting material. The pair may become more destructive as well; female budgerigars rip up their sandsheets at this stage, and may become far more territorial than usual. Nest boxes for budgerigars must all be fixed at approximately the same height when they are breeding in a colony together, because otherwise, they are likely to start fighting for possession of the higher boxes. This applies wherever birds of the same species are being housed in a colony.

✦ LEFT
One of the more obvious signs of breeding activity will be increased contact between the members of the pair, with the cock often feeding the hen as a prelude to mating.

✦ BELOW LEFT
Mating will usually occur on a perch, with the hen remaining still while the cock bird hops on to her back. The perches themselves must always be secure, so that the birds can balance without difficulty.

Hens of seed-eating species will nibble more determinedly at the cuttlefish bone in their quarters to raise their calcium intake, which will be vital for the eggshells in due course. Having chosen a nest site, they will spend progressively longer periods of time sitting there, immediately prior to egg-laying. In the case of budgerigars, the increase in the size of the hen's droppings before this event is a warning that the appearance of the eggs is imminent. This is important. Watch the hens carefully at this stage because birds may become egg-bound and require emergency treatment.

In some cases, it is quite easy to tell when the birds are coming into breeding condition because of a

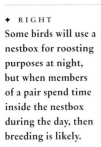

✦ RIGHT
Some birds will use a
nestbox for roosting
purposes at night,
but when members
of a pair spend time
inside the nestbox
during the day, then
breeding is likely.

✦ BELOW RIGHT
Many cock birds, like
this male peafowl,
will provide a display
at the start of the
breeding season.

change in their appearance. In the
case of hen budgerigars for example,
their ceres turn a much darker shade
of brown as the time for egg-laying
approaches. Cock golden song
sparrows develop a black bill as they
come into breeding condition, but the
most spectacular colour change is seen
in the case of many of the weavers and
whydahs originating from Africa.
The plumage of cocks of these species
are transformed at the start of the
breeding period. Male whydahs grow
long tail plumes, which are used in
their display, while their weaver
counterparts are temporarily
transformed from their typical rather
dull, sparrow-like appearance into
stunningly beautiful birds.

Out of all birds, however, the
peacock is best-known for its display,
with its magnificent breeding train
taking several years to develop to its
full extent. At the start of the
breeding period, the peacock uses
his magnificent plumes to attract and
maintain his harem of hens and also to
intimidate other males. In the case of
pheasants and quails as well, males can
become very aggressive towards other,
especially as the time for breeding
approaches, and it essential to ensure

they are kept apart, because they will
seriously injure or possibly even kill
each other. Solid partitions between
flights will stop these birds from
attempting to fight through mesh.
You should also regularly check the

double-wiring in adjacent flights
housing parrots, to ensure that any
cock birds cannot reach the toes of
their neighbours, as they too are likely
to become more aggressive at this
stage of the year.

INCUBATION

Assuming all proceeds normally, the eggs should be laid on a daily or, for parrots, alternate day basis. The hen will not start to incubate them immediately. It is quite usual for two or even three eggs to be laid before she starts to incubate them in earnest. This ensures that the chicks hatch at roughly the same time, improving their chances of survival because there will be no age gap between the chicks in the nest.

Canary breeders have capitalized on this, removing the eggs in sequence as they are laid and replacing them with dummy eggs until the fourth morning, when the final egg of the clutch is due to be laid. When assessing the likely date of hatching, based on the incubation period, bear this in mind; the incubation period for the first eggs laid in a clutch is likely to be extended accordingly.

The number of eggs laid in a clutch varies quite widely, ranging from one or two, in the case of pigeons and doves, through to a dozen or more, in the case of pheasants and quails. There may be greater variability in some species than others – budgerigars lay anything from two to eight or

more eggs in a clutch. In many species, such as canaries, the hen sits alone, but in others, such as the cockatiels and most cockatoos, incubation duties are synchronized betweeen the pair.

The cock birds will sit for much of the day, with the hen taking over in the late afternoon and remaining on the nest through the night, until the following day.

◆ LEFT
A pair of Norwich canaries. Only the hen incubates, but she may not sit tightly on the nest until at least two eggs have been laid. Canaries usually lay four eggs in a clutch.

◆ BELOW LEFT
A pair of citron-crested cockatoos defending their nest box. These and other white cockatoos are unusual amongst parrots in that incubation duties are shared by members of the pair.

◆ BELOW RIGHT
A white-capped pionus parrot hen incubating. Avoid any disturbance: a hen may damage her eggs as she hurriedly tries to leave the box.

HATCHING

Once the chicks hatch, you will hear them calling for food, usually as dusk approaches, and you may also see discarded eggshells on the floor of the birds' quarters, often deposited some distance away from the nest itself. Do not disturb the birds unless you suspect that something is seriously wrong; you may cause the nest and chicks to be abandoned, especially with nervous birds such as pigeons and doves, and many finches.

Adjust the birds' food to include more dietary protein at this stage, to meet the growth requirements of the chicks. So strong is the desire for livefood in the form of small, easily digested invertebrates, such as micro-crickets, that other equally nourishing alternatives may be ignored. Waxbills, for example, are unlikely to rear chicks successfully in the absence of livefood, in contrast to the nuns, which are more amenable to rearing foods such as eggfood. This can be obtained from many pet stores, and can usually be offered to the birds straight from the packet, without having to be mixed with water. Scrupulous hygiene is vital at this stage; the young chicks must not be offered sour food.

◆ LEFT
There can be quite a difference in budgerigar chicks when they hatch, as the eggs are laid on alternate days.

◆ BOTTOM RIGHT
As an alternative to using an artificial incubator, broody domestic poultry hens, especially bantams, are sometimes used to hatch the young of similar birds, such as pheasants.

◆ LEFT
Feeding in a dark nest is difficult, so some chicks have light edges to their bills and luminous mouth markings, which help the adult birds find them.

◆ BELOW LEFT
A hatching pheasant. The chicks of ground birds hatch in a more advanced state of development than those which live and nest in trees.

HATCHING CANARY CHICKS

1 The eggs of all canaries are speckled, and those of the different breeds cannot be distinguished from each other. Patterns are individual to the eggs.

2 When they hatch, canary chicks are totally dependent on the hen. She will brood them to maintain their body temperature, and feeds them on demand.

3 These chicks are begging to be fed. Weak or sickly chicks will not be able to lift their heads in this way, and so they will not be fed by the hen.

4 The wide gape of the chicks ensures that they swallow their food. Food passes to the crop of the neck, and the chicks cease begging when this is full.

The young of ground-dwelling species, such as pheasants, hatch in a more advanced state of development than those of tree-nesting birds, but they are still vulnerable, especially if they become wet at any stage. Rearing foods are vital to their well-being.

One of the best ways of monitoring the progress of chicks in the nest is to note the amount of food being consumed. It may be possible to take a quick glance at parrot chicks in the nest, provided that you do not disturb the sitting bird. If it leaves the nest

when you open the aviary, this will provide the ideal opportunity. Putting fresh food in place will distract the adult birds. Following this routine over a number of weeks will ensure that the birds do not become stressed by your presence.

REARING FOODS

◆ BELOW
Fresh supplies of rearing foods are especially
important for canaries when they have chicks.
There are a number of different brands on the
market for this purpose.

The nutritional requirements of all birds will change at different stages of the year, and especially during the breeding season, when their need for protein rises dramatically. The extra protein is needed to meet the growth requirements of their chicks. Young finches, for example, are likely to have left the nest within just a fortnight of hatching, and the adult birds may have reared five chicks, or even more, during this period. As a result, many finches in the wild become highly insectivorous at this stage, and this is reflected by the behaviour of their aviary counterparts. Members of the waxbill group, in common with most softbills, will only rear their chicks if they are provided with an almost constant supply of livefood at this time. Young crickets are ideal for the purpose, being available in different sizes. They are also far more easily digested than mealworms, which can pass through the body of a young chick unaltered, leaving it at serious risk of starvation.

The use of egg food at this time is also recommended, even prior to when the chicks have hatched, so that the adult birds can gain a taste for it. Eggfood is especially popular with canaries, as well as other finches, and is often eaten by softbills and many parrots, such as cockatiels and Australian parakeets. Budgerigars, too, are likely to benefit if this type of food is provided for them when they have young chicks.

Although some bird breeders still mix up their own softfoods to feed to chicks during the rearing period, it is far more commonplace today for packeted recipes to be used, and many of those on the market provide a good nutritional balance. Whichever brand you choose, however, do not change it suddenly during the rearing period, as this can lead to severe digestive upsets in the young birds. Equally, good hygiene is vitally important – clear up any spilt eggfood after each feed, replacing the containers twice daily and washing them with a detergent before rinsing them off thoroughly, drying and refilling.

PREPARING AND GIVING REARING FOODS

1 Mixing up rearing food for canaries. Some foods of this type are available pre-prepared. If adding water, aim for a smooth consistency.

2 As the time for weaning approaches, breeders will often add in blue maw seed, which is a good way to wean the birds on to solid food.

3 Give additional feeds to a young chick in the nest if you suspect that it may not be acquiring sufficient food from its mother.

RINGING

If you want to ring the birds while they are still in the nest, this needs to be carried out when they are a few days old. Generally, only exhibition stock is close-rung in this way, but there may be legal requirements in some countries for native species to be banded as a means of identifying birds bred in captivity.

Ringing can be carried out quite easily. Group the three longest toes together and slide the ring over these, up to the ball of the foot. Then, with the small toe kept parallel and in contact with the leg behind, it should be possible to slide the ring over the toe and up the leg. Check that the ring can move freely up and down the leg. If the chick is too old when you try to ring it, the band will be too small to fit over the ball of its foot, but avoid disturbing the adult birds in the nest any more than is necessary.

Club members usually obtain their rings from the society to which they belong. Ring manufacturers advertise in bird-keeping publications. Split-type rings can be useful for identification purposes – to mark a cock finch that is singing and would be impossible to pick out later in the year, for example. These split rings clip easily on to the bird's leg.

Celluloid rings are ideal for finches and most smaller softbills; aluminium rings are used for budgerigars; stainless steel is preferred for bigger parrots.

Identification of parrots, by means of micro-chipping, is widespread as a means of deterring thieves. The tiny micro-chip with its unique code is implanted into the bird after fledging, and provides a permanent marker. It is activated when a reader is passed over the bird's body.

RINGING A COCKATIEL CHICK

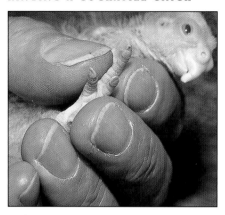

1 It is vital to fit a closed ring before the foot itself is too big for the band to pass over it. Start by grouping the three longest toes together.

2 Next, slide the band over these particular toes, up to the ball of the foot. Note the year of hatching and the individual ring number.

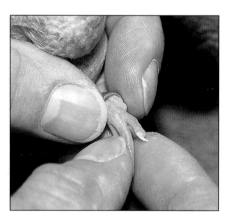

3 Gently slide the ring onwards over the foot, keeping the short back toe parallel with the leg at this stage. Do not rush this procedure.

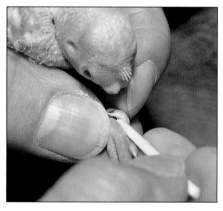

4 The ring needs to be moved over this toe. Use the blunt end of a matchstick to free the toe. The ring should now move freely over the leg.

As another means of identification, some laboratories carrying out DNA sexing will retain a blood sample of a bird, taken for sexing purposes. This then means that in the future, if the bird is stolen and recovered, it will be possible to prove its identity on the basis of a comparison between the stored DNA sample and a fresh sample. While avian thefts have increased significantly over recent years, this approach offers some hope in the battle against crime of this type.

In the case of budgerigars in particular, you should keep a periodic check on the legs of all your birds which are fitted with a closed band, to ensure that the leg is not swelling around the ring. This is potentially very serious, if it is not recognized early on, partly because it becomes very difficult to remove the ring. This task should be carried out by an avian vet using specialist tools, and it may be necessary to anaesthetise the bird. There is no known reason as to why budgerigars are especially susceptible, nor indeed as to why this happens. It is more common in the case of birds which have been rung for some time, rather than those which have recently been fitted with rings.

FLEDGING

The period during which young birds leave the nest can be a dangerous time, especially for doves – they leave prematurely, before they are fully able to fly, and have to be watched to ensure they do not become saturated and chilled in heavy rain.

Parrot chicks are normally more developed when they fledge. The risk to them is more from the power of their own flight; Australian parakeets, in particular, are very wild when they fledge, and they can kill themselves by flying hard and fast directly at the aviary mesh. It helps to have screened this area, to show that there is a barrier. The young birds will soon settle down, when transferred to separate accommodation.

Australian parakeets, especially young cock birds, are also at great risk of being attacked by their father, keen

to nest again, and so seeking to drive away other males. It is therefore a good idea to remove the first-round chicks as soon as possible, once you are certain that they are capable of feeding on their own.

In other cases however, it may be better to leave the birds together with their parents for a longer period, provided that the aviary is big enough to accommodate the family group.

There are a number of dangers facing a bird which has recently left

the nest, even in the confines of an aviary. Young pigeons and doves, in particular, will both fledge before they are able to fly, and if they disappear into undergrowth, they may not be seen by their parents, with the cock bird usually assuming responsibility for attending to their needs at this stage. Young finches, too, are highly vulnerable in wet weather, as their soft plumage can easily become waterlogged, leaving the young birds at risk from hypothermia.

✦ LEFT
Young birds are often duller in terms of their plumage than adults, as in the case of these star finches. It can take anything from a few months to several years for the chicks to attain full coloration.

✦ RIGHT
Young parrot chicks may return to their nest box at night or even during the day, after they have emerged for the first time. Watch for any signs of aggression from the adult pair.

BREEDING PROBLEMS

At each stage in the breeding cycle, problems can arise, some of which will require rapid intervention on your part to save a bird's life.

The first problem that may arise is that the birds may simply show no desire to go to nest. There can be a number of causes, ranging from an incompatible partner to inadequate nesting facilities, so start by reviewing your management of the birds. Try offering other nest sites, in the shelter as well as under cover in the flight. Look at the birds' diet – perhaps a supplement would help to encourage breeding activity. Some birds, even budgerigars, need to be within sight and sound of others of their kind if they are to breed successfully. This can apply to many finches. In the case of bigger parrots, try swapping their partners. The result can be spectacular, with hens going to nest successfully within a few weeks, having failed to make any attempt to nest over previous years.

◆ LEFT
The destructive nature of larger parrots such as cockatoos means that they may destroy their nest box by gnawing at it. Here, the entrance hole has been protected. Check for sharp edges on the metal sheeting, as the birds could cut their tongues or feet badly.

The egg-laying period can create its own problems – notably egg-binding which is a potentially fatal disorder. This occurs when a hen cannot expel the egg from her body and so it forms a blockage, usually in the lower part of the reproductive tract. Chilling, immaturity or old age, and a calcium deficiency are all possible causes of egg-binding. Muscular activity is depressed by the cold, as it is by a deficiency of calcium, while if the egg is abnormally large or has a soft rubbery shell (which can also be a reflection of a lack of calcium), it is more likely to be retained in the body.

The earliest indication of egg-binding is likely to be when the hen

◆ ABOVE AND RIGHT
Feather plucking of chicks in the nest can be a problem, often in the case of the more prolific parrots. Red lories are shown here. The plumage of plucked chicks regrows once they have left the nest.

◆ BELOW
In the case of nervous pairs, or those which
instinctively do not sit tight on their eggs, a
simple heat source in the form of a heat pad
may be required in the nest box.

is seen unexpectedly out of the nest
box, and appears to be unsteady on
her feet. Her condition will rapidly
worsen, and she will lose her ability
to perch, ending up huddled on
the floor. Emergency veterinary
treatment is necessary under these
circumstances, with an injection of
calcium borogluconate frequently
being given to improve muscular
contractions, and force the egg out
of the reproductive tract.

Should this fail, however, more
radical action – possibly surgery – will
be required to remove the obstruction.
Birds start to recover rapidly from
egg-binding, but they should be
prevented from laying again until they
are fully recovered, which may not be
until the next breeding season. In the
meantime, try to discover why the
problem arose, paying particular
attention to the bird's diet.

Although egg-binding is most
likely to strike at the start of a clutch,
any eggs laid beforehand can be
fostered. This also applies if any pairs
abandon their nest, but it is important
that the eggs are placed under pairs
that laid at roughly the same time, to
ensure the chicks will be of a similar
age when they hatch.

With pheasants and quails, which
do not always prove to be good sitters,
it may be necessary to invest in an
incubator in order to hatch the eggs.
Regular turning is essential during the
incubation period, and it will help if
the incubator incorporates a turning
device. Specialist suppliers of such
equipment can be found through the
columns of bird-keeping magazines,
while, in an emergency, a broody
bantam may be borrowed to hatch
pheasant eggs successfully.

Even in a good breeding season,
not all the eggs will hatch. This may
be because they were not fertilized
at the outset; often the hen retreats
immediately into the nest box, and so
mating does not take place. These are
described as clear eggs because it is
possible to see through them when
they are held up in front of a bright
light. Those eggs that contain well-
developed embryos that died late in
the incubation period are opaque, and
live eggs have a delicate network of
blood vessels.

◆ LEFT
Sometimes the nest
location may be in an
inappropriate site, as
here, where it is very
close to the covered
aviary roof. The heat
beneath will be very
fierce, especially in
warmer climates.

Chilling can be a cause of losses of fertile eggs, while problems with humidity, particularly in incubator surroundings, may have this effect as well. The shell is not actually a solid barrier but consists of many thousands of microscopic pores through which water evaporates during the incubation period. This allows an air-space to form at the blunt end of the egg, and enables the chick to start breathing air about 48 hours prior to hatching. If the rate of evaporation is inadequate, however, the chick will effectively drown in the shell. Another cause of death can be if the shell is heavily contaminated; bacteria pass through the pores and overwhelm the chick's immune system.

Most pairs will feed their chicks without problems, with this task being

undertaken by the hen at first. If the chicks call persistently from within the nest, however, and you discover that something is wrong, you may need to take over, which is not something to be undertaken lightly. It will be a time-consuming occupation. Special hand-rearing foods must be mixed for each feed as instructed on the package. Good hygiene is particularly important. The use of a probiotic preparation, if not incorporated into the rearing food, is advisable to increase the chicks' resistance to infection. A teaspoon with bent sides makes a good feeding nozzle. Wipe the chicks' bills after each feed to prevent any food deposits hardening and distorting the growth of the bill.

Keep the chicks warm in a brooder, gradually reducing the temperature as they grow older and start to feather up. Solid food should be introduced to their diet at this stage, gradually replacing their rearing food. Regular weighing is the best way to monitor progress, bearing in mind that chicks lose weight as they near fledging age.

Feather-plucking of chicks in the nest is a problem confined to budgerigars and lutino cockatiels. There is usually no prior warning. One or both adult birds denude their offspring within a few hours, usually just as the feathers over the back and wings have emerged; in all other respects, they remain exemplary parents. There is nothing that can be done and the plumage will be starting to regrow by the time the chicks leave the nest. Unfortunately, this does appear to be an inherited vice, and such birds are best homed as pets, rather than being kept as part of a breeding programme.

✦ ABOVE

The overwhelming desire of the cock bird to breed may lead to displays of aggression, as shown by this red-winged parakeet. It might be necessary to separate the pair for a short period.

HAND-REARING

1 Spoon feeding is usually a safer and easier method of feeding young parrots. The edges of the spoon are bent inwards to funnel the food down towards the chick's mouth.

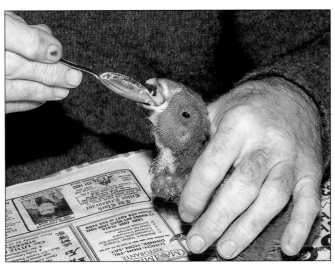

2 It is usually possible to see the crop, located at the base of the neck, filling up in this case. Allow the chick to feed at its own pace, and do not rush this process.

3 It is much harder to control the rate of food output if you are using a syringe of any type for hand-feeding. There is also the possibility of a blockage in the nozzle which could create problems.

4 Once they become used to the routine, most young birds will feed without problems. Difficulties are most likely to re-emerge at the start of the weaning period.

Sudden death of young birds can sometimes occur in the post-fledging period, and it is virtually impossible to establish the cause without an autopsy. This can be very valuable, however, to the extent of saving the lives of other birds and alerting you to a health problem in your stock which may otherwise have gone undetected.

In the case of young Australian parakeets and peach-faced lovebirds, which appear unwell soon after they fledge, or are found dead, it is likely that the problem is intestinal worms. The effects of these parasites, acquired while the chicks were picking around in the droppings of the adults, are far more severe at this early stage in life.

Similarly, young budgerigars, which die soon after fledging, are often the victims of the protozoan disease trichomoniasis, having acquired the parasite responsible while being fed by their parents. Treatment of the adult breeding stock will help to prevent further losses, once the cause of the problem has been ascertained.

COLOUR EXPECTATIONS

◆ BELOW
A light-green dominant pied budgerigar cock,
seen on the left, and a light-green hen. The hen
is out of condition, as shown by her pale, rather
than dark, brown cere.

It is possible to predict the likely outcome of pairings of different colours, based on the laws of genetics. The green budgerigar is dominant over other colours, which means that if a blue is paired with a green, all the offspring will be green but will carry the blue character in their genetic make-up, as shown by the first pairing in the table below. These birds are known as splits (indicated in the tables by the use of an oblique line). When paired together, they should produce a percentage of blue chicks, as shown by the second and third pairings. All such combinations occur randomly, so these are average figures. It is rather like tossing a coin and calling "heads"

or "tails". The results tabled are only a guide but will average out over an increasing number of pairings.

Accurate record-keeping is vital when it comes to colour breeding and managing an exhibition stud. It is

important to have a stock register for such birds, so that you can track their origins and ancestry over a period of time. This will help you to determine which birds should be paired together in the future, and will give you the opportunity to maximise the number of chicks of a particular colour being bred perhaps, or those which are likely to produce youngsters with the best show potential.

The stock register itself will list all the birds which you have in your collection, giving information about their origins, ring numbers, show wins and similar information. It is linked with nest cards on the breeding cages,

◆ BELOW
An opaline olive cock bird, seen on the left, and a young light-green hen. The opaline characteristic is always sex-linked in its mode of inheritance.

COLOUR EXPECTATIONS

- Green x blue >
  100% green/blue

- Green/blue x green/blue >
  50% green/blue + 25% blue +
  25% green

- Green/blue x blue >
  50% green/blue + 50% blue

- Green/blue x green >
  50% green/blue + 50% green

- Blue x blue > 100% blue

SEX-LINKED MUTATIONS

The lutino and cinnamon mutations are sex-linked in their mode of inheritance in budgerigars, as they are in most other birds. The mutation responsible for the change in colour is confined to the sex chromosomes, which determine the individual's gender. This has a direct bearing on the colour expectancy table, because hens have one of their sex chromosomes shorter than the other. This means that, unlike cocks, they cannot be split for a sex-linked mutation. The likely outcomes from the various pairings are therefore:

- Green cock x lutino hen >
  50% green/lutino cocks +
  50% green hens

- Lutino cock x green hen >
  50% green/lutino cocks +
  50% lutino hens

- Green/lutino cock x lutino hen >
  25% green/lutino cocks +
  25% lutino cocks + 25% green hens + 25% lutino hens

- Green/lutino cock x green hen >
  25% green cocks +
  25% green/lutino cocks +
  25% green hens + 25% lutino hens

- Lutino cock x lutino hen >
  50% lutino cocks + 50% lutino hens

It is impossible to distinguish split birds by sight from normal greens, but if you want to breed a sex-linked recessive mutation, it is better to choose a cock bird of this type rather than a hen, to give a realistic chance of producing sex-linked chicks. The other advantage of this particular pairing is that it is possible to sex the chicks while they are still in the nest – all the green offspring will be male.

DOMINANT MUTATIONS

The dominant pied mutation, as seen in the budgerigar, is a typical example of dominant mutations. Having one dominant pied bird in a pair means that a percentage of the offspring are likely to be dominant pied. Visual distinction between single and double factor is not usually possible in this case.

- Double factor pied x green =
  100% single factor pied

- Single factor pied x green =
  50% single factor pied +
  50% green

- Single factor pied x double factor pied =
  50% single factor pied +
  50% double factor pied

- Single factor pied x single factor pied =
  50% single factor pied x
  25% double factor pied x
  25% green

- Double factor pied x double factor pied =
  100% double factor

which gives details about the adult pair; the date the first egg was laid; when it is due to hatch; the number of eggs in the clutch; the number of chicks which hatch and any deaths during the rearing period; their colour and ring numbers; and the date when they fledged.

When a pair have finished breeding, these details can be transferred to a breeding register, which enables you to monitor the breeding progress of particular birds – exhibition hopefuls, for example – and the chicks which are retained in the stud are listed in due course in the stock register. You can purchase registers in printed form, or as computer programmes. Printed nest cards are also available, although alternatively, you can simply write or print these yourself.

✦ RIGHT
A young cobalt dominant pied cock seen with a young light-green hen. Although the barring on the forehead of both birds will recede at the first moult, the pied markings on the cock will remain constant.

THE BIRD GROUPS

WAXBILLS AND RELATED SPECIES

This family of finches is widely distributed across Africa, Asia and Australia. Many species are popular avicultural subjects, to the extent of being fully domesticated in some cases, such as the zebra finch. From a bird-keeping standpoint, they can be broadly divided into three categories. There are the African waxbills, so called because the red colour of their bills resembles sealing wax. The second category consists of the nuns or mannikins, found mainly in Asia and also in parts of north Africa. Their plumage is relatively subdued, comprising various shades of brown, black and cream. Finally, there are the Australian grassfinches, which are widely distributed across that continent.

◆ OPPOSITE

The Gouldian finch is one of the most colourful finches in the world, as well as one of the most commonly-kept in bird-keeping circles.

◆ LEFT

Lively and active by nature, this star finch is a typical example of its group. Such birds show to best effect in aviary surroundings, rather than in cages.

WAXBILLS

These small finches, averaging 10–13 cm (4–5 in) long, have been popular with both novice and experienced bird-keepers for many years. Waxbills make delightful occupants of a planted aviary in mixed- or single-species groups, although housing the birds in flocks of single species provides the greatest chance of breeding success. Blue waxbills are best housed in single pairs, unless the aviary is particularly large, because the cock bird of the dominant pair is likely to bully similarly coloured birds, especially during the breeding season.

BLUE WAXBILLS

There are three different species of blue waxbill, all of which are represented in aviculture. The most colourful, and also the easiest to sex, is the red-cheeked cordon bleu (*Uraeginthus bengalus*), so called because of the distinctive red cheek patches of the cock bird. In common with other members of the group, its underparts are an attractive sky-blue colour, offset against light brown upperparts. Hens are paler in colour, and they also lack the red areas on the sides of the head. A rare colour change has been recorded in some cock birds of this species; they have yellowish-orange rather than red cheek patches. The red-cheeked cordon bleu inhabits northern parts of Africa.

In the blue-capped cordon bleu (*U. cyanocephala*), the blue plumage is more extensive and covers the entire head of the cock bird. Hens show some brown feathering on the top of their heads, with brown present on the centre of the abdomen. This species is found in north-eastern Africa.

The third member of the genus is known as the cordon bleu or the blue-breasted cordon bleu (*U. angolensis*). It has grey plumage on the abdomen, with hens being paler than cocks in colour. The cordon bleu originates from southern parts of Africa.

All three blue waxbills require careful acclimatization before they can be allowed access to an aviary in temperate areas. Do not allow them

BREED BOX	
Length	13 cm (5 in)
Incubation period	12 days
Fledging period	21 days
Clutch size	3–6 eggs

outside until all risk of frost has passed, and preferably when the weather is more settled. Problems are most likely to arise at this stage if the birds cannot find easy access to food, so it is worthwhile confining them beforehand in the aviary shelter, where food and water should be located.

Blue waxbills require a foreign finch seed mixture that contains various millets and other small seeds such as niger. They also feed readily on fresh grass seeds, chickweed and millet sprays. Livefoods such as micro-crickets are vital for the rearing of chicks. The birds seek out insects at this stage and the chicks will be neglected if these are not available.

Heated accommodation is essential for the blue waxbills during the cold, dark winter months, with artificial lighting to increase the length of the feeding period. A large flight cage will serve the purpose, but an indoor flight will provide the birds with more space and can help to keep them fitter.

✦ BELOW
Waxbills such as this attractive pair of red-cheeked cordon bleus require careful management at first, but may then live for a decade or more.

RED-EARED WAXBILLS

✦ BELOW
Red-eared waxbills are hard to sex outside the breeding season. Two birds preening each other does not signify they are a pair, because they are social birds by nature.

The majority of waxbills have more brown feathering in their plumage than the blues, such as the red-eared waxbill (*Estrilda troglodytes*) which occurs in northern Africa, south of the Sahara. Sexing can be difficult outside the breeding season, when the underparts of cock birds become a more colourful shade of pink. The red patches on the sides of the head are

BREED BOX

Length	10 cm (4 in)
Incubation period	12 days
Fledging period	21 days
Clutch size	4–5 eggs

not helpful because of a similar species, the St Helena waxbill (*E. astrild*), which has almost identical facial markings, although the brown barring on its body is more prominent. The most obvious difference is that the red-eared waxbill has a blackish rump, extending over the surface of its tail feathers.

Breeding results are usually better if a group of red-eared waxbills are housed together, so if you make a mistake when picking out pairs, this is not necessarily significant. As the breeding season approaches, the cock bird displays to his intended mate, holding a blade of nesting material in his bill. Pairs usually prefer to construct their own nests, although

they may occasionally use a covered nesting basket. The nest is woven using grass stems, coconut fibre and similar material, and is quite bulky. There is an obvious opening on the top, leading into a chamber that remains empty, with a concealed entrance into another chamber below. The first chamber is referred to as the cock's nest, and is designed to distract any predators, who will find the nest apparently empty.

ORANGE-CHEEKED WAXBILLS

A species with very similar requirements to the red-eared waxbill is the attractive orange-cheeked waxbill (*E. melpoda*). Relatively long, straggly claws help these birds to maintain a grip on thin branches in the wild, where they inhabit reedy areas, but within the confines of the aviary they can be hazardous. It is, therefore, important to clip the claws back

BREED BOX

Length	10 cm (4 in)
Incubation period	12 days
Fledging period	21 days
Clutch size	4–6 eggs

before the start of the breeding season, so that the birds do not become caught up in their quarters.

The broad orange cheek patches enable this species to be identified without difficulty, but recognizing true pairs on the basis of differences in their plumage is very difficult. Hens may have paler coloration overall, but this is not entirely reliable. The display of the cock bird provides the best way of distinguishing between the sexes. He swaggers along the perch, swinging his tail from

side to side, with a piece of nesting material in his bill; he also sings quite loudly. Seclusion is very important for breeding success because these waxbills can be nervous when nesting.

✦ BELOW
The characteristic orange feathering on the cheeks of these waxbills starts to develop from the age of about six weeks.

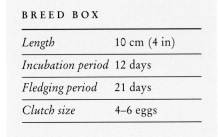

LAVENDER FINCHES

✦ BELOW
Lavender finches often become
quite tame in aviary surroundings.
They are agile birds, clambering up
and down branches like tits.

The lavender finch (*E. caerulescens*) is less colourful than some waxbills but it is still very attractive, with a bluish-grey body, offset against the red of the rump and the tail feathers. Hens can often be difficult to distinguish but may be paler.

Lavender finches generally agree well in groups, but they may show a tendency to pluck each other's feathers if housed in cages. When transferred to a flight or aviary, their plumage soon grows again. Pairs nest reliably in a well-planted aviary, particularly if provided with a box bush (*Buxus*).

A closely related variety, the black-tailed lavender finch (*E. perreini*), is distinguishable by the colour of its tail feathers, which are black in colour, rather than reddish.

✦ LEFT
Black-tailed lavender finches are not often seen in collections. They should be looked after in the same way as the lavender finch. Note the black bill and tail.

BREED BOX

Length	10 cm (4 in)
Incubation period	12 days
Fledging period	19 days
Clutch size	3–5 eggs

FIREFINCHES

Firefinches are so-called because the cock birds are predominantly red. The hens are mainly brown, so sexing is quite straightforward. The red-billed firefinch (*Lagonosticta senegala*) is probably the most widely kept of its group. Firefinches need very careful management at first, and it is essential

that they have heated winter-time accommodation. Pairs breed readily. Arrange the aviary so that the plants are under cover, because this lessens the risk of a nest site being chosen

that may later be flooded. It also helps if the flight itself is enclosed on one side with tongue-and-groove timber, to give these small birds protection against wind and rain.

BREED BOX

Length	10 cm (4 in)
Incubation period	12 days
Fledging period	19 days
Clutch size	3–5 eggs

✦ RIGHT
A cock red-billed firefinch displays its unmistakable colour. Chicks of both sexes are a similar shade of greyish-brown at first.

GOLDEN-BREASTED WAXBILLS

Another colourful waxbill that ranges over much of Africa to the south of the Sahara is the golden-breasted waxbill (*Amandava subflava*). It is the smallest member of the group, averaging about 7.5 cm (3 in) in size. The underparts are orangey-yellow in colour. They have a reddish eye stripe and brownish wings, with barring running down the sides of the body. Hens lack the eye stripe and are a duller shade.

Golden-breasted waxbills are one of the most adaptable members of the genus, to the extent of nesting in finch nesting baskets or boxes in breeding cages. Nesting material should be provided to enable the birds to line their nests. In view of the small size of these waxbills, cage fronts must be of a foreign finch design with suitably narrow bar spacing.

Both adult birds share the task of caring for the chicks, which should start to hatch after an incubation period of approximately 12 days. Small livefoods, including whiteworm and aphids, are vital for rearing the chicks. The young will stay in the nest for up to three weeks, and will continue to return here for a period after they have fledged.

✦ ABOVE RIGHT
This pair of golden-breasted waxbills shows the brighter colours of the cock bird. Note also that only the cock bird has the red eye stripe.

BREED BOX	
Length	7.5 cm (3 in)
Incubation period	12 days
Fledging period	21 days
Clutch size	4–6 eggs

CUT-THROAT FINCHES

The cut-throat finch (*Amadina fasciata*) is one of the largest members of the group at approximately 12.5 cm (5 in) long. This species is instantly recognizable by the bright red patch across the throat of the cock bird.

Cut-throats are not generally recommended as companions for smaller waxbills because they tend to be aggressive, particularly when breeding. They can be housed in groups of the same species, on their own or with other birds of similar size such as Java sparrows.

Breeding is relatively straightforward, particularly as pairs can often be persuaded to use nest boxes, which they will line with nesting material. Do not provide nesting sites while the weather is still cold because hen cut-throats are vulnerable to egg-binding, which can arise as a result of chilling. It is vital to provide cuttlefish bone or a calcium supplement to ensure the eggshells are properly formed. In addition to livefood, cut-throats may also be persuaded to take a proprietary egg food, which should be supplied fresh each day.

BREED BOX	
Length	12.5 cm (5 in)
Incubation period	12 days
Fledging period	21 days
Clutch size	3–5 eggs

✦ LEFT
The characteristic red throat marking that distinguishes the male cut-throat is very dramatic. The depth of the brown colour elsewhere on the body, and the markings themselves, may vary between individuals.

RED AVADAVATS

The red avadavat or tiger finch (*Amandava amandava*) has a wide range across southern Asia, from India to parts of China and Indonesia. It is easy to tell when these birds are coming into breeding condition

BREED BOX

Length	10 cm (4 in)
Incubation period	12 days
Fledging period	19 days
Clutch size	4–6 eggs

✦ LEFT
The cock bird of this pair of red avadavats is more darkly coloured than the hen. These birds construct a large domed nest in vegetation, often quite close to the ground.

because this is when cock birds develop their rich red feathering, offset against dark brown wings. Those originating from the eastern part of the species range are sometimes called strawberry finches, and are recognizable by their brighter red underparts and small white spots on the wings. Hens are duller in colour but pairs are similar in appearance outside the breeding season. These birds may develop black patches of plumage. This is known as acquired melanism. It will disappear when the birds are transferred to more spacious surroundings and are given a more varied diet.

NUNS

These relatives of the waxbills are found in Africa and Asia. They are highly social by nature, and good breeding results are most likely if the birds are kept in flocks comprising a single species. The birds' claws grow quickly, and may need to be clipped back to prevent the birds from becoming caught up in their aviary surroundings.

SILVERBILLS

The silverbill (*Lonchura malabarica*) is one of the most widely distributed species of nun, ranging from northern parts of Africa across Asia as far as the Indian subcontinent. Like other members of this group, silverbills' plumage is predominantly brown; the Asian form is distinguished from its African relative by its black rump. It is impossible to sex these finches visually, but cocks can be recognized by their song. They are very easy birds to cater for, living well in groups. Pairs

BREED BOX

Length	10 cm (4 in)
Incubation period	12 days
Fledging period	21 days
Clutch size	4–8 eggs

nest readily, often using a finch nesting basket or nesting box. Indian silverbills are especially prolific, laying clutches of up to 10 eggs and rearing two broods of chicks in a season. Pairs nest quite successfully in breeding cages, feeding on a mixture of millets

✦ LEFT
Pairs of African silverbills generally nest readily. They are not dependent on livefood for rearing their chicks.

and similar seeds. Egg food is usually taken when there are young in the nest, helping to raise the protein level of the birds' diet.

BENGALESE OR SOCIETY FINCHES

The most widely kept member of this group is a bird that does not occur in the wild. The Bengalese, better known in North America as the society finch (*L. domestica*), is thought to be a fertile hybrid, developed from pairings of the striated munia (*L. striata acuticauda*) in China more than 300 years ago. A number of different colour mutations are established, including chocolate, fawn, pied and crested forms.

Bengalese are popular exhibition birds, usually being shown in matched pairs rather than as individuals. They are highly valued as foster parents in view of their steady natures, and are used to rear Gouldian finches, among others.

Visual sexing is impossible, so the only straightforward means of recognizing pairs is by the song of cock birds. It is

◆ LEFT
The self chocolate variety of the Bengalese or society finch, as seen here, is closest to the ancestral form of this domesticated finch.

◆ RIGHT
This is the fawn mutation of the Bengalese. These birds are called society finches in North America because of their sociable natures.

useful to band birds that you know are cocks. Celluloid rings that clip around the leg are invaluable for this purpose; they can be fitted at any age and are produced in a range of colours so you can distinguish individuals easily. In spite of their small size, Bengalese may live for seven years or more. These finches are highly recommended if you are keen to keep small birds in the home, with pairs often breeding well in suitable cages.

◆ LEFT
This is a chestnut and white Bengalese finch. The markings of these pied birds are variable; pairing two matching individuals is not necessarily a guarantee that their offspring will be similarly marked.

BREED BOX

Length	13 cm (5 in)
Incubation period	12 days
Fledging period	21 days
Clutch size	5–6 eggs

TRI-COLOURED NUNS

The tri-coloured nun (*L. malacca*) ranges eastwards across Asia to the Philippines and Indonesia. It is a popular species, invariably looking very sleek, and agreeing well with other birds as part of a mixed collection. Because of the problem in sexing these birds visually, starting out with a small group offers the best hope of obtaining at least one true pair. The birds' claws often become straggly, and need to be carefully trimmed back prior to releasing them into an outdoor aviary.

Once acclimatized, these birds are relatively hardy, but they still need a sheltered aviary and heated accommodation if the winter is harsh. Good breeding results are most likely to be obtained in a planted flight with stands of bamboo of suitable size helping to provide a secure nesting environment for them. The hens lay between three and five eggs, with incubation lasting 12–13 days. The young fledge when they are about three weeks old. Livefood plays very little part in the diet of these birds when they have chicks, so it is often easier to rear them than waxbills.

BREED BOX

Length	10 cm (4 in)
Incubation period	13 days
Fledging period	20 days
Clutch size	3–5 eggs

✦ ABOVE
The combination of cream, black and chestnut-brown plumage marks out the tri-coloured nun. These finches are reasonably hardy once acclimatized.

MAGPIE MANNIKINS

The magpie mannikin (*L. fringilloides*) is one of the best known of the African mannikins in bird-keeping circles. Its requirements are identical to the tri-coloured nun's. Pairs of magpie mannikins can be aggressive when ready to nest and, in view of

✦ RIGHT
The magpie or pied mannikin is found in Africa rather than Asia. The name comes from the fact that its plumage is predominantly black and white.

their powerful bills, it is better to keep them on their own rather than mix them with waxbills. It is also not a good idea to keep individual mannikins of different species together because they may pair up and produce unwanted hybrid offspring. If they are to be kept in a group on their own, take care that the birds are not overcrowded, as this can greatly reduce the likelihood that they will breed successfully.

Although magpie mannikins are so-called because of their predominantly black

BREED BOX

Length	13 cm (5 in)
Incubation period	12 days
Fledging period	21 days
Clutch size	4–6 eggs

and white plumage, resembling a magpie, young birds of this species are much browner in colour when they first leave the nest. It will take several months for them to moult into adult plumage, after which they will be indistinguishable from their parents, unless they have been ringed. Band the young birds with split rings soon after fledging for this reason.

JAVA SPARROWS

The Java sparrow or rice bird (*Padda oryzivora*) is the largest member of the group, averaging about 15cm (6in) long. The white form has been kept in the Orient for centuries, but other colour forms have been developed over recent years. The most common is an attractive fawn variety, and there are greys and fawn pieds. Cock birds have a very pleasant song.

Java sparrows should be mixed only with companions of similar size such as weavers, or possibly cockatiels, if not being kept in a group or on their own. Often only the dominant pair will breed, but the presence of others of their kind seems to encourage breeding activity.

BREED BOX	
Length	15 cm (6 in)
Incubation period	13 days
Fledging period	27 days
Clutch size	4–6 eggs

♦ ABOVE
The Java sparrow originates from south-eastern Asia. Visual sexing is difficult, although cocks may sometimes be picked out by their larger bills. Their song provides a more reliable indicator of their gender.

AUSTRALIAN GRASSFINCHES

This group of finches includes highly coloured birds such as the Gouldian and parrot finches. A number of species are commonly bred, and they are easy birds to look after, although foster parents may be needed to hatch and rear the chicks. Cage-breeding is practised with Australian grassfinches, which has helped to establish colour varieties: pairings can be controlled to maximize the chance of young of a specific colour.

PARROTFINCHES

The most widely bred species is the blue-faced parrotfinch (*Erythrura trichroa*) from New Guinea. The blue on the sides of the head is less evident in hens.

A commercial foreign finch seed mix, augmented with greenstuff, egg food and

♦ BELOW
This is a true pair of blue-faced parrotfinches, but separating the sexes by sight is very difficult. Young birds moult into adult plumage at about five months old, showing little sign of blue feathering on their heads up to this point.

BREED BOX	
Length	13 cm (5 in)
Incubation period	14 days
Fledging period	23 days
Clutch size	4–5 eggs

small livefoods, is recommended once the chicks have hatched. Soaked seed, especially millet sprays, is valuable at this time as well. Pairs can be nervous and are most likely to nest in a planted flight, where they may rear two rounds of chicks in rapid succession.

GOULDIAN FINCHES

Australia is home to a group of finches that rivals the parrotfinches in colour. The Gouldian finch (*Chloebia gouldiae*) is unusual in that it occurs in three head colours in the wild – red, black and yellow (in reality, more of an orange tone). Hens are paler than cock birds, which develop a reddish tip to the bill as they come into breeding condition. Such is the interest in Gouldian finches that a number of distinctive colour varieties have been created. These can affect the head coloration or the plumage on the breast or the body, and sometimes the entire body. Among the most popular variants are the white-breasted and lilac-breasted forms, along with the blue-backed, although many breeders still regard the natural colours as the most attractive.

In spite of having been bred for many generations, these beautiful finches need to be kept warm, and they must be overwintered in heated accommodation in temperate areas.

Pairs are usually put in cages to breed. Some breeders keep Bengalese as well as Gouldian finches, in case foster parents are needed. Gouldian finches are susceptible to air-sac mites, minute parasites that live in the airways, and these interfere with their breathing, causing wheezing and loss of condition. It is possible to treat cases of air-sac mite with ivermectin, but it is also necessary to break the cycle of transmission. Adult birds pass the mites to their chicks when they feed them; by fostering the eggs before they hatch, there will be no risk of the young Gouldians

being infected, provided that they are subsequently kept away from any older birds that could be carrying the parasites.

Gouldian chicks are very drab compared with adult birds. They acquire their adult plumage from the age of about six weeks onwards, and

✦ ABOVE
The Gouldian finch is often called Lady Gould's finch in North America. It was named by the Victorian explorer John Gould after his wife Elizabeth because of its stunning beauty. This is the black-headed form.

✦ LEFT
The orange- or yellow-headed Gouldian finch is the rarest variety in the wild. It is the dilute form of the red-headed.

BREED BOX	
Length	13 cm (5 in)
Incubation period	14 days
Fledging period	21 days
Clutch size	4–5 eggs

this can be a difficult time for them. It is important not to wean the chicks too early, as this may increase the risk of them suffering from the condition often described as "going light", that is, weight loss across the breastbone. It may be caused by the birds not eating enough to maintain their body weight, or it could be the result of an infection. If you have the misfortune to start losing Gouldian chicks, it is important to have the birds autopsied so that the underlying cause can be identified and the remaining chicks can be treated.

✦ RIGHT
When male Gouldian finches, such as the red-headed one seen here, come into breeding condition, cock birds develop a cherry-red tip to their bills. The variety is genetically recessive to the black-headed form.

STAR FINCHES

Another Australian grassfinch well represented in bird-keeping circles is the star finch (*Neochmia ruficauda*), which is found on the eastern side of the continent. The white markings extending from the head, down the chest and on to the flanks are thought to resemble a star, hence its name. It is sometimes called the red-tailed grassfinch – red coloration is clearly visible on the rump and tail. Red plumage is also present on the head, merging with the bright red colour of the bill.

The hen's head colour is paler than the cock bird's, but this is not an entirely reliable guide because young birds of both sexes are similarly coloured. Pairs may nest in a breeding cage equipped with a nest box or in aviary surroundings, where they prefer to construct their own nest. Expect two or even three rounds of up to four chicks each to be reared in succession.

BREED BOX

Length	10 cm (4 in)
Incubation period	13 days
Fledging period	21 days
Clutch size	4–6 eggs

✦ BELOW
In this pair of star finches, the subdued colour of the hen contrasts with the more brightly coloured cock. These grassfinches will usually rear their young on soft food, so there is no need to provide small invertebrates for them.

MASKED GRASSFINCHES

The masked grassfinch (*Poephila personata*) originates from northern and eastern parts of Australia. The mask is a distinctive shade of black, with the wings and underparts being predominantly brown. White and black areas of plumage are present on the rear of the body. The cock's song is the best way of distinguishing the sexes.

Feeding requirements are basically identical to those of other finches, but they do not necessarily need invertebrates to rear their chicks.

Masked grassfinches are lively and rather nervous by nature; breeding successes are more likely in flights than in cages. It is worthwhile keeping a few pairs of Bengalese so the grassfinches' eggs can be fostered if the nest is abandoned.

◆ LEFT
Visual sexing is virtually impossible for masked grassfinches. These birds prefer a well-planted aviary that provides them with seclusion if danger threatens.

BREED BOX

Length	13 cm (5 in)
Incubation period	13 days
Fledging period	21 days
Clutch size	4–5 eggs

In common with other related Australian species, it is a good idea to provide them with a source of granulated charcoal. The finches use this as a deodorizer, scattering it in the bottom of the nest. No one knows why this strange behaviour has arisen – one theory is that it may deter flies from the nest site.

ZEBRA FINCHES

The most widely kept of the Australian finches is the zebra finch (*P. guttata*), so-called because of the black and white stripes on the sides of the cock bird's body. The hen is duller by comparison, although some have white feathering. The sexes can also be distinguished by the bill – the cock bird's is a brighter red.

The first dark-eyed white mutation appeared in 1921. It can be separated from the chestnut-flanked white (often referred to as the "cfw") because cocks of this latter colour retain the characteristic markings on the sides of their bodies.

Pied zebra finches, i.e. ones that show both white and coloured areas in their

BREED BOX

Length	10 cm (4 in)
Incubation period	12 days
Fledging period	20 days
Clutch size	4–6 eggs

◆ ABOVE
The zebra-like markings of the cock zebra finch can be clearly seen in this individual. Hens are significantly duller in their overall colour.

plumage, are bred in a variety
of colours – the pied mutation has
been combined with other mutations
such as the fawn, where the body
colour is brownish rather than grey.
In terms of solid colours, cream and
silver forms have occurred, while more
localized changes in coloration over
recent years have led to the creation of
varieties such as the orange-breasted
and the black-breasted.

Mutations have not been confined
to changes in colour. A crested form
of the zebra finch can be
linked with any colour.
The crest forms a
circular area of
feathering in

✦ ABOVE
The markings of the cock bird can be clearly
seen in this exhibition pair of chestnut-flanked
white zebra finches.

✦ ABOVE
In the fawn mutation of the zebra finch, it is
easy to distinguish the sexes. The grey plumage
has been replaced by a warmer shade of brown.

Pairs of Zebra finches will usually
settle well in the home, although their
constant cheeping can be a drawback.
Outdoors, the cheeping is not loud
enough to upset neighbours.

Pairs breed well in either aviary or
cage surroundings, using a nest box
or nesting basket. Once the pair have
started to lay, do not provide further
nesting material; they may start to
build over their eggs. Chicks should
start to hatch after approximately
12 days, and fledge when they are
about three weeks old. Adult birds
may lay two or even three clutches
in rapid succession; remove nesting
facilities at this stage to prevent them
from becoming overtaxed.

The young mature from about
three months onwards, but it is not a
good idea to allow them to breed until
they are at least six months of age and
fully mature.

the centre of the head. Rarer than this
is the yellow-beaked variety, with the
legs and feet also being paler in colour.

Zebra finches are easy birds to
maintain. Their basic diet is mixed
millets and canary seed, augmented
with greenstuff and soft food. A
vitamin and mineral supplement,
sprinkled over the moist greenstuff,
helps to compensate for the dietary
deficiency in seed. Zebra finches live
well in groups, and with other finches
of similar size; they can also be housed
with small doves and cockatiels. They
are relatively hardy but they do need
protection from the elements, so
encourage them to roost in the
aviary shelter, particularly when
the weather is bad.

✦ LEFT AND RIGHT
Note the black area
of plumage in the cock
bird of this pair of black-
breasted zebra finches.

WEAVERS AND WHYDAHS

Weavers will often develop amazingly colourful plumage at the onset of the breeding season. Cock whydah birds can be recognized by their magnificent tail plumes, and are known as widow birds because black predominates in their plumage at this time of the year. Whydahs and weavers are frequently polygamous, their plumage serving to attract harems of hens. Cock weaver birds construct the most ornate nests in aviary surroundings, just as they do in the wild, when provided with suitable materials such as dried grass and thin twigs. Whydahs often do not bother to build a nest; the hens seek out particular waxbills' nests and lay their eggs there, taking no part in the rearing of their offspring.

✦ OPPOSITE
The male red bishop undergoes a striking transformation in appearance at the start of the breeding season. For the remainder of the year, his plumage is drab.

✦ ABOVE LEFT
The village weaver is an active, robust bird that is easy to keep and quite hardy, once acclimatized. Cock birds weave ornate nests to attract potential mates.

WEAVERS

The weaver group is so-called because of the way the cock birds construct their ornate nests, weaving them from strands of grass and other foliage materials. Nests are often suspended from bushes, or even from the aviary mesh itself. Weavers make fascinating aviary occupants, although they are not suitable companions for smaller birds, such as waxbills. For successful breeding, house the cocks in the company of several hens rather than in pairs.

RED BISHOPS

◆ LEFT
The cock bird of this pair of orange weavers is in his breeding plumage. Colour feeding at the time of the moult can help to maintain the intensity of the orange feathering, although this is not always necessary.

The red bishop (*Euplectes orix*) is one of the most spectacular members of the weaver group. Cock birds develop a magnificent ruff of brilliant orange plumage around the neck when they come into breeding condition, and this is offset against the black feathering elsewhere on the body. The mantle over the back is of a browner

BREED BOX

Length	15 cm (6 in)
Incubation period	14 days
Fledging period	15 days
Clutch size	2–7 eggs

shade, with orange around the vent. Hens, in comparison, are basically brown in colour, with some darker streaking, especially on the underparts. There are a number of different forms of the red bishop species, which ranges widely across much of northern Africa, to the south of the Sahara.

A planted aviary is recommended for breeding, and will provide the cock with plenty of opportunity to weave its nests. It is important to keep two or three hens with each cock – a single hen is likely to be persecuted by her would-be suitor, and this will make successful breeding unlikely.

VILLAGE WEAVERS

The village weaver (*Ploceus cucullatus*) has very similar requirements to the red bishop. Cocks develop rich yellowish underparts offset against a blackish head when in breeding condition. When out of colour, they resemble hens, but with more black streaking on their bodies. It is advisable to keep cock birds apart because they may fight, especially during the breeding period. Hens lay clutches of up to four eggs, which should hatch after a fortnight. The young leave the nest at two weeks old.

BREED BOX

Length	17.5 cm (7 in)
Incubation period	14 days
Fledging period	15 days
Clutch size	2–4 eggs

◆ LEFT
The male village weaver's strong, conical bill helps these birds to build their nests effectively, acting rather like a sewing needle. The bill can also be used to devastating effect to bully smaller companions.

RED-BILLED WEAVERS

In spite of being one of the commonest birds in the world, successful breedings of the

BREED BOX

Length	13 cm (5 in)
Incubation period	14 days
Fledging period	18 days
Clutch size	2–4 eggs

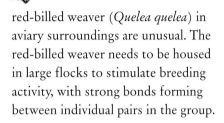

◆ LEFT
The attractive colour of the male weaver's breeding plumage is clearly shown here in contrast with the hen. The male bird's feet, too, are more brightly coloured.

red-billed weaver (*Quelea quelea*) in aviary surroundings are unusual. The red-billed weaver needs to be housed in large flocks to stimulate breeding activity, with strong bonds forming between individual pairs in the group.

When not in breeding condition, the colour of the hen's bill is yellowish rather than red. The cock bird's bill is always red, and his body colouring, from the plumage to the feet, will differentiate him from the hen.

WHYDAHS

The breeding requirements of these birds are specialized, but otherwise they are easy to keep. Cock birds are often advertised with the letters "IFC" after the name, indicating that they are in full colour at this time.

◆ FAR RIGHT
The amazing appearance of the male Fischer's whydah, with its elongated tail plumes, has led to these birds sometimes being known as straw-tailed whydahs.

FISCHER'S WHYDAHS

Fischer's whydah (*Vidua fischeri*), from East Africa, is a typical example of this group. The tail feathers of the cock bird grow to a length of 20 cm (8 in), which is approximately double that of its body. Hen birds usually lay their eggs in the nests of the purple grenadier waxbill (*Uraeginthus ianthinogaster*), a relative of the cordon bleu, or the red-eared waxbill. Some of these birds must therefore be housed with Fischer's whydahs in a large aviary if breeding is to be successful.

BREED BOX

Length	10 cm (4 in)
Incubation period	12 days
Fledging period	21 days
Clutch size	3 eggs

SENEGAL COMBASSOUS

The Senegal combassou or village indigo bird (*V. chalybeata*) uses the nests of the Senegal firefinch for its eggs, but if a cock is housed with several hens in an aviary on their own, the hens may construct their own nests.

BREED BOX

Length	13 cm (5 in)
Incubation period	12 days
Fledging period	14 days
Clutch size	3 eggs

◆ LEFT AND ABOVE
A cock Senegal combassou moults into breeding plumage by shedding its lighter coloured feathers. The resulting dark blue colour is why these whydahs are also known as village indigo birds.

CANARIES AND RELATED FINCHES

Canaries are descended from finches that live on the Canary islands, off the west coast of Africa, and after over 500 years of selective breeding, cage and aviary varieties are far removed from their wild relatives. The characteristic that first attracted people to the canary was the singing ability of the cock birds. This is at its best in the springtime at the start of the breeding period, but the birds sing throughout the year, except during the moult, which occurs after the breeding season in late summer.

✦ OPPOSITE
A pair of green singing finches. These birds are less distinct in colour than their close relation, the canary, and, in spite of their name, they sing less well; they are less popular as pets as a result.

✦ ABOVE LEFT
The Fife fancy is one of the group of type canaries, bred primarily for its appearance rather than its singing prowess. They are available in a wide range of colours.

CANARIES

The canary's early development took place in the Harz Mountain area of Germany. The birds were valued for their song, and young cock birds were trained to mimic the sound of the mountain streams of the region. This tradition is still reflected in the show bird standard. The origins of other varieties, bred for looks and posture, can be traced back to Holland and Belgium. From there, they spread to different localities in Europe and the breeds evolved in isolation. This is reflected in the breed names, which echo the area where they were developed. For instance, an influx of Flemish refugees, fleeing religious persecution in Belgium, led to the development of the Norwich canary in the East Anglia region of England. These chunky birds are still seen in shows in that area.

It is fashion that dictates a breed's rise or fall in popularity. The Scotch fancy was common in Scotland in Victorian times but is now scarce. As a posture breed, the bird's shape had made it popular, but the form had to be adopted at shows, and the difficulty in training the birds became a factor in their decline when tastes moved on.

BREED BOX

Length	10.5–20 cm (4^1/$_4$–8 in)
Incubation period	14 days
Fledging period	14 days
Clutch size	4 eggs

✦ ABOVE
Wild canaries are far less colourful than their domesticated relatives. In fact, they are very rarely kept outside their native islands.

✦ LEFT
The green singing finch (*Serinus mozambicus*), a close relative of the canary, is found over a wide area of mainland Africa, and has an attractive song. It needs similar care in aviary surroundings. Hens can be identified by the black spots across the throat. They have been known to live for 20 years or more.

Among the most popular international breeds today are the Border fancy, which was developed in the Border district between England and Scotland, and its smaller compatriot, the Fife fancy, which was developed as a result of concerns that the Border was becoming too large.

Another newcomer with an established following is the Gloster, a breed created in the 1920s in the English county of Gloucestershire by crossing crested roller and Border fancy canaries. As the result of the lethal factor associated with crested mutations, crested birds are not paired together but with non-crested individuals. The crested form of the Gloster is called the corona, the non-crested form, the consort. These birds are bred in a wide range of colours, including green, blue (which is actually a greyish variant) and white, as well as variegated forms.

Many breeds have changed in appearance down the centuries. The Yorkshire fancy, which was developed in the coal mining communities of northern England, used to be popularly regarded as slim enough to slip through a wedding ring, and early illustrations from the 1850s portray these

◆ ABOVE
The stocky build of the Norwich is the reason these canaries are sometimes called the John Bull of the canary fancy, after the popular figure of English folklore. This particular canary is a buff-feathered hen.

◆ RIGHT
This example of a top Border fancy canary shows the relatively small, rounded head, as well as the rounded back and chest that are characteristic of the breed. The wing tips meet at the base of the back.

◆ LEFT
This curved posture is the typical stance of the Scotch fancy. The way the bird holds its head forward emphasizes the length of its neck. When being exhibited in a show cage, these canaries hop back and forth in a characteristic manner, keeping their wings closed. This movement is called "travelling".

◆ LEFT
This Fife fancy canary shows the typical yellow colour that is closely associated with these birds, although canaries are bred in a wide range of colours. The lack of any dark markings on its body means that it is described as a clear yellow.

◆ RIGHT
The crest of the Gloster corona should be even, and must not obscure the eyes. The neck should be relatively thick. This is a variegated bird, which has both dark and light areas in its plumage.

◆ BELOW
The Gloster consort matches the corona in all respects, apart from its lack of a crest. This particular individual is described as three parts dark because of the extent of the variegation in its plumage.

canaries as being very thin but tall. Today, although the Yorkshire has retained its stature, sometimes being dubbed the "guardsman of the fancy", it has become a heavier breed.

The oldest and undoubtedly the most unusual breed of canary is the lizard. Its origins have been lost, but the earliest published account of canary variants, published in the early 1700s, lists birds with very similar markings. It got its name from the rows of markings running down the sides of its body, which approximate to the scales of a reptile. Lizards may have a clear area of plumage on the head, called a cap. If this is complete, the bird is described as clear-capped, but if it is divided up with darker feathering, it is called broken-capped. Those lizards without caps are known as non-capped.

HYBRID CANARIES
There are those who believe that the lizard is not of pure canary descent, and suggest that it may have been hybridized with a native finch early in its development. They point to the fact that its markings are highly unusual, and cite the development of the red factor canary as evidence that such crosses can be made successfully. This radical change in the canary's colour came about in the 1920s, as a result of a breeding experiment with the aim of creating canaries with pure red feathering. It provided the stimulus for the development of what are often termed "coloured canaries".

The red coloration was introduced as the result of crossings between canaries and a related finch, the black-hooded red siskin (*Carduelis cucullata*), that inhabits the northern part of South America. The resulting hybrids proved fertile, and so it was possible to create a strain of such birds, but they still retain an orange shade to their plumage rather than being pure red, and the distinction between the two feather types that exist in all canaries is clearly evident. Generally, the buff form is described as frosted, compared with the non-frosted (yellow) variety. This is a reflection of the distribution of colour

♦ **RIGHT**
This beautiful clear yellow Yorkshire fancy canary shows the height of these birds. They must adopt an upright stance in the show cage with no tendency to slouch. Yorkshire canaries measure approximately 17 cm (6¹/₂ in) long.

♦ **BELOW**
This is a clear-capped lizard canary. These birds are described as having a silver feather type, corresponding to buff in most other breeds. The yellow-feathered counterpart in the lizard is known as the gold.

FEATHER LUMPS

The characteristic known as feather lumps has become a problem for the Gloster as well as for the Norwich canary. Feather lumps are caused by the repeated pairings of buff-feathered birds – a process called double buffing – in order to increase their overall size. The practice can result in the plumage becoming so soft that feathers cannot emerge properly from their shafts. The feathers will actually grow back under the bird's skin, causing painful and unsightly swellings that do eventually drop off, although recurrences over successive moults are common. The long-term solution to prevent feather lumps is to incorporate birds of yellow, rather than buff, feather type into the breeding programme.

Norwich canaries with lumps can be used to produce mules. The risk of feather lumps makes the Norwich birds unsuitable for breeding with each other, but using them in this way means the characteristic will not be passed on.

♦ **BELOW**
Black-hooded red siskins were used in the development of the red factor canary. They are kept in their own right and require similar care to canaries, but they are scarce in aviculture and strictly protected in the wild. The hen is far less colourful than the cock, but this characteristic is not seen in their canary descendants, for which sexing depends on the cock's song.

pigment within the individual feathers; the lack of pigment around the edges of soft-feathered, frosted birds causes them to appear paler.

Domestic canaries have been crossed with any number of other finches to produce hybrids. When a canary is bred with a European finch, such as a goldfinch, the resulting offspring are described as mules. Mules are valued for their appearance or song, but development of a strain is impossible because they are normally infertile. It is usual practice to pair a hen canary with a cock finch because the canary will prove to be a steadier parent.

The hens originally bred from pairings between canaries and black-hooded red siskins were infertile until the third generation. Today, the fertility of red canaries such as this intensive clear red is normal.

FEEDING

Canaries are straightforward to look after, with few special requirements, although they can be very wasteful in their feeding habits. The main ingredients in their seed mix are red rape and plain canary seed, augmented with other items such as niger, gold of pleasure, hemp and linseed. Greenstuff such as chickweed should be offered regularly, along with egg food, particularly when the birds are breeding. Provide greenstuff regularly in small amounts, rather than only occasionally in large amounts, to avoid any risk of causing diarrhoea.

During the moulting period, a slightly different diet is required, because this is when new feathers will take up colour pigments. Red factor canaries should be offered a diet based mainly on groats and niger, rather than a regular canary seed mix, to reduce the uptake of yellow pigment into their plumage, which will turn it a shade of orange. Egg food should be withheld and a colouring agent administered via the drinking water at this time.

Colour feeding will improve the intensity of the bird's coloration, but it is not permitted for all breeds. Liquid colour agents and soft foods produced for this purpose are available from birdseed suppliers and pet stores. Be sure to follow the manufacturer's instructions exactly – overdosing on liquid colour will spoil the appearance of the bird's plumage until the next moult. This will mean a disastrous showing season, and you may unwittingly put the bird's health at risk.

BREEDING

Pair up canaries in the spring, and provide each pair with a nesting pan lined with felt stitched in at the bottom. Make sure nesting material is available. Move the cock bird to another location after a fortnight; he plays no further part in the breeding process. It is standard practice to remove the eggs as they are laid,

The new colour canary group consists of many different varieties. Colour is the paramount feature. This particular individual is an intensive rose bronze, with the bronze input darkening the bird's plumage.

Mules are popular exhibition subjects. This particular lightly marked goldfinch mule won the overall supreme award out of nearly 10,000 birds of all varieties entered at the British National Exhibition of Cage & Aviary Birds. More mules have presently achieved this honour than either canaries or budgerigars, in spite of their relative scarcity.

replacing them with dummy eggs. On the fourth morning, put back the three eggs laid previously and remove the substitutes. This ensures that the chicks hatch together, approximately 13 days later, increasing their chances of survival. If the chicks are to be close-rung, this should take place at six days old: the circular band can be slid up their legs over the toes.

During the breeding period, even before the chicks have hatched, a regular supply of egg food should be

◆ LEFT
Aviary-bred goldfinches are very popular for breeding mules because of their colourful appearance. They will usually mate readily with hen canaries if they are paired together on their own.

◆ BELOW
The Parisian frill is one of the largest of all canaries, measuring approximately 20 cm (8 in) in length. The distinctive pattern of the feathering is set down in the show standard for the breed.

offered to the hen. Pre-mixed egg foods are a better option than those which need to be mixed with water, because they are of a standard consistency. Provide a fresh supply once or twice daily, in a clean container. Most hens produce two rounds of chicks in succession. Reintroduce the cock bird when the young are roughly 18 days old, and provide a second nesting pan.

Once the chicks start to feed on their own, sprinkle tiny blue maw seed on top of the egg food to help wean them on to seed. Soaked seed is valuable at this stage, being softer than seed straight from a packet, although any prepared in this way must be discarded at the end of the day, particularly in hot weather, before it turns mouldy. Young canaries can usually be removed from the breeding cage when they are three weeks old. They often live for nine years or more, and sometimes for over 15 years. The young birds should be transferred to an indoor flight at first, before being released into an outdoor aviary when the weather is good.

◆ ABOVE
Canaries with frilled plumage are popular in mainland Europe, where there are a number of distinctive varieties. The North Dutch frill is considered to be the ancestor of all today's frilled breeds. Red coloration has been introduced to this breed, creating canaries with a very distinctive appearance. They need to be colour-fed.

151

QUAILS AND PHEASANTS

This group of birds is quite nervous by nature, and so will benefit from being kept in a planted aviary environment. They can also be highly aggressive, with the colourful plumage of cock birds actually serving as a threat to other males of their own kind, which is why they must be kept strictly apart from each other. Screening between adjacent aviaries at eye-level is particularly vital, to prevent the birds from attempting to fight through the double layer of mesh separating them. They are often housed in trios comprising a cock and two hens, rather than in pairs. A single hen may end up being persecuted by her mate, to the extent that the pair have to be separated to safeguard her health.

◆ OPPOSITE

The magnificent display of the cock Indian peafowl is one of the most amazing sights in the natural world. These birds need plenty of space and are surprisingly noisy.

◆ ABOVE

Pheasants will spend much of their time on the ground and need to be housed in planted aviaries, which offer them a good amount of seclusion.

QUAILS

The quail group of birds will live happily on the floor of the aviary. An opening cut at low level, allowing the birds to move easily from the shelter into the flight and back, ensures the quails can seek protection from the elements when necessary, and is therefore very important. Such an opening can be easily fitted in the main door. Quails should be given their food inside the shelter for the extra protection offered; special quail feeders prevent the birds from scattering their food around on the floor. Small seeds, notably assorted millets, should form the basis of their diet, augmented with livefood such as small mealworms and soft food.

Quails are relatively hardy birds but they dislike damp conditions, and it is important that their quarters are well-drained to avoid risk of flooding. A concrete base is not entirely suitable because the birds are likely to suffer calluses on their feet from walking constantly over a hard and potentially abrasive surface. Coarse gravel is a more suitable option; it helps to have an area of grass in the flight as well, where the birds can scratch around, and to incorporate plants for cover. These conditions encourage successful breeding, although it is often the case that quails ignore their eggs, which must then be transferred to an incubator for hatching.

CHINESE PAINTED QUAILS

The Chinese painted quail (*Coturnix chinensis*), often referred to as CPQ, is the most widely kept species of quail. These birds measure just 13 cm (5 in) in length and will not disturb other birds, even small finches, when sharing their quarters. They show far less tendency to fly than others of the species, and do not seek to perch off the ground. In spite of their small size, male Chinese painted quails can be very aggressive. It is advisable to keep them in small groups rather than in pairs, running a cock with at least two and up to four hens. A single hen will be persecuted by her intended mate,

BREED BOX	
Length	13 cm (5 in)
Incubation period	18 days
Fledging period	not applicable
Clutch size	7–10 eggs

particularly at the onset of the breeding season, and will probably be severely feather-plucked.

The chicks are tiny, not much bigger than bumble bees, and are able to run around almost immediately after hatching. Egg food and blue maw seed is the rearing food, along with soaked millet sprays.

Several colour forms of the Chinese painted quail have been established; the most commonly kept is the silver variant – birds of both sexes have a distinctly silvery tone to their plumage but they can still be sexed easily.

◆ LEFT
In this pair of Chinese painted quails, the cock can be distinguished by its blue and reddish-chestnut coloration, while the hen is brownish.

JAPANESE QUAILS

The Japanese quail (*Coturnix coturnix*) is slightly larger in size than the Chinese painted, but similar in its requirements. These quails have been bred in a range of different strains as domestication has occurred.

BREED BOX	
Length	17.5 cm (7 in)
Incubation period	18 days
Fledging period	not applicable
Clutch size	12 eggs

✦ ABOVE
Like other quails, hatching eggs in incubators over many generations has adversely affected the parenting instincts of Japanese quail, to the extent that they may be reluctant to incubate their own eggs.

BOBWHITE QUAILS

The bobwhite quail (*Colinus virginanus*) from North America is an attractive species, measuring about 23 cm (9 in) in length. It is important to remember that these quails are rather nervous birds and their aviary must be designed accordingly to ensure their safety. If alarmed, they will fly up almost vertically, which means that not only may they badly injure their heads on the roof of their quarters, but they can also cause other aviary birds above them to panic, with potentially fatal consequences.

BREED BOX	
Length	23 cm (9 in)
Incubation period	21 days
Fledging period	not applicable
Clutch size	12–20 eggs

✦ ABOVE
The male bobwhite quail shown here has brighter markings than the hen, with more whitish areas on the head.

ORNAMENTAL PHEASANTS

These magnificent birds look truly spectacular when housed in spacious aviary surroundings, but bear in mind that cocks are particularly aggressive and should not be housed together. In fact, it is not a good idea to keep pheasants of the same species in adjacent flights because the cock birds will try to reach each other through the mesh. Double-wiring on both sides of the aviary framework will help to prevent direct physical contact. It would also be worthwhile to build up the base of the aviary, so that there is a solid barrier extending up the sides. This will discourage aggression by ensuring that the birds cannot see their neighbours.

LADY AMHERST'S PHEASANTS

Among the most widely kept species of pheasant is Lady Amherst's (*Chrysolophus amherstiae*), which is known to originate from China, Tibet and Myanmar (formerly Burma). The cock bird is particularly striking in appearance, thanks to its red, metallic green, blue, white and barred feathering; the hen is duller in coloration. Like most other pheasant species, these birds are polygamous so, when breeding, a cock bird should be kept in the company of two or three hens in a well-planted flight which allows the females sufficient shelter and space to incubate their eggs. Each clutch comprises 10 or more eggs. Should a hen refuse to sit, the eggs can be transferred under a broody bantam, which will usually hatch the eggs satisfactorily without any problems.

BREED BOX	
Length	173 cm (68 in)
Incubation period	23 days
Fledging period	not applicable
Clutch size	10–12 eggs

✦ BELOW
The beautiful Lady Amherst's pheasant is named after the wife of a British ambassador. When displaying, the cock bird spreads his collar to emphasize the colour of his mantle.

GOLDEN PHEASANTS

The golden pheasant (*Chrysolophus pictus*) is perhaps even more spectacular in appearance than Lady Amherst's. Shades of gold, orange and chestnut-red, along with browns and metallic green areas, dominate in the case of mature cock birds of this species. They are smaller than Lady Amherst's, with cock birds averaging up to about 112 cm (44 in) in length. Hens are mainly brown in colour. Young male golden pheasants resemble hens, and it is likely to take two years for cock birds to develop their breeding finery.

The incubation period lasts for about 23 days, with hens laying in a scrape on the ground. Once the chicks have hatched, smaller seeds such as

◆ RIGHT
The golden pheasant is one of the most widely kept of all pheasants. Breeding may be best accomplished by introducing the cock to the quarters of the hens and removing him once egg-laying begins, to minimize the risk of aggression.

millets should be provided, along with starter crumbs and some livefood. Feeding the adult birds is completely straightforward; a pheasant seed mix is ideal and they will also eat greenstuff and invertebrates.

A variety of colour mutations includes Gighi's yellow golden pheasant, named in part after the Italian professor who helped to establish it. It is, in effect, a dilute mutation with the overall intensity of the colour being reduced.

Dark-throated and salmon varieties have also been developed but are not very widely kept.

BREED BOX

Length	112 cm (44 in)
Incubation period	23 days
Fledging period	not applicable
Clutch size	10–12 eggs

HIMALAYAN MONALS

In terms of iridescence, few birds have more striking plumage than the cock Himalayan monal (*Lophophorus impeyanus*). Bronze, blue, green and gold are just some of the colours that are apparent. Hens are very easy to identify by their streaked brownish coloration, with a white area of feathering under the throat. Originating from reasonably high altitudes, Himalayan monals are used

◆ RIGHT
This pair of Himalayan monals demonstrates that, as with most pheasants, these birds can be sexed easily, although it is often possible to confuse young birds of both sexes with the adult hens.

BREED BOX

Length	71 cm (28 in)
Incubation period	27 days
Fledging period	not applicable
Clutch size	5–6 eggs

to cold weather but dislike prolonged damp, dank conditions. A large, densely planted enclosure reduces the risk of a serious attack on the hen by her intended mate, while also giving her greater security in which to raise her offspring.

The clutches are rarely of more than six eggs and, as a result, breeders often remove the first clutch soon

after laying, with the aim of encouraging the hen to lay again soon afterwards. Incubation takes around 27 days and the young are able to walk almost immediately after hatching. In the case of birds in immature plumage, look for traces of black feathering on the throat; this indicates a young cock. It takes two years for these birds to acquire full adult plumage.

SATYR TRAGOPANS

The satyr tragopan (*Tragopan satyra*) is another member of the pheasant family originating from the Himalayan region. White spots encircled in black are a feature of these birds. Their tails are quite short. Cock birds are larger than hens, measuring about 71 cm (28 in) on average, with more colourful skin around their eyes.

✦ LEFT
The cock satyr tragopan has lappets, or inflatable wattles, around the throat which are filled with air as part of his display. They can reach a length of up to 15 cm (6 in).

BREED BOX

Length	71 cm (28 in)
Incubation period	28 days
Fledging period	not applicable
Clutch size	5–6 eggs

A major difference between tragopans and the other pheasants is that they are much stronger fliers, and this needs to be reflected in the design of their quarters, with a good choice of perches being provided. A nesting platform in a secluded part of the aviary must also be provided, as hens lay off the ground. It is advisable to keep a cock with two or three hens to avoid the risk of one on its own being persecuted. They lay six eggs in a clutch, and these should hatch after an interval of around 28 days. A diet as offered to other pheasants suits them well, but tragopans will also eat fruit and berries readily. They are vulnerable to frostbite like many pheasants and should be encouraged to roost under cover.

INDIAN BLUE PEAFOWL

One of the best-known members of the pheasant family, the Indian Blue Peafowl (*Pavo cristatus*) is polygamous by nature. This means that a cock bird has a harem of several hens, which are much smaller in size, averaging 90 cm (3 ft) in length. As the size of these birds precludes them from being kept in all but the largest aviary, they are usually allowed to roam at liberty in a secure garden during the daytime. Often, they are

BREED BOX

Length	2.34 m (92 in)
Incubation period	28 days
Fledging period	not applicable
Clutch size	4–8 eggs

✦ LEFT
The long train of a mature peacock is comprised of up to 150 feathers, with those in the centre of the train being the longest. The spots evident when the plumes are fanned out for display purposes are known as "eyes" or "ocelli".

then shut in a large outbuilding with perches at night, where they will be safe from foxes and other predators. Feeding is very straightforward, with grains helping to augment foods which the birds gather while foraging. The peahen will usually make dense undergrowth her choice of nesting site. The young develop slowly and it will be three years before cocks even start to develop their magnificent train of plumes. There is a white form of the Indian peafowl, as well as pied birds, but these do not match the beauty of the natural form.

Javanese Green Peafowl

✦ BELOW
The striking head coloration of the Javanese green peafowl helps to distinguish these birds. They can be susceptible to enteric parasites, causing a disease known as blackhead.

The Javanese green peafowl (*Pavo muticus*) originates from south-east Asia, ranging from Thailand over the Malay peninsula down to Java. It is less commonly seen than the Indian blue peafowl (*Pavo cristatus*), and is distinguished by having blue and yellow areas on the head, and green rather than blue feathering on the neck. Cocks can sometimes prove aggressive towards people in defence of their hens, and must be approached carefully because they have sharp spurs on their legs which can easily inflict cuts and scratches.

Clipping the wings of cock birds may restrict their domain, but they can still jump more than 1.8 m (6 ft). These birds are really only suitable for owners with large gardens. A typical clutch comprises six eggs, which hatch after 28 days. The young develop slowly and may be brooded until they are at least eight weeks old.

BREED BOX

Size	100 cm (39 in)
Incubation period	28 days
Fledging period	not applicable
Clutch size	6 eggs

Red Junglefowl

The red junglefowl (*Gallus gallus*), which is widely distributed across southern parts of Asia, is in fact the main ancestor of today's domestic poultry breeds. These birds need similar care to peafowl, but junglefowl are much stronger fliers, which must be borne in mind if they are allowed out to roam in a garden. Cockerels must be kept apart because they can be exceptionally aggressive. They are also very noisy, and close neighbours will not relish the crowing of one or more of these birds at the crack of dawn each day. Red junglefowl are polygamous by nature. If hens refuse to incubate their own eggs, a broody bantam can normally be relied upon to undertake this task. Hatching typically takes between 18 and 21 days.

BREED BOX

Size	60 cm (24 in)
Incubation period	20 days
Fledging period	not applicable
Clutch size	6 eggs

✦ RIGHT
Junglefowl originate from wooded areas, as their name suggests, and they are less nervous when housed in planted flights which provide them with cover. This should encourage hens to incubate their own eggs.

SOFTBILLS

The name of this large and diverse group of birds derives not from the texture of their bills – which are not soft and may inflict a painful bite if the bird manages to grab hold of a finger – but from their nutritional needs, in that hard seed does not feature in their diet. Softbills are fed on softbill mix, as well as on fruit, invertebrates and, in some cases, nectar. The housing needs of softbills can vary widely, but the size of the birds gives a valuable insight into their relative hardiness. Smaller individuals, such as sugarbirds, are not sufficiently hardy to live outdoors throughout the year in temperate areas, and will require additional heating and lighting through the winter period. Softbills can be kept as part of a mixed collection, but they may not always agree amongst themselves; much will depend on the species concerned.

✦ OPPOSITE
Levaillant's barbet is an attractive African bird easily maintained on a diet of fruit, insects and softbill food. Like most softbills, these are aviary rather than pet birds.

✦ ABOVE LEFT
Touracos are unusual softbills in that they feed to a large extent on plant matter. Caring for softbills takes more time than finches because of their dietary needs.

SMALL SOFTBILLS

Softbills are a very diverse group of birds. They are distinguished in terms of their dietary needs rather than their zoology – their bills are not actually soft – and there are three recognized sub-divisions, based on the dietary requirements of the different species. There are the nectivores, which rely mainly on nectar to meet their nutritional needs; the frugivores, feeding largely on fruit; and the insectivores, which eat mainly invertebrates. These categories serve only as a general indication of feeding requirements; all softbills require a wide variety of foodstuffs in order to remain in good health and to breed successfully.

The size of these birds is significant in terms of their care. The smaller softbills are less hardy than larger members of this group and will always require heated winter accommodation in temperate areas. Additional lighting, to extend the feeding period to twelve hours, will be important in latitudes where shortened daylight hours occur throughout the winter.

A planted aviary is recommended, and they must have a water container or small pool for bathing purposes, as well as separate water for drinking. Good hygiene is vital for nectivores in particular; sour nectar can rapidly cause serious intestinal upsets. Dirty drinkers are likely to give rise to the fungal infection known as candidiasis. An affected individual will often hold its bill ajar, and a cheesy growth within, a characteristic of the infection, is evident on closer inspection. Treatments include using a specific anti-fungal preparation, but beware because an outbreak can spread rapidly from drinkers.

SUNBIRDS

The requirements of hummingbirds may be too specialized for most bird-keepers, although some dedicated fanciers do keep and breed them successfully, but there are a number of other attractive nectivores that are more straightforward to care for. The sunbirds, for example, are often considered to be the Old World hummingbirds' equivalents. They share a number of characteristics, including iridescence on their plumage in many cases, and long, narrow, pointed bills to probe into flowers for nectar. However, sunbirds cannot feed in flight while hovering, but must perch for this purpose. Sunbirds found in Asia have a reputation for being difficult to keep because they are more insectivorous in their feeding habits than some of their African relatives.

In most cases, sexing is relatively straightforward because cocks are usually more brightly coloured than hens. The difficulty stems from identifying the species or age of hens

✦ RIGHT
In breeding plumage, the cock malachite sunbird is a magnificent dark green, whereas the hen is olive-brown above with yellowish grey underparts. Out of colour, the cock can still be recognized by his two elongated central tail feathers.

correctly; in most cases they are all very similar. It helps to refer to a specialist field guide with coloured photographs showing the prime distinguishing features of species.

BREED BOX	
Length	15 cm (6 in)
Incubation period	14 days
Fledging period	14 days
Clutch size	1 egg

MALACHITE SUNBIRDS
The malachite sunbird (*Nectarinia famosa*) is one of the most distinctive African species, with the long tail feathers of the cock bird accounting for about half its total length of 15 cm (6 in). Like others of their type, these sunbirds feed on a diet of nectar, and small insects such as young crickets; sometimes the birds will take a fine-grade insectivorous food and sponge cake soaked in nectar.

In aviary surroundings, the hen will build a large, suspended nest, often in a clump of bamboo, using a range of materials, including spiders' webs and moss. A single egg will be laid inside the nest. Young fledgling sunbirds are similar in size to their parents but they do have noticeably shorter bills.

PURPLE SUGARBIRDS

✦ BELOW

Purple sugarbirds are relatively straightforward to look after and, compared with sunbirds, are easy to breed as well. They are keen bathers, like most small nectivores.

The purple sugarbird (*Cyanerpes caeruleus*) originates from northern parts of South America. It feeds mainly on nectar, although diced fruit and a fine-grade softbill food should also be provided daily, along with livefood such as crickets. Sexing is very easy – males are purple in colour whereas hens are mainly green. Young birds resemble hens, but odd purple feathers on the head enable young cocks to be identified before they have fully moulted. Pairs may build a nest within a nesting basket or small nest box. There is a similar species called the red-legged sugarbird (*Cyanerpes cyaneus*), the cocks of which only gain their purplish plumage for the duration of the breeding season.

BREED BOX

Length	10 cm (4 in)
Incubation period	12 days
Fledging period	14 days
Clutch size	2 eggs

BLUE DACNIS

The blue dacnis (*Dacnis cayana*) is found over a wide area of Central and South America. It has similar habits to the purple sugarbird, although its bill is shorter. Cocks are an attractive combination of blue and black, while hens are green. As in the case of other small softbills, these birds are not hardy and they will require protection from the elements.

BREED BOX

Length	13 cm (5 in)
Incubation period	12 days
Fledging period	14 days
Clutch size	2 eggs

✦ BELOW

In this pair of blue dacnis, the cock bird is on the right. Pairs can be housed with other non-aggressive birds of similar size. However, in a relatively small enclosure, they should be kept apart from others of their kind because cocks may fight viciously.

TANAGERS

Tanagers are widely distributed in the Americas and are closely allied to the honeycreepers, although fruit rather than nectar is the mainstay of their diet. They are relatively easy to keep, eating a wide range of fruit and berries, and are quite able to use their stout bills to nibble chunks out of an apple rather than requiring it to be cut up into tiny pieces for them. Sprinkle a low-iron soft food over their fruit, which should be provided fresh each day along with a few invertebrates such as waxworms or mealworms.

Breeding is possible, particularly in a densely planted flight, but unfortunately, it is very difficult to sex tanagers visually. Cocks often have bolder heads than hens, but minor variations in appearance between individuals are likely to be due to them originating from different parts of their range.

Euphonias, such as the orange-crowned euphonia (*E. saturata*), are an offshoot of the main tanager group

◆ RIGHT
Euphonias are small, stocky birds about 10 cm (4 in) long, and they have a pleasant song. This is a cock orange-crowned euphonia, from north-western South America.

BREED BOX

Length	10–20 cm (4–8 in)
Incubation period	15 days
Fledging period	19 days
Clutch size	2–5 eggs

and they can usually be sexed more easily. The cock is an attractive shade of violet, offset against rich yellow on the crown and underparts. Hens in comparison are predominantly greenish; an olive shade above and yellower on the underparts. They typically lay clutches of up to five eggs, and these should hatch after an incubation period of about 15 days. Livefood is important for rearing purposes, with the young fledgling feeding on its own at three weeks old.

◆ ABOVE
Tanagers from high altitudes, such as the mountain species, are relatively hardy, but the smaller *Tangara* species such as the emerald spotted (*T. guttata*) require heat during the winter months.

ZOSTEROPS

◆ BELOW
Zosterops are lively, social birds that can be kept in small groups or in the company of birds of similar size. The chestnut-flanked variety (*Z. erythropleura*) is often available.

The zosterops or white-eye (*Zosterops palpebrosa*) is one of a number of small softbills of Asiatic origin popular among bird-keepers. These birds need a constant supply of nectar as well as diced fruit, softbill food and small invertebrates. Like most nectivores, white-eyes are keen bathers and it is important that their liquid food is provided in a sealed container rather than an open pot; otherwise, the birds are likely to attempt to bathe in it and their plumage will inevitably become sticky as a result.

As the time for breeding approaches, cock birds start to sing and hens search for spiders' webs and other materials with which to construct their nests. The incubation and rearing periods last for about 12 days each and pairs may rear two clutches of chicks in rapid succession. Small livefoods such as crickets are necessary for the growth of the chicks. Zosterops must have snug winter-time accommodation, indoors out of the cold.

BREED BOX

Length	10 cm (4 in)
Incubation period	12 days
Fledging period	12 days
Clutch size	2–4 eggs

RED-HEADED TITS

Red-headed tits (*Aegithalos concinnus*) are another group of very active small softbills. They thrive on a varied diet but are insectivorous, so small crickets and fine-grade softbill food should feature prominently in their diet. Their small size and natural curiosity mean that they must have a fine covering of mesh over their flight, with no gaps, to prevent the possibility of escape. A planted flight suits them well, but these tits are not hardy and should be housed in warm surroundings during the winter time.

For breeding purposes, provide a small nest box or covered basket along with nesting material, sited in a well-planted area of the aviary. Pairs can be quite prolific. Hens lay up to six eggs in a clutch and they should hatch after a period of 14 days. Small livefoods such as aphids are necessary when the young are being reared.

◆ RIGHT
Red-headed tits are best kept in a group, certainly at first, if breeding is the aim. As visual sexing is impossible, this gives the best chance of obtaining at least one true pair.

BREED BOX

Length	10 cm (4 in)
Incubation period	14 days
Fledging period	14 days
Clutch size	5–6 eggs

BLACK-CHINNED YUHINAS

The black-chinned yuhina (*Yuhina nigramenta*) may not be as colourful as some softbills, but its attractive crest and lively personality help to compensate for that. These birds measure about 10 cm (4 in) long. Nectar, fruit diced into small pieces and small livefoods such as micro-crickets form the basis of their diet.

Yuhinas build a cup-shaped nest, well-hidden in vegetation. When displaying, the male lowers his crest and dances with his wings outstretched in front of the hen. Pairs are best housed away from others of their own kind because they persistently squabble at this stage of the year. Three eggs form a typical clutch, and this is incubated mainly

✦ RIGHT
This is a pair of black-chinned yuhinas. Males can be recognized when in breeding condition not just by their larger crests, but also by their song, although this is not very loud.

BREED BOX

Length	10 cm (4 in)
Incubation period	13 days
Fledging period	15 days
Clutch size	3–4 eggs

by the hen for 13 days. The young fledge after a similar interval. Small livefoods that can be easily digested by the chicks are vital for rearing purposes. Egg food should also be provided. When they leave the nest, the young are paler in colour than the adult birds.

PEKIN ROBINS

The pekin robin (*Leiothrix lutea*) has a wide distribution across southern parts of Asia. There may be minor differences in plumage between individuals and, unfortunately, there is no clear-cut way of distinguishing the sexes by sight. Once in breeding condition, however, cocks have a magnificent song.

Pekin robins make an ideal introduction to keeping softbills. They are very easy to care for, taking a varied diet that may even include some millet seed. They are also relatively hardy once acclimatized, but must still have good protection during bad weather. Some provision for heating in their quarters is advisable. The main drawback of keeping pekin

BREED BOX

Length	15 cm (6 in)
Incubation period	14 days
Fledging period	14 days
Clutch size	4 eggs

robins in a mixed collection is that they can be disruptive during the breeding season, stealing the eggs of other birds that are sharing their accommodation. They build cup-shaped nests. The incubation and fledging periods last for about 14 days each. A pair may have more than one round of chicks in the summer, when the cock's melodious song will be frequently heard.

✦ LEFT
In spite of its similarity in shape, the pekin robin is not actually a robin; nor is it confined to China. As well as insects, these birds eat large quantities of egg food when rearing their chicks.

MEDIUM-SIZED SOFTBILLS

Not all softbills are colourful, but their interesting habits and attractive song compensate for lack of vivid plumage. Most of the species included in this section are relatively hardy, once properly acclimatized, but this may take a couple of years and it is important to have contingency plans in the event of severe weather – a flight attached to a well-insulated and heated birdroom, for instance. The birds can be shut inside, if necessary, although they do not need to be confined in cages. Softbills in general are very lively birds, and they will need to be housed in spacious surroundings if their feather condition is not to deteriorate through inadequate flight exercise.

GREATER HILL MYNAHS

The greater hill mynah (*Gracula religiosa*) is widely kept as a pet. Although unrivalled for the clarity of their speech, these members of the starling clan are messy by nature, and so are usually accommodated in box-type cages. It is important to start out with a young mynah as a pet. These are often advertised as "gapers" because of their habit of begging for food. They can be easily recognized by the flat, bare, yellow patches of skin on the sides of the head which are known as wattles; and their plumage lacks the iridescence of adults.

There are various subspecies of different sizes. Pairs can only be recognized with certainty by being sexed. Breeding is not too difficult. Provide a large nest box lined with twigs. The hen lays two or three eggs which hatch after 15 days. At this stage, the adult birds become much more insectivorous than usual, with the chicks ultimately fledging at about a month old. It is not uncommon for two clutches to be reared in succession. Early chicks should be removed when they are independent.

BREED BOX	
Length	30 cm (12 in)
Incubation period	15 days
Fledging period	28 days
Clutch size	2–3 eggs

◆ LEFT
The powers of mimicry of the greater hill mynah may exceed those of parrots in some respects. They are less reluctant to talk in front of strangers, and also mimic sounds such as a ringing telephone with greater clarity.

CHINESE CRESTED MYNAHS

◆ BELOW
The Chinese crested mynah is a robust softbill
that is hardy and easy to care for, even if you
have no previous experience of these birds. It
may become tame in aviary surroundings.

Other members of the starling clan are popular as aviary birds rather than as household pets, although hand-raised chicks can become very tame and may learn to say a few words. The Chinese crested mynah (*Acridotheres cristatellus*) is a typical example. This bird is widely distributed in south-east Asia. Visual sexing is largely impossible, although hens may sometimes be recognized by their smaller crests. Pairs need to be kept apart, especially from smaller companions, because they can become very aggressive at the start of the breeding season.

Their requirements are virtually identical to those of the greater hill mynah. A low-iron softbill food is recommended to protect against the risk of iron-storage disease, which affects the liver. Diced fruit and livefood such as mealworms should feature as part of their daily diet.

A typical clutch comprises four or five eggs, with incubation taking 18 days. The chicks leave the nest just over three weeks later.

BREED BOX

Length	25 cm (10 in)
Incubation period	18 days
Fledging period	23 days
Clutch size	4–5 eggs

EMERALD STARLINGS

Iridescence is a feature seen on the plumage of many starlings, particularly those of African origin. The emerald starling (*Lamprotornis iris*) from West Africa is a typical example of this group; its predominantly green colour looks especially striking in bright sunlight, as do the reddish-purple areas of plumage. Visual sexing is not possible. This bird ranks as one of the smallest of the glossy starlings. Like other members of the group, it is a keen bather, which helps to keep its plumage looking sleek.

◆ RIGHT
The impressive coloration of the emerald starling is most clearly apparent in sunlight. In duller surroundings, it tends to merge into the background.

BREED BOX

Length	20 cm (8 in)
Incubation period	14 days
Fledging period	23 days
Clutch size	2–4 eggs

ROYAL STARLINGS

Most African starlings are relatively hardy once properly acclimatized, but one of the most spectacular members of the group, the royal starling (*Cosmopsarus regius*) from the north-eastern part of the continent, needs heated winter-time quarters in temperate areas. This bird measures at least 35 cm (14 in), its magnificent, slender tail feathers accounting for about half of this figure. The golden yellow feathering on the lower chest and underparts is especially striking, contrasting with the iridescence elsewhere on the plumage, notably the violet area above and the green feathering over the back and wings.

Royal starlings need a spacious flight with perches sited well away from the mesh to prevent damage to

BREED BOX

Length	35 cm (14 in)
Incubation period	14 days
Fledging period	22 days
Clutch size	4–6 eggs

their tail feathers. They are more insectivorous in their feeding requirements than most other starlings and often spend time hunting for invertebrates on the floor of their enclosure. This may leave them vulnerable to tapeworms, as well as gapeworms which cause breathing distress. If a royal starling looks slightly off-colour, one of these

✦ RIGHT
For obvious reasons, the royal starling is also known as the golden-breasted starling. Although insectivorous, these birds often eat fruit, especially berries of various types.

parasites may well be the reason – an avian vet will be able to advise you on the best course of action.

RUFOUS-BELLIED NILTAVAS

One of the more colourful softbills which needs careful management when first acquired is the rufous-bellied niltava (*Niltava sundara*). This is a member of the flycatcher clan, and a native of southern Asia. Sexing is very straightforward – only the cock shows the amazing violet, blue and rich

BREED BOX

Length	17.5 cm (7 in)
Incubation period	14 days
Fledging period	14 days
Clutch size	4 eggs

chestnut coloration, while the hen is olive-brown. The birds can be housed with smaller softbills such as zosterops. A good quality insectivorous softbill food and a range of invertebrates are essential, along with berries and fruit.

With careful acclimatization, these flycatchers are relatively hardy but are best housed in accommodation where heat is available, if necessary. Breeding in a well-planted aviary is possible, especially if there is running water to attract midges. Squabbling may be observed between a pair at the outset.

These birds usually choose a nest site high up in the aviary, and are happy with an open-fronted nest box, using moss and similar materials. A constant supply of small livefoods is vital for breeding success.

✦ LEFT AND RIGHT
Sexing the rufous-bellied niltava presents no problems because the sexes differ significantly in coloration. These birds can be susceptible to foot problems, so ensure they have a good supply of fresh springy branches as perches, and that all the perches are clean.

169

MAGPIE ROBINS

Magpie robins (*Copsychus saularis*), also known as dhyal thrushes, are found across southern Asia and the Philippines. There are differences in markings between the various forms but generally adult cocks are a combination of black and white in colour, while hens display less contrast in their plumage and are greyer overall.

BREED BOX

Length	20 cm (8 in)
Incubation period	13 days
Fledging period	17 days
Clutch size	5 eggs

The melodic calls of the cock birds are most likely to be heard in the early morning and late afternoon, especially during the breeding season. The hen builds a cup-shaped nest, either directly in the vegetation of the flight, often favouring stands of bamboo, or in an open-fronted nest box. Magpie robins will often become very tame in aviary surroundings, especially when nesting, and many will be persuaded to take livefood from the hand. The hen will lay five eggs in a clutch. Incubation lasts for around 13 days and the young chicks will start to fledge from between two and three weeks after hatching.

✦ ABOVE
The immaculate appearance of the magpie robin, coupled with its fine song, has helped to make this species popular with softbill enthusiasts.

BLACK BULBULS

The black bulbul (*Hypsipetes madagascariensis*) is a typical representative of another not-very-colourful group of birds which, in the case of the cock bird, has an attractive song. This is the way to distinguish between the sexes. As the name indicates, these bulbuls are greyish-black in colour. In south-eastern Asia, there is a form which has a white head.

Although recognizing a pair is difficult at the outset, breeding is quite likely to take place, particularly in a planted aviary. A nest of twigs is constructed in the branches of a bush or tree, and lined with softer material. The hen sits alone, with the chicks hatching about 12 days later. The young leave the nest after about two weeks. Bulbuls are easy to cater for, taking a more

BREED BOX

Length	25 cm (10 in)
Incubation period	13 days
Fledging period	13 days
Clutch size	3–5 eggs

omnivorous diet than the magpie robin, including more finely chopped fruit and berries. Small livefoods such as crickets should be supplied during the rearing period, when egg food will also be taken. Bulbuls are reasonably peaceful by nature and can often be kept satisfactorily as part of a mixed collection. They are relatively hardy once acclimatized.

✦ LEFT
The black bulbul is one of the Asiatic species best known in bird-keeping circles, and is more widely kept than its African relatives. Their care is straightforward.

GREY LAUGHING THRUSHES

The laughing thrushes are so-called because of their calls, with some species proving to be talented songsters. They are a robust group of Asiatic softbills, popular in bird-keeping circles because they are hardy and easy to look after. They usually have to be housed on their own because of their predatory nature – hence their alternative name of jay thrush. The grey laughing thrush (*Garrulax maesi*) is a typical member of the group, recognizable by its silvery-grey ear coverts. It originates from southern and central areas of China, where it inhabits mountain forests. Unfortunately, there is no reliable way of distinguishing pairs visually, but their care is straightforward; a mixed diet including plenty of livefood, such as mealworms, suits them very well.

Dense bamboo undergrowth encourages breeding, with the birds becoming shyer at first during this period. Four eggs, hatching after 13 days, form a typical clutch. Keep disturbances to a minimum or the adult birds may eat their chicks.

BREED BOX	
Length	28 cm (11 in)
Incubation period	13 days
Fledging period	21 days
Clutch size	4 eggs

✦ ABOVE
Laughing thrushes are highly active birds, bold and brash by nature. They can strike up a strong bond with their keeper in aviary surroundings. If housed as a group, beware that the weakest individual is not bullied by its companions.

Making them hunt for livefood by scattering it on the floor of the aviary may provide a distraction in the case of a pair known to attack their chicks.

BLACK-HEADED SIBIAS

The black-headed sibia (*Heterophasia capistrata*) originates in the Himalayan area of Asia, which makes it relatively hardy once settled in its surroundings. These sibias will thrive in a planted aviary and can become quite tame, often to the point of feeding on mealworms from the hand. Visual sexing is not possible, and this can be a major handicap to breeding attempts.

Conifers are a good choice of plant for sibias. They may even use pine needles to form the outer structure of their nests, lining the interior with softer materials. It will take about two weeks for the eggs to hatch, with the chicks leaving the nest after a similar period. Pairs are best housed on their own for breeding purposes, and should not be mixed with smaller companions who may be bullied, particularly when nesting is imminent.

BREED BOX	
Length	25 cm (10 in)
Incubation period	14 days
Fledging period	14 days
Clutch size	4 eggs

✦ BELOW
The black-headed sibia cannot be sexed by sight, but breeding has proved possible in aviary surroundings. A pair is most likely to breed if housed on their own once they show signs of nesting behaviour.

LEVAILLANT'S BARBETS

Bill shape can give an indication of potential aggression, although in the case of barbets, their stocky bills have another important function – tunnelling into rotten wood or excavating nesting chambers in the ground. Even so, it is advisable to keep these attractive birds on their own, and never with smaller companions. Some can prove to be aggressive in the company of their own species. Sexing is difficult, although hens may be less brightly coloured overall.

Barbets form a large group, with distribution in parts of Africa, Asia and South America. It is important to find out the range of a particular species because this has a definite bearing on its requirements. Those from tropical forest areas are generally much more frugivorous in their feeding habits than those from the scrubland of southern Africa, such as Levaillant's barbet (*Trachyphonus vallianti*), which take a more insectivorous diet.

A deep nest box, preferably covered with bark around the entrance hole, is recommended. The hen may lay up to five eggs, which take two weeks to hatch. Fledging occurs about three weeks later. A greatly increased supply of livefood is essential for rearing purposes, in addition to the regular offerings of fruit, berries and a low-iron softbill food or soaked mynah pellets.

Barbets need adequate protection from the cold and damp during the winter, and it is advisable to house them in a birdroom where heating and lighting are available through this period. Their strong bills can, however, inflict serious damage on woodwork.

BREED BOX

Length	20 cm (8 in)
Incubation period	14 days
Fledging period	22 days
Clutch size	3–5 eggs

SPECTACLED MOUSEBIRDS

Mousebirds are a group of African softbills that are highly social by nature and thrive in a well-planted flight, although they may damage some of the vegetation. The spectacled mousebird (*Colius striatus*) measures about 30 cm (12 in) overall, with its long tail accounting for approximately three-quarters of its total length.

There are a number of different subspecies, and there is no means of distinguishing the sexes visually.

Pairs build large, bulky nests, often well-disguised in vegetation, made of dry grass and moss. Three eggs form the typical clutch. They hatch in two weeks and the incubation is shared by both adult birds. The chicks develop very quickly and often leave the nest at about 10 days old, before they can fly, clambering around using their feet and bills. Mousebirds are very easy to feed on a diet of fruit, softbill food and berries, along with livefood and greenstuff such as chickweed. They are not hardy and need to be housed in warm, dry surroundings during the winter.

BREED BOX

Length	30 cm (12 in)
Incubation period	14 days
Fledging period	10 days
Clutch size	3 eggs

◆ RIGHT
A spectacled mousebird shows its climbing abilities. The coloration of these birds and the way in which they clamber quietly around the branches is the reason for their unusual common name.

LARGE SOFTBILLS

Unlike the smaller softbills, members of this group, especially those which originate from the more temperate latitudes, are relatively hardy after they have been properly acclimatized in their surroundings. However, all species will still require a heated, well-lit shelter during the colder winter months. A number of species of large softbill may be at risk from frost-bite in some climates, if they are allowed to remain out in the flight. Most large softbills are aggressive by nature, and should be accommodated in individual pairs rather than in large, mixed groups. Do not attempt to keep large softbill species in the company of smaller companions.

RED-BILLED TOUCANS

The toucans represent one of the best-known and most spectacular groups of larger softbills. They originate from parts of Central and South America. Thanks to a much better understanding of their needs in recent years, breeding success in private collections has become more commonplace. First and foremost, it is vital to use only a low-iron softbill food, or preferably softbill pellets, to safeguard against the premature demise of the birds from iron-storage disease. This is a dietary-induced illness which is almost impossible to cure by the time the symptoms have become apparent. Diced fruit should also figure prominently in their diet, along with livefood such as large crickets or mealworms, and even pinkie, or dead day old mice. Under no circumstances should pairs of toucans be housed with smaller companions, as these are likely to be seized and eaten.

It is not uncommon for a male toucan to persecute the hen intently at the start of the breeding period if she is not immediately responsive. It may be advisable to remove the male to separate accommodation until the hen is showing obvious signs of nesting activity. The red-billed toucan (*Ramphastos tucanus*) hen lays two or three eggs, incubating them for about 20 days. The young leave the nest at around eight weeks of age. A varied diet, including plenty of livefood, is necessary throughout this period.

♦ RIGHT
A red-billed toucan shows the characteristic markings on its bill. It is virtually impossible to sex these birds visually, although hens may be slightly smaller than cocks. The bill itself is lightweight, with a honeycombed structure.

BREED BOX

Length	50 cm (20 in)
Incubation period	20 days
Fledging period	56 days
Clutch size	2–3 eggs

RED-BILLED HORNBILLS

Hornbills are sometimes regarded as the Old World equivalent of toucans, although their bills are not generally as highly coloured or as broad. The red-billed hornbill (*Tockus erythrorhynchus*) is the most widely kept member of the group, originating from Africa. Its small size, in comparison with other hornbills, makes it suitable for a garden aviary. In contrast to toucans, these hornbills are much quieter, with the male uttering a bubbling call when excited. Sexing is reasonably straightforward; the cocks have a swollen area, described as a casque, on the top of their bill.

Although primarily insectivorous by nature, these birds eat a range of foods, including low-iron mynah pellets, diced fruit which they swallow whole, and berries of various types.

The breeding habits of these birds are fascinating, and involve the hen being walled up inside the nest by her mate for some of the time, to protect her from predators such as snakes. Damp mud and clay should be provided for this purpose. The hen lays four or six eggs and ten weeks later, the young hornbills emerge. In the meantime, the male feeds his mate through a slit in the mud wall, although towards the end of the nesting period, when the young require more food, the hen may break outside to assist in feeding the brood.

For much of the remainder of the year, hornbills are very inactive, sitting with their heads hunched down on their shoulders. This is a normal posture and not a cause for concern. Although hardy, it is absolutely vital that hornbills are made to roost in a warm shelter when the temperature outside is set to fall below freezing, because these birds are prone to frost-bite, which will cause the loss of toes and can lead to difficulty in perching.

◆ LEFT
The speckled patterning over the wings is a feature of the red-billed hornbill and related species from Africa.

BREED BOX

Length	45 cm (18 in)
Incubation period	not applicable
Fledging period	70 days
Clutch size	4–6 eggs

◆ BELOW
The red-billed hornbill may appear to have eyelashes, but these are modified feathers rather than hairs. Cock birds have longer, bigger bills than hens.

RED-BILLED BLUE PIES

Many members of the crow family are predominantly black and white, but the red-billed blue pie (*Urocissa erythrorhyncha*) is a spectacular exception to the rule. It has cobalt-blue markings, while the bill, legs and feet are reddish in colour. The sexes are similar, although in most cases cock birds will have brownish irises.

◆ ABOVE
The brilliant blue coloration of the red-billed blue pie may differ in depth between individuals. There is also a yellow-billed form that is less commonly seen in collections.

BREED BOX

Length	60 cm (24 in)
Incubation period	17 days
Fledging period	21 days
Clutch size	3–6 eggs

A pair of these corvids should be kept on their own in a spacious aviary. They need plenty of branches so they can hop from one to another, with uncluttered areas offering substantial flying space as well. Provide the birds with a large wicker basket, as commonly sold in garden centres for houseplants, for them to use as a nesting platform, and they will construct a loose assortment of twigs and sticks on top of it. The hen lays three to six eggs and these should hatch after about 17 days. For the first week or so, there is a real risk that the chicks may be cannibalized by the adult birds. This is more likely to occur if all the food is provided within easy reach. It is therefore a good idea to scatter livefood around the flight to keep the adults actively searching for it. The young birds grow rapidly and are ready to leave the nest by three weeks of age. Once they are feeding independently, they should be transferred to separate quarters.

HARTLAUB'S TOURACOS

This distinctive group of African birds feeds largely on fruit, berries and greenstuff, which should be chopped into pieces. Chickweed, dandelions and cress, which can be grown very easily at home, are just some of the possible options. Sprinkle on a low-iron softbill food.

Cocks can be very spiteful towards intended partners, so it is better to start out with a genuine proven pair if possible. Hartlaub's touraco (*Tauraco hartlaubi*) is one of the most commonly bred species. It originates from parts of Tanzania and Kenya. A densely planted aviary reduces the likelihood of aggression during the breeding season, with touracos building a platform-type nest on a suitable support. The two eggs hatch after a period of three weeks, and the young fledge when they are about a month old.

Although hardy, touracos need adequate protection during periods of cold weather because they are susceptible to frostbite.

◆ LEFT
The red pigment in the flight feathers of Hartlaub's touraco is derived from a copper-based compound, and is unique in the animal kingdom. These birds are also unusual in not having a fixed perching grip, which means they can grip with three toes in front of the perch and one behind, or in a 2:2 configuration.

BREED BOX

Length	40 cm (16 in)
Incubation period	21 days
Fledging period	28 days
Clutch size	2 eggs

AUSTRALIAN PARAKEETS

These parakeets were the first group of parrots to be bred successfully on a regular basis in aviary surroundings. It happened during the later years of the 1800s, before the requirements of such birds were well understood, which shows their adaptability. They are very easy to maintain on a diet of seed and greenstuff, although the best results are obtained by offering a wider range of foodstuffs. A mixture of millets and plain canary seed, augmented by a little sunflower seed and groats, will suffice for the smaller species, such as the grass parakeets. The percentage of thicker-shelled seeds, such as small pine nuts and safflower, should be increased for other members of the group.

Pairs should be housed separately from other birds. Never introduce a hen to a cock at the start of the breeding season because she may be attacked if she does not immediately respond to his advances. Pairs start to breed at the onset of spring. Provide a nest box lined with either wood shavings or softwood offcuts, which the larger species will be able to whittle away to form an absorbent nest lining. Visual sexing is possible in most cases. Most pairs of Australian parakeets are quite prolific, and will have two clutches of eggs in succession.

✦ OPPOSITE
The splendid grass parakeet, also called the scarlet-chested because of the rich red plumage evident on the cock's breast, is an ideal choice for a garden aviary.

✦ LEFT
As the popularity of some parakeets such as the splendid has grown, so colour mutations have emerged in breeding stock. This is a blue form of the species, with the hen on the right.

BUDGERIGARS

The budgerigar (*Melopsittacus erithacus*) is the most popular pet bird in the world. These attractive Australian parakeets were first brought to Europe during the 1840s, and before the end of that century were being bred on a tremendous scale. Some breeding establishments in France housed as many as 100,000 birds.

Part of the reason for the budgerigar's popularity is its friendly nature, coupled with its powers of mimicry. These small parakeets rank among the champion chatterboxes of the avian world; some individuals are able to build up vocabularies of 500 words or more, which is far more than most members of the parrot family, with the exception of the African grey parrot. But whereas greys can be rather shy mimics, the budgerigar is quite willing, in most cases, to run through its repertoire in front of strangers.

Their calls are not loud and, unlike many parrots, budgerigars are not very destructive by nature, so they are quite easy to house in aviary surroundings, in flights made from 19 gauge mesh. Budgerigars are also quite hardy, and provided that they have a dry and well-lit shelter where they can retreat when the weather is bad, they do not require artificial heating or lighting.

One of the other major reasons underlying the popularity of the budgerigar is the range of colour varieties which have been developed. There are literally millions of possible combinations, taking into account the range of colours, markings and crested forms which now exist. This makes them popular exhibition birds and they are bred especially for that purpose. Budgerigars are judged by set standards and exhibition birds are significantly larger than their pet and aviary counterparts. Ordinary budgerigars will breed well when housed as a group, but their exhibition counterparts are usually separated in breeding cages, where the parentage of the chicks can be guaranteed.

If you are interested in exhibiting budgerigars, you must have a separate birdroom with space for breeding cages, and a training area for the birds prior to the show season. Heating and lighting will be needed because exhibition budgerigars are bred during the late winter in northern temperate areas.

The breeding period in aviaries is usually restricted to the warmer months of the year. Budgerigars are naturally prolific birds and in order to discourage them, nest boxes must be removed before winter. Hens breeding at this stage are particularly vulnerable to egg-binding, and the overall results are likely to be unsatisfactory.

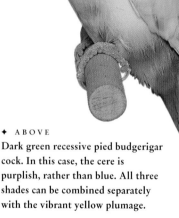

✦ ABOVE
Dark green recessive pied budgerigar cock. In this case, the cere is purplish, rather than blue. All three shades can be combined separately with the vibrant yellow plumage.

PET BUDGERIGARS

When it comes to choosing a budgerigar as a pet, it is the age of the bird rather than its coloration that is significant. Talking ability does not depend on variety, nor is it true that only cock birds will talk. Hens can be effective mimics but their natural calls are often slightly harsher in tone than the males'. The major drawback of having a hen as a pet is that she is likely to become very destructive at

✦ ABOVE
Light green and sky blue budgerigars. Both these birds are cocks, as shown by the blue ceres above the bill. Light green is the budgie's natural colour.

✦ **ABOVE**
The albino hen budgerigar
is pure snow white in colour,
although birds can show a slight
blue suffusion in some lights.

COMMON FORMS OF BUDGERIGAR

Greens	These include the light green, which is the colour of the wild budgerigar. There are also dark greens and olive greens, created by the dark factor being superimposed on the light green colouring.
Blues	The sky blue is the lightest shade. The cobalt and mauve are the dark factor forms. The violet is also a member of this group, and is one of the most sought-after of all budgerigar colours, particularly the yellow-faced form. This local colour change can be combined with the other blue colours, as well as the grey mutation, to create equivalent yellow-faced varieties.
Pieds	There are two distinct forms of pied, which can be distinguished both visually and genetically. The Australian dominant pied is larger than its Danish recessive counterpart, and has black eyes with obvious irises, whereas the eyes of the Danish form are simply plum-coloured. The markings of pieds are variable, but the colour combinations are typically either yellow and green or white and blue.
Lutino and albino	These are pure yellow or white respectively, with red eyes.
Opaline	The heads are more lightly marked than normal, with a clear area forming a V-shape at the top of the wings.
Cinnamon	The wing markings are brownish rather than black.
Clearwings	The collective term used to describe the wing marking colours corresponding to (yellow wing) green and (whitewing or slightly darker greywing) blue series budgerigars.
Spangle	A mutation with pale centres to the feathers on the back and wings. Double factor spangles are of a decidedly paler shade than single-factor birds.
Crests	These occur independently of colour. Three types are recognized – tufted, full-crested and half-crested forms.

certain times once she is mature and coming into breeding condition. It may not be just the sandsheet at the bottom of her cage which she rips up. Outside her quarters, the hen may strip wallpaper, or nibble at flaking paintwork, sometimes poisoning herself with fatal consequences.

Hens do not need to be paired up in order to lay eggs. If she does lay, do not remove the eggs because this will simply encourage her to produce more, just like a chicken. This will drain the hen's body reserves of calcium and other minerals, leaving her at greater risk of suffering from egg-binding, with the shell of the egg being rubbery rather than firm. Cock budgerigars, too, may develop behavioural difficulties when they come into breeding condition. This usually takes the form of regurgitating seed to a favoured toy or mirror. Such

BREED BOX

Length	20 cm (8 in)
Incubation period	18 days
Fledging period	35 days
Clutch size	4–6 eggs

✦ **BELOW**
The violet is highly sought-after because of its colour. It is possible to create other varieties involving this colour, such as violet pieds.

behaviour can be distinguished from the illness known as sour crop because the budgerigar constricts its pupils and appears very alert rather than off-colour. Even so, action needs to be taken to prevent weight loss; removing the object for two or three weeks should allow this phase to pass.

It is quite difficult to sex young budgerigars when they are between six and nine weeks old, which is the best time to obtain one as a pet. The cere of cock birds, i.e. the area above the bill encircling the nostrils, tends to be more prominent and of a deep purplish shade at this age, compared with hens. Once a young budgerigar starts to moult for the first time, at about 12 weeks old, sexing becomes

✦ RIGHT
It is in the darker colours of the budgerigar that the impact of the spangle character is most apparent, as shown by this grey individual.

✦ ABOVE
The opaline mutation, seen here in combination with sky-blue, affects the budgerigar's body markings, rather than the coloration itself. It is sex-linked character in terms of its mode of inheritance.

much more straightforward because the cere shows its adult coloration. The cere colour of hens is always brown; that of cock birds is generally blue, although for the lutino, albino and recessive pied varieties it remains purple. The depth of brown coloration in hens varies through the year, becoming much darker at the start of the breeding season.

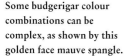

✦ ABOVE
Some budgerigar colour combinations can be complex, as shown by this golden face mauve spangle.

When selecting a budgerigar, there are a number of tell-tale indicators which can be used to confirm the bird's age. In the first place, in a young bird, the barring on the head, associated with most varieties, extends right down to the cere without an intervening area of clear plumage, which is why young birds are described as barheads. The spots on the face are generally less pronounced, while there is no white iris around the eyes, as seen in adult budgerigars of most varieties. There may also be a dark tip to the upper bill in chicks that have recently fledged.

Most young budgerigars are instinctively tame, and by placing your hand parallel with the perch, it should not be too difficult to persuade a fledgling to step on to your outstretched finger. Before finalizing your choice, however, ask to see the wings held open. Any missing flight feathers along the back edge may indicate the feather ailment French Moult, which is caused by a virus. Although in mild cases the feathers will regrow normally, in more severe cases the bird's ability to fly will be permanently handicapped.

AVIARY BIRDS

If you are seeking budgerigars for a colony aviary, you will need to obtain these prior to the start of the breeding season. The introduction of any birds after this time will be disruptive and can result in severe fighting between hens for possession of a nest box. Even in an established group, this can be a problem. It is essential to provide twice as many nest boxes as pairs, and position them so that they are all at the same height. Before the start of

the breeding season, ensure that there are the same number of cocks and hens in the aviary. Even so, budgerigars are promiscuous, and cocks will often mate with other hens once their own partner is incubating eggs on her own.

Although budgerigars are mature by six to nine months old, it is usual not to allow pairs to nest until they are at least a year old. Hens will then breed reliably until they are five or six, by which time their clutch size is likely to be declining, although cock

✦ ABOVE
Crested varieties of the budgerigars have also been developed. This is a full circular created grey cock bird. A crest can be combined with any variety.

◆ LEFT
Opaline grey-green dominant pied cock. This particular mutation is larger in size than the recessive pied and has more prominent cheek spots, as well as black eyes with white irises.

birds can remain fertile for most of their lives. Hens typically lay four to six eggs, which hatch after a period of 18 days. Young budgerigars fledge at about five weeks old, by which time the hen will have probably laid again. Pairs should be restricted to two clutches of chicks in succession. Budgerigars do not need nesting material; instead, they lay on wooden concaves, usually supplied with the nest box. It is useful to have a spare concave so that you can change these over when one becomes soiled, scrubbing off the used one and leaving it to dry.

When seeking breeding stock, it is impossible to age budgerigars once they have moulted into adult plumage unless they are fitted with a closed ring around one leg, engraved with the year in which they hatched; "00", for example, indicates a bird hatched in 2000. The only other possible clue may be the condition of the feet and legs. If these are heavily scaled, this is often indicative of an older bird.

When buying aviary stock, check the bill for signs of scaly face mites, which leave mini snail-like tracks in the first instance, before progressing to the characteristic coral-like encrustations at the sides of the bill. Similar signs may be evident on the legs as well. These parasites spread very rapidly in aviary surroundings, and are hard to eliminate. Treatment is quite straightforward, though, so if you want a particular budgerigar that is infected with these parasites, go ahead provided that you can keep the bird apart until it has fully recovered.

You should also check the bill to ensure that the upper and lower portions are properly aligned. This is an inherited weakness with no cure. The bill will have to be trimmed back regularly, so it is preferable not to buy such birds.

EXHIBITION STOCK

You are unlikely to find birds of exhibition quality at your local pet store. You will probably have to seek out an established exhibitor in order to obtain suitable birds. Such breeders can be tracked down in your neighbourhood through the national budgerigar organization in your country, or through the advertisement columns of the bird-keeping journals. Set yourself a budget and remember that it is better to buy a few birds of good quality than more birds of mediocre quality. Do not expect to purchase the best birds in the stud. Follow the breeder's advice – most are genuine and keen to help novices. It helps to specialize in a particular colour variety; most leading studs have acquired their reputations in specific areas because it is easier to concentrate on developing the required features associated with one single variety.

◆ ABOVE
In the case of the yellow-face cinnamon sky blue, the wing markings are transformed from black to a warm shade of brown. The throat spots are also brown.

◆ ABOVE
The rich buttercup yellow lutino and the snow-white albino are both red-eyed varieties due to the lack of the black pigment melanin in their bodies. Their feet are pink.

GRASS PARAKEETS

The grass parakeets are the most widely kept birds out of the entire group of Australian parakeets. Their relatively small size and characteristic quiet nature mean they are easy to accommodate even in a fairly small garden. They are quite hardy, although they can be vulnerable to intestinal roundworms. This is a reflection of the length of time they spend foraging for food on the floor of the flight; in this way they easily pick up the microscopic roundworm eggs. These are attractive birds and several stunning colour mutations have been established.

SPLENDID GRASS PARAKEETS

Some breeders consider the splendid grass parakeet (*Neophema splendida*) to be even more attractive than the turquoisine. The cock bird has a bright scarlet area on its chest, offset against the brilliant blue coloration of the head. Hens, in comparison, have green chests. The best-known mutation is the sea-green or dilute blue, in which the scarlet of the cock's breast is transformed to a salmon shade, with the green areas having a decidedly bluish hue. A pure blue form, with a white breast in the case of the cock, has also been established. Although hardy, these and other grass parakeets require a well-lit aviary shelter and may suffer respiratory problems during foggy weather.

✦ LEFT
The splendid grass parakeet is so-called because of its striking appearance. Only the cock has the red feathering on the breast. This is a good choice for a garden aviary.

✦ BELOW LEFT
The traditional blue form of the splendid grass parakeet retains a green hue to its plumage. A hen bird is shown here.

✦ BELOW
The pure blue form of the splendid grass parakeet is less common than the greenish variant. The cock is shown on the left. Note the white and slight salmon coloration.

BREED BOX

Length	20 cm (8 in)
Incubation period	19 days
Fledging period	30 days
Clutch size	5–6 eggs

TURQUOISINE GRASS PARAKEETS

✦ BELOW
This is an orange-bellied example of the
turquoisine grass parakeet, a cock bird as shown
by the red areas on the wings. Mutations are
widely available in this group of parakeets.

The turquoisine grass parakeet
(*N. pulchella*) originates from the
south-east of Australia. Sexing is
straightforward with cocks having
red patches on their wings.

The incubation period lasts
approximately 19 days. Great care
needs to be taken when the young
fledge at around four weeks old
because they are usually very nervous
and can injure themselves by flying
into the aviary mesh, not appreciating
the presence of a barrier. Growing
climbing plants, such as nasturtiums
(*Tropaeolum majus*), at the end of the
flight opposite the shelter, can help to
highlight the obstruction.

The yellow form of the turquoisine
is perhaps the most striking colour
mutation. It is also possible to
introduce the scarlet-bellied
characteristic into such strains,
adding to their beauty. As with
most other grass parakeets, pairs
should be housed on their
own, rather than in groups.

BREED BOX	
Length	20 cm (8 in)
Incubation period	19 days
Fledging period	30 days
Clutch size	5–6 eggs

BOURKE'S PARAKEETS

Bourke's parakeet (*N. bourkii*) has one
of the most distinctive colour schemes
of all parrots. It is of a greyish-brown
shade with pink underparts. This latter
feature has been developed in the rosa
form, which displays very strong pink
coloration. Sexing is harder in this
species than for other grass parakeets;
hens tend to lack the blue frontal band
seen on the heads of cocks, and have
whiter heads as a result. Like other
species, Bourke's parakeets are
normally more active towards dusk
than during the day.

BREED BOX	
Length	23 cm (9 in)
Incubation period	19 days
Fledging period	28 days
Clutch size	4–5 eggs

✦ LEFT
In the case of the rosa, the
underlying pink colour is more
prominent than usual. It is not
possible to influence the depth
of this colour by dietary means
in these or other parrots.

✦ ABOVE
Bourke's parakeet
has unusual
coloration. These
are active birds, like
other grass parakeets,
and are unsuitable as
household pets, but
they will thrive in
aviary surroundings.

RED-RUMPED PARAKEETS

A popular Australian parakeet is the red-rumped (*Psephotus haematonotus*), which measures about 28 cm (11 in) long. Cocks can be easily sexed by their bright green colour; the hens are much greyer and lack the distinctive red feathering on the rump. It is better to purchase young birds if possible, rather than attempting to pair up adult birds. Some cocks can be very aggressive and may even kill their male chicks prior to fledging. Young birds hatched in the spring will breed during the following year.

Incubation lasts approximately 18 days, with the young fledging after four or five weeks in the nest. They should be removed as soon as they are feeding independently, by which time the adult pair is likely to be starting to nest again.

A number of mutations have been established, including blue and lutino forms and a pied.

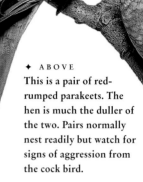

✦ ABOVE
This is a pair of red-rumped parakeets. The hen is much the duller of the two. Pairs normally nest readily but watch for signs of aggression from the cock bird.

BREED BOX	
Length	28 cm (11 in)
Incubation period	18 days
Fledging period	32 days
Clutch size	4–6 eggs

✦ LEFT
The lutino form of the red-rump is a relatively new mutation, being mainly pure yellow with red eyes.

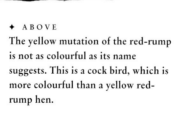

✦ ABOVE
The yellow mutation of the red-rump is not as colourful as its name suggests. This is a cock bird, which is more colourful than a yellow red-rump hen.

BLUE BONNET PARAKEETS

The blue bonnet parakeet, or *P. haematogaster*, is less common than the red-rump, but requires similar care. The red patch on the cock's abdomen is usually larger and more richly coloured than in hens. These birds can be quite playful by nature, which is not a trait commonly associated with Australian parakeets.

BREED BOX	
Length	28 cm (11 in)
Incubation period	21 days
Fledging period	37 days
Clutch size	4–5 eggs

✦ ABOVE
The unusual name of the blue bonnet comes from the blue feathering on the sides of its head.

ROSELLA PARAKEETS

Rosella parakeets may be identified without difficulty thanks to the scalloped markings on their backs, a feature unique to these birds. Unsurprisingly, the most colourful species are the most widely kept, such as the crimson rosella, also called Pennant's parakeet (*Platycercus elegans*). While adult birds are brick-red, the young are usually greenish in colour. Visual sexing in the case of rosellas is impossible; DNA sexing will be required.

The eastern (*P. eximius*) or golden-mantled rosella (GMR) is another widely bred species. These birds are prolific, with hens often laying six or seven eggs in a clutch and rearing all the chicks successfully. It takes approximately 26 days for the eggs to hatch, and the young parakeets leave the nest box when they are about five weeks old. On occasions, pairs may be double-brooded, and these parakeets can live for over 20 years.

✦ BELOW
The blue mutation of Pennant's parakeet has become readily available over recent years.

✦ RIGHT
Pennant's parakeet is also known as the crimson rosella, thanks to the colour of its plumage. Prolific and hardy, these are popular aviary birds.

BREED BOX

Length 25–30 cm (10–12 in)	
Incubation period 26 days	
Fledging period	35 days
Clutch size	5–7 eggs

✦ RIGHT
Eastern rosellas rank among the most colourful species, showing the characteristic scalloped markings which help to distinguish members of the rosella group.

BARNARD'S PARAKEETS

Barnard's parakeet (*Barnardius barnardi*) is a close relative of the rosellas, sharing with them the characteristic of tail feathers that do not taper along their length. This is why this group of Australian parakeets are known collectively as broadtails. They need the same care as other Australian parakeets, and an equally lengthy flight of at least 3.6 m (12 ft) with perches at either end, in view of their active nature.

Sexing can be difficult; hens tend to have a greenish tinge to the blue mantle area on the back. Incubation of the four to six eggs lasts 19 days, with the young fledging about five weeks later.

BREED BOX	
Length	33 cm (13 in)
Incubation period	19 days
Fledging period	35 days
Clutch size	4–6 eggs

✦ ABOVE
Barnard's parakeet is one of the less common Australian species in aviculture, although its care creates no special problems. It is a close relative of the rosellas.

PRINCESS OF WALES'S PARAKEETS

The stunning pastel coloration of the Princess of Wales's parakeet (*Polytelis alexandrae*) is distinctive. They average about 45 cm (18 in) long. The hen is distinguished from the cock bird by her mauvish-grey crown, and by the paler red colour of her bill. These parakeets have loud calls, which may lead to difficulties in urban areas. Although friendly by nature, Princess of Wales's parakeets are too lively to keep as pets in the home.

BREED BOX	
Length	45 cm (18 in)
Incubation period	19 days
Fledging period	35 days
Clutch size	4–6 eggs

Colour mutations have been established and, of these, the blue form is the most common seen.

✦ ABOVE
The Princess of Wales's parakeet has a reputation for egg eating. Placing dummy pigeon eggs in the nest of a pair that are destroying their eggs may cure them of this behaviour.

✦ FAR LEFT
This is the blue form of the Princess of Wales's parakeet. Note the spatules on the ends of the flight feathers, indicating a mature cock bird. These sometimes break off.

BARRABAND'S PARAKEETS

Barraband's parakeet (*Polytelis swainsonii*) is related to the Princess of Wales's parakeet and is about the same size. Sexing is easy as the cock birds display yellow plumage on the throat.

BREED BOX

Length	40 cm (16 in)
Incubation period	19 days
Fledging period	35 days
Clutch size	4–6 eggs

Hens lay four to six eggs in a clutch, often preferring a natural log, rather than a deep nest box. Young birds look similar to adult hens but cocks may be more colourful at this stage, and only young males will sing, starting at just a few months old. It will take two years for the young to attain maturity.

✦ RIGHT
Barraband's parakeet can be sexed very easily once the birds are mature, but sexing youngsters is much harder.

PILEATED PARAKEETS

The pileated parakeet (*Purpureicephalus spurius*) is unusually coloured, with deep mauve feathering on its chest. Hens are significantly duller in coloration. In south-western Australia, where these birds originate, they use their distinctive bills to extract the seeds of the eucalypt called marri, which features prominently in their diet. They eat a regular seed in aviary surroundings, but with their powerful bills can be very destructive. They should be housed in a strong aviary, clad with 16 gauge mesh. When they fledge, young pileated parakeets are much smaller than the adult birds and are predominantly green in colour. Their underparts are a greyish shade of mauve, and there are only odd scattered red feathers on their heads and undertail coverts. They will moult into adult plumage from the age of about a year old. Some young pileated parakeets have been known to breed in their first year, before they have acquired their adult plumage. Regular deworming, as in the case of other Australian species, is recommended.

BREED BOX

Length	35 cm (14 in)
Incubation period	19 days
Fledging period	35 days
Clutch size	4–6 eggs

✦ RIGHT
The long bill is a particular feature of the pileated parakeet: it is a reflection of its feeding habits.

AUSTRALIAN KING PARAKEETS

The male Australian king parakeet (*Alisterus scapularis*) is stunningly attractive. The hen is comparatively subdued with more green plumage on the head and chest. These birds need a long flight and a deep nest box, or hollow log, equipped with a suitable

BREED BOX	
Length	43 cm (17 in)
Incubation period	21 days
Fledging period	56 days
Clutch size	4–5 eggs

ladder to ensure that they can move in and out. The box should be located in a secluded part of the aviary. The hen lays a clutch of four or five eggs, which should hatch after three weeks.

◆ ABOVE
This is a cock Australian king parakeet. A large aviary with plenty of flying space is needed for these birds, along with a deep nest box.

The young will fledge at about two months old. However, you must be patient because it can take Australian king parakeets a couple of years to settle in their quarters after a move, before going to nest.

CRIMSON-WING PARAKEETS

Male crimson-wing parakeets (*Aprosmictus erythropterus*) are, as the name suggests, crimson in colour. Hens are mainly dull green. It is better to start out with young birds because older cock birds may be aggressive towards their potential mates. Provide a deep nest box, or hollow log, with a ladder for ease of access. The hen lays a clutch of three or six eggs, which should hatch after three weeks. The young fledge at six weeks old.

BREED BOX	
Length	30 cm (12 in)
Incubation period	21 days
Fledging period	42 days
Clutch size	3–6 eggs

◆ BELOW
The characteristic wing coloration of the crimson-wing is clearly seen in this cock bird.

◆ RIGHT
Crimson-wings require a relatively deep nest box, with a secure ladder giving them easy access to the interior. The structure must be well supported in the aviary because of its weight.

RING-NECKS AND RELATED PARAKEETS

The 14 species in the psittaculid group are widely distributed across north Africa through the Middle East and across Asia to parts of China. Those which are confined to islands, such as the Blyth's Nicobar parakeet (*Psittacula caniceps*) and Layard's parakeet (*P. calthorpae*), are essentially unknown in bird-keeping circles, and the Mauritius or echo parakeet (*P. echo*) ranks among the rarest parrots in the world. Others have a long avicultural history, and are widely kept and bred.

The psittaculid parakeets range from about 30 cm (12 in) to 50 cm (20 in) in length, with their long and flamboyant tails typically accounting for half the measurement. Although the young birds invariably resemble the hens, the dark stripes extending down the face from the sides of the cock's bill mean that distinguishing the sex of the adult bird is straightforward, especially as there will often be differences in plumage between the male and female of a species.

RING-NECKED PARAKEETS

The ring-necked parakeet (*P. krameri*) has the distinction of being the most widely distributed species of parrot in the world today. The African type (*P. k. krameri*) was highly prized by the Romans. The birds were housed

BREED BOX

Length	38 cm (15 in)
Incubation period	24 days
Fledging period	49 days
Clutch size	4–5 eggs

in cages made of ivory and silver, and slaves made responsible just for their care. Previously, the ancient Greeks had fallen under the charm of the Indian type (*P. k. manillensis*). Distinguishing between these two types is quite easy; the African is slightly smaller in body and has a darker upper mandible with a black tip, rather than bright red as in the Indian. Also, the head of the African is a paler shade of green.

✦ ABOVE
The African ring-necked parakeet (*above*) differs from its Indian relative (*above right*) in its overall coloration.

✦ RIGHT
The coloration of the bill provides an obvious means of distinguishing between the African and Indian forms of the ring-necked parakeet.

✦ ABOVE
Sexing adult ring-necks is straightforward thanks to the collar of the cock bird, but it may take two years for this feature to become apparent in young birds.

Ring-necks are relatively hardy birds once established in their quarters, but they must have adequate protection from the cold because they can be vulnerable to frostbite. It is possible to keep two pairs together in a large aviary, but both pairs should be introduced at the same time. There is no strong pair bond between cock and hen, with very little direct contact being observed between them outside the breeding period.

LEFT
The blue form of the Indian ring-neck is widely kept, making it one of the most popular colour forms.

◆ RIGHT
The primrose is one of the rarer colours. This one is a hen. It can take two years or more for ring-necks to start breeding, so establishing new colours is inevitably a slow process.

This makes it feasible to swap partners, although persuading a young cock to mate with an older hen can be difficult; he may not be confident enough to take this step. Ring-necks often roost in nest boxes throughout the year, and in the northern hemisphere they are among the earliest birds to start nesting. In mild weather, hens may lay as early as February. To protect against a sudden cold snap, however, make the nest boxes from thick timber and site them in a sheltered part of the aviary.

For all psittaculid species, the nest box needs to be deep, with a ladder attached inside, below the entrance hole, to give access to the base. Line the box with wood shavings and pieces of softwood battening that the birds can whittle away to make a nest lining.

Colour mutations have become widely established in the Indian type over recent years, and some of these are highly valued in India. They include the lutino form, in which the green plumage is replaced by yellow, and the cock's black facial feathering by white. The pinkish area encircling the neck is retained, appearing more prominent against the yellow plumage,

while the red upper bill is unaffected. The elegant blue mutation is very popular. The pink of the cock's collar has become modified to white, while the bill retains its red coloration. Hens are pure blue rather than green. Breeders have combined these colours to create a pure white albino with red eyes; the cocks have no collar. Other colour variants include pied, cinnamon and dark factor forms, as well as grey and grey-green. With mutation ring-necks, DNA testing enables those birds that are important for the future of the breeding programme to be identified at an early stage.

ALEXANDRINE PARAKEETS

The Alexandrine (*P. eupatria*) is closely related to the ring-necked parakeet, but is slightly larger with a more powerful bill. Alexandrines tend to nest later in the year than ring-necks, with hens laying clutches of two or three eggs. It takes up to three years for young cock birds to moult into adult plumage, but thanks to DNA techniques, it is possible to

distinguish the sexes well before this stage. With the Alexandrine, it can be very difficult to distinguish between genuine colour mutations and those created by hybridization with ring-necks. Hybrid birds are identifiable by their small size, when compared with true Alexandrine mutations, except in the case of the blue, where the red on the wings is replaced by white.

BREED BOX

Length	50 cm (20 in)
Incubation period	28 days
Fledging period	49 days
Clutch size	2–3 eggs

◆ ABOVE AND LEFT
The Alexandrine parakeet makes an impressive aviary occupant, although pairs can be destructive. The hen bird lacks the neck collar.

DERBYAN PARAKEETS

The largest member of the psittaculid group is the Derbyan parakeet (*P. derbiana*), which is known to originate from the Himalayan region, ranging from north-east Assam through to south-eastern Tibet. The cock bird is particularly striking and easy to identify, thanks to the deep mauve shade of the underparts offset against the greenish wings, and orangish-red upper bill. Hens have black bills. These attractive parakeets are very hardy, but their loud calls and destructive nature mean that housing them satisfactorily may well be impossible in some locations.

Derbyans breed later than other psittaculid parakeets, perhaps because they originate from what can be a bitterly cold part of the world. Hens rarely lay before early summer in northern temperate areas. A typical clutch has two or three eggs and incubation takes about 26 days. The young leave the nest after about seven weeks. Increased amounts of roughage and fruit, as well as soaked seed, should be offered when they are rearing their chicks. Derbyans often show a particular fondness for pine nuts as part of their seed mix; these form part of their natural diet in the wild.

BREED BOX

Length	50 cm (20 in)
Incubation period	26 days
Fledging period	49 days
Clutch size	2–3 eggs

✦ ABOVE
The Derbyan is the largest member of the group, and needs suitably robust accommodation. The cock bird is the more colourful of the pair.

MOUSTACHED PARAKEETS

The moustached parakeet (*P. alexandri*) is found over a wide area of south-east Asia. Sexes can be identified by bill colour – the hen's bill is black. There are a number of distinct types. In the Javan (*P. a. alexandri*), the hen has a pinkish bill, and pale pink breast feathering. Measuring approximately 33 cm (13 in) long, these parakeets have never been especially popular, possibly because they are rather noisy. They can also be quite destructive.

BREED BOX

Length	33 cm (13 in)
Incubation period	23 days
Fledging period	50 days
Clutch size	3–4 eggs

✦ RIGHT
This pair of moustached parakeets show the broad black stripe around the bill, the reason for the common name of these parakeets.

LONG-TAILED PARAKEETS

In contrast with other members of the group, the long-tailed parakeet (*P. longicauda*) is not hardy, requiring very careful acclimatization and protection from frostbite on cold winter nights. The cock birds' narrow, elongated tail feathers measure up to 20 cm (8 in) long. Hens have brown rather than red bills, and a green rather than a black stripe extending back on the sides of the head. Mealworms may be eaten avidly as a rearing food.

BREED BOX

Length	40 cm (16 in)
Incubation period	26 days
Fledging period	55 days
Clutch size	2–5 eggs

✦ RIGHT
Long-tailed parakeets are not as hardy as other members of the psittaculid group, and this must be reflected in their accommodation.

PLUM-HEADED PARAKEETS

The plum-headed parakeet (*P. cyanocephala*) is one of the most popular members of the group, probably due to its quiet nature, and soft, relatively musical calls. Averaging 35 cm (14 in) long, these parakeets are also very docile, even when breeding, and they can be housed in a spacious flight in the company of non-aggressive softbills or finches.

Although the sex of adult birds can be distinguished at a glance (by head colour), young cock birds with their grey heads resemble adult hens in appearance. Close inspection may reveal odd plum-coloured

BREED BOX

Length	35 cm (14 in)
Incubation period	23 days
Fledging period	43 days
Clutch size	4–6 eggs

feathers, but obtaining a true pair of plum-heads can sometimes prove to be difficult.

Pairs nest readily, but in northern temperate areas it is a good idea to discourage them from breeding until April by withholding the nest box. This increases the likelihood of success. Hen plum-heads usually stop brooding their offspring – which can number up to six – before they are fully feathered, and this can lead to losses if there is a sudden cold snap. Even if this happens, or indeed their eggs fail to hatch, plum-heads are unlikely to show any interest in breeding again until the following year, and will abandon the nest box.

✦ LEFT
The plum-headed parakeet is an ideal choice for a garden aviary. Quiet, colourful and graceful in flight, these birds are justifiably popular.

CONURES AND RELATED PARAKEETS

"Conure" is the name given to some parakeets found in Central and South America that were formerly classified as *Conurus*. There are two major groupings, the aratinga conures, which make up the numerically bigger group, and the pyrrhura conures. Pyrrhuras are known as scaly-breasted conures because of the markings on their chest; aratingas are characteristically noisy and destructive.

Feeding conures is straightforward. A complete diet will prevent dietary deficiencies that could compromise breeding activities, but successful breeding is also possible on a seed-based diet, augmented by a supplement, plus vegetables and fruit. Millets, canary seed, groats, flaked maize, sunflower, safflower, pine nuts and hemp in restricted quantities should feature in the seed mixture.

BLUE-CROWNED CONURES

◆ BELOW
The blue-crowned conure is one of the larger *Aratinga* species, averaging 35cm (14in) long, with a powerful bill and loud voice.

The blue-crowned conure (*Aratinga acuticaudata*) occurs over a huge area of South America, from eastern Colombia in the north, southwards to parts of Paraguay, Uruguay and Argentina. It can be instantly identified by its coloration, with blue feathering apparent on the head, offset against the prominent white patch of skin encircling each eye. The remainder of the plumage is greenish, apart from the undersides of the tail feathers which have a reddish hue. Young birds have less blue on their heads, where it is restricted to the forehead and the crown. They can develop into affectionate, personable pets if obtained at an early age, although their talking abilities are rather limited.

BREED BOX

Length	35 cm (14 in)
Incubation period	26 days
Fledging period	52 days
Clutch size	3–4 eggs

WHITE-EYED CONURES

The white-eyed conure (*A. leucophthalmus*) is widely distributed across South America. Individual markings are a feature of the aratingas, and this is exemplified by the white-eyes. These birds are mainly green in colour, with red plumage evident along the leading edge of the wings. Scattered red feathers on the sides of the face and the head

◆ LEFT
The bare white skin around the eyes accounts for the name of the white-eyed conure, although this particular feature is associated with a number of other species as well.

enable birds to be recognized. It is not true to say that cocks are more brightly coloured than hens. Young white-eyed conures have a duller coloration, having yellow rather than red wing markings.

BREED BOX

Length	33 cm (13 in)
Incubation period	26 days
Fledgling period	53 days
Clutch size	2–4 eggs

Nest boxes must be provided throughout the year for roosting. The nest box should be about 30 cm (12 in) square and 45 cm (18 in) in depth. These conures are not especially popular in bird-keeping circles, probably because of their rather subdued coloration.

GOLDEN-CROWNED CONURES

The golden-crowned or peach-fronted conure (*A. aurea*) is found in the southern part of South America, ranging from Brazil to parts of Bolivia, Paraguay and Argentina. Although it measures just 25 cm (10 in) in length, it has a loud call, particularly if it is

BREED BOX

Length	25 cm (10 in)
Incubation period	26 days
Fledging period	50 days
Clutch size	3–4 eggs

disturbed for any reason, and its bill is powerful enough to inflict damage on any exposed, easily accessible timber in the aviary. There is a tendency for people to believe that the more colourful individuals are cock birds, but this is not borne out by DNA sexing.

Young peach-fronted conures have pale rather than black bills on fledging, with an area of yellow feathering immediately above the cere merging into orange.

A whitish upper bill is the feature of Petz's or the orange-fronted conure (*A. canicularis*), a Central American

✦ ABOVE
Immature golden-crowned conures are duller in colour than these adults, and it will take between two and three years for them to reach maturity.

species that can be confused with the golden-crowned, although the two species are widely separated in terms of their distribution.

SUN CONURES

The dazzling sun conure (*A. solistalis*) aroused tremendous interest in the early 1970s when breeding stock became available for the first time. Since then, they have become well established in aviculture. In the wild, they are generally to be found north of the Amazon, on the eastern side of South America, extending from Venezuela to Brazil.

✦ LEFT
When they fledge, sun conures have greenish backs and a greenish tone to their underparts. Their distinctive coloration takes two years to develop over successive moults.

BREED BOX

Length	30 cm (12 in)
Incubation period	26 days
Fledging period	50 days
Clutch size	3–4 eggs

Sun conures measure about 30 cm (12 in) long. They have proved to be hardy birds but their calls can be disturbing. This is their major draw-back and likely to preclude them from being kept on a colony basis, as they are in some public collections. Sun conures can look particularly

spectacular as a breeding flock. The diversity in markings between individuals is clearly apparent; some are of a much more fiery shade than others, with a decidedly orange hue over much of their plumage. This does not appear to be an inherited characteristic, and both predominantly yellow and orange coloured chicks can occur in the same nest.

Young sun conures can develop into superb pets, and may be taught to whistle and repeat a few words. In the home, however, it is important to spray them regularly because otherwise they may be prone to feather-plucking, which can be a difficult habit to break. Toys and branches to gnaw will help to keep them occupied, and so prevent them from plucking their feathers out of boredom. Sun conures have a life expectancy of over 20 years.

FIERY-SHOULDERED CONURES

The chest markings of the fiery-shouldered conure (*Pyrrhura egregia*) are not especially prominent, and neither are the brown ear coverts, but the bare white skin encircling the eye is clearly evident, as is the fiery orange colour in the shoulder area on the wings. Young birds are not as brightly coloured as adults; their wing markings are less prominent.

Most pyrrhuras nest readily in aviary surroundings, if conditions are suitable. The successful establishment of the fiery-shouldered conure in barely a decade is proof of that. They will even breed successfully in indoor flights, provided that they have

BREED BOX	
Length	25 cm (10 in)
Incubation period	23 days
Fledging period	51 days
Clutch size	4–5 eggs

adequate seclusion. Hens lay four or five eggs in a clutch, and incubation lasts 23 days. The young fledge at about seven weeks old. They should be transferred to separate accommodation as soon as they are feeding independently.

◆ ABOVE
The fiery-shouldered conure is a relative newcomer on the avicultural scene. It was totally unknown in collections until 1988, but is now quite widely kept and bred.

SLENDER-BILLED CONURES

The unusual slender-billed conure (*Enicognathus leptorhynchus*) occurs in the wild at the tip of South America, in Chile. It resembles other members of the pyrrhura group both in the barring on its underparts and in overall coloration. However, it is significantly larger, measuring approximately 40 cm (16 in) overall, and instantly recognizable by its long, thin upper bill, which protrudes some distance over the lower mandible, and from which it takes its name.

BREED BOX	
Length	40 cm (16 in)
Incubation period	26 days
Fledging period	49 days
Clutch size	4–6 eggs

Virtually unknown in aviculture until the mid-1970s, pairs have proved to be good nesters, with the result that stock of this species is readily available. Young birds can become great companions, especially if hand-reared. Hens lay four to six eggs, and incubation lasts for 26 days. The young birds fledge at about seven weeks old. Hard-boiled egg is a popular rearing food, along with assorted greenstuff and soaked seed.

Aviaries for these conures should incorporate an area of grass, where the birds can dig for food using their bills, which are an adaptation to help them find food in their rather harsh native habitat. Even young slender-billed conures will very nearly have full-grown bills when they leave the nest. Young birds are best identified by the bare skin around their eyes, which is white in colour, rather than grey.

◆ ABOVE
Slender-billed conures use their distinctive elongated bills to dig for corms and roots. They should be housed in aviaries that incorporate an area of lawn for this reason.

195

BROTOGERIS PARAKEETS

The brotogeris group of parakeets occurs in parts of Central and South America. They average about 23 cm (9 in) in length, and are highly social birds, with breeding results most likely to be obtained when they are housed in small groups rather than as individual pairs. These parakeets can be quarrelsome, however, so it is important to have only sexed pairs and to introduce all members of the group to their aviary at the same time. Provide more nest boxes than pairs. Reintroducing any individuals that have been removed will be fraught with difficulty, although young birds that have been bred in the aviary will normally be accepted without problems. Brotogeris parakeets can be fed the same as conures, although fruit should form a more significant part of their diet.

CANARY-WINGED PARAKEETS

The canary-winged parakeet (*Brotogeris versicolurus chiriri*) is the most widely kept member of the brotogeris group. These birds are

BREED BOX	
Length	23 cm (9 in)
Incubation period	26 days
Fledging period	45 days
Clutch size	4–5 eggs

hardy once properly acclimatized, usually preferring to roost in a nest box rather than on a perch. The bright canary-yellow feathering on the edges of the wings, and the lime-green body colour distinguish it from the closely related white-winged parakeet (*B.v. versicolurus*), which is a darker shade of green. As with other brotogeris parakeets, there is no means of distinguishing the sexes by sight. Also, do not assume that two birds which preen each other are a true pair as this is not necessarily the case.

✦ ABOVE
In spite of their relatively small size, canary-winged parakeets are likely to prove destructive in aviary surroundings and may also be very noisy on occasions.

TOVI PARAKEETS

The tovi parakeet (*B. jugularis*) is also known as the orange-chinned parakeet. It is otherwise mainly green, aside from the bronzy brown plumage on the wings. While adult birds can be

BREED BOX	
Length	17.5 cm (7 in)
Incubation period	26 days
Fledging period	42 days
Clutch size	4–6 eggs

shy, young birds will develop into friendly pets. Hens lay between four and six eggs in a clutch and incubation lasts about 26 days. The chicks leave the nest at about six weeks old. Soaked seed and plenty of fruit should be offered regularly, particularly when pairs are breeding. These small parakeets are quite hardy once acclimatized.

✦ RIGHT
The highly social nature of brotogeris parakeets in general is shown by these tovis. Within colonies, however, strong pair bonds usually exist between individual members.

LINEOLATED PARAKEETS

The lineolated parakeet (*Bolborhynchus lineola*) has a wide distribution across much of Central America extending into northern South America. Its small size – it averages little more than 15 cm (6 in) in length – and quiet, gentle nature have led to the lineolated becoming very popular over recent years. This popularity has increased still further, thanks to the development of various colour mutations, including blue, lutino and dark factor variants.

BREED BOX

Length	15 cm (6 in)
Incubation period	18 days
Fledging period	35 days
Clutch size	4–5 eggs

Pairs of these parakeets may sometimes be persuaded to breed in a spacious double budgerigar breeding cage, lined with coarse wood shavings, although results are likely to be better if they are housed in a flight. Hens lay four or five eggs, which hatch after 18 days. The young leave the nest at five weeks old.

✦ ABOVE
The lineolated parakeet is also known as the barred parakeet because of the variable black coloration on its plumage. Although cock birds are sometimes more heavily barred than hens, this is not always the case.

A diet of smaller seeds, such as millets, augmented with fresh foods suits these parakeets very well. Soft food may also be eaten, and is especially useful for breeding birds.

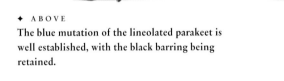

✦ ABOVE
The blue mutation of the lineolated parakeet is well established, with the black barring being retained.

MONK PARAKEETS

Although colour mutations are generally scarce among New World parakeets, they do occur with monk or quaker parakeets (*Myiopsitta*

BREED BOX

Length	28 cm (11 in)
Incubation period	26 days
Fledging period	45 days
Clutch size	5–7 eggs

monachus). Blue and yellow colour mutations have been recorded. These parakeets are also unusual in that they use their nest for roosting. It is possible to allow them to build their nest if you can provide a raised platform and a supply of twigs from apple and sycamore trees. Colonies of birds may amass huge structures. In an aviary, the pair may breed in nest boxes. These birds nest more readily when housed in groups, due to their highly social nature: bear this in mind when planning a breeding programme.

✦ ABOVE
The grey-breasted parakeet is another name for the monk or quaker parakeet. These birds must be housed in flights covered in 16 gauge mesh.

COCKATIELS

With their crests, and in their breeding behaviour, cockatiels
(*Nymphicus hollandicus*) resemble cockatoos, but they also have
a number of characteristics that are more typically associated
with Australian parakeets, and these have helped to ensure their
widespread popularity as aviary birds. For many years, the cockatiel
was overshadowed by its better-known Australian relative, the
budgerigar, but during the later years of the 20th century it achieved
worldwide popularity in its own right, thanks particularly
to the emergence of colour mutations.

◆ OPPOSITE
The red-eyed silver is one of the less
common mutations, shown here in the
company of a white-faced cock bird.

◆ ABOVE LEFT
The white-faced cockatiel cock bird
has a pure white face. The hen's facial
plumage is greyish.

COCKATIELS

The original grey form of the cockatiel is easy to recognize – predominantly grey with white patches on the wings. Cock birds have prominent yellow areas on the sides of their faces, with circular orange patches of plumage there as well. Adult hens are less distinctive. Their facial plumage is greyer, although the undersurface of their tail feathers is clearly barred with yellow.

Cockatiels are popular both as pets and aviary birds, but it is important to start out with a genuine youngster if you are seeking a companion bird. If possible, start off with a hand-raised chick. Recently fledged chicks resemble hens, although it is possible to identify them by the pinkish tinge to the cere above the bill, incorporating the nostrils. Young birds' tail feathers are shorter than adults' when they are weaned and ready to be rehomed.

Young cockatiels can be nervous to start with, but they settle down quickly and will become very tame. Many people prefer cock birds as pets because of their attractive whistling calls, but unless the young cockatiels are sexed by means of DNA, it is impossible to distinguish the sexes until the cocks start singing at around three months of age. Cockatiels can live well into their teens, and have been known to live into their late twenties in some more exceptional cases.

Although cockatiels have a similar history of domestication to the budgerigar, becoming well known and widely bred from the 1840s onwards, it was not until a century later that the first mutation – the pied – became established. Pieds have variable areas of light and dark plumage, and the pattern of distribution is random and highly individual. Those having extensive solid areas of colour are often described as lightly variegated.

It was the emergence of the lutino mutation in Florida during the late 1950s that first focused attention on the cockatiel. These birds are a striking pale lemon shade all over, with orange cheek patches. Visual sexing is still possible but harder than with the grey: the barring under the hen's tail feathers is not clearly defined against the white background.

BREED BOX

Length	30 cm (12 in)
Incubation period	19 days
Fledging period	35 days
Clutch size	5–6 eggs

Feather-plucking is known to be a problem with various strains of lutino cockatiels: signs include having a slightly bald area behind the crest. If buying a new cockatiel, it helps to start out with young birds because you can be certain that they have not been feather-plucked. Nothing can be done once the feathers have been removed, other than waiting for them to grow back again. Take particular care with the housing of recently fledged cockatiels in this condition if the climate is anything but warm, because they are vulnerable to being chilled until their plumage has regrown.

Another highly attractive cockatiel mutation is the cinnamon, in which the grey plumage has become brownish. The cocks are a darker shade of brown than the hens, and the mutation is sex-linked in its mode of inheritance, the same as the lutino.

✦ ABOVE
Grey is the usual colour of cockatiels, as shown by this pair. Cockatiels breed well in aviaries, while young birds can develop into excellent companions.

✦ RIGHT
Sexing cockatiels is quite straight-forward. The cock bird's head is predominantly yellow, while the hen's is much greyer.

◆ BELOW
It is possible to combine the cinnamon characteristic with other mutations, as shown by this primrose cinnamon pied. In this case, the pied areas have a fairly pronounced yellow tone.

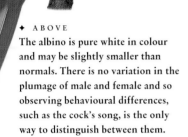

◆ ABOVE
The albino is pure white in colour and may be slightly smaller than normals. There is no variation in the plumage of male and female and so observing behavioural differences, such as the cock's song, is the only way to distinguish between them.

An unusual colour change occurred in Germany with the emergence of the pearl mutation. The centres of the individual feathers have lost pigment, and are thus paler than the edges. In the cock birds, this feature tends to become obscured with maturity. The pearl mutation is not linked with a particular colour and so can be seen in association with other forms as well, although it is less distinctive in the case of lutinos.

The emergence of the white-faced mutation is particularly significant. All yellow and orange pigmentation has disappeared from the feathering. As a result, cocks can be distinguished by their pure white heads; the hens' heads are greyish-white. By combining this mutation and the lutino, it has been possible to create the albino, which is pure white in colour with reddish eyes.

The silver mutations of the cocka-tiel occur in two forms, a dominant version which is fairly common, and a rare recessive form, with red eyes.

Recent mutations have resulted in changes to the ear patches, but these are not common.

With so many different mutations and varieties, it is not surprising that there is growing interest in exhibiting cockatiels, particularly in North America, where judging standards are well established.

Cockatiels are very easy to look after. Feed them on a budgerigar seed mix, augmented by some sunflower and safflower seeds, groats and a little hemp. Alternatively, offer a complete diet. If you are using seed, add a supplement to combat Vitamin A deficiency, which can contribute to chick mortality in the nest. Offer greenfood, apple and soft food regularly, particularly during the breeding period.

One of the less obvious charms of the cockatiel is its very gentle nature. Cockatiels can be kept with finches, quails, doves and non-aggressive softbills, although their size in a small flight can be upsetting to very small birds. You can also keep cockatiels on a colony basis, although breeding results are never as good as when they are housed in individual pairs. This is because they will share nest boxes, and the number of eggs laid is too great for a single bird to brood, increasing the likelihood of fatal chilling.

Both parents share incubation and brooding duties. As they grow older, the chicks hiss menacingly in the nest when they are disturbed. Pairs should be restricted to rearing two broods in a season. Remove the nest box in the autumn or they may attempt to breed right through the winter.

◆ LEFT
The markings of pied cockatiels are highly individual and not just in the feathering. In this individual, some dark pigment is retained on the bill. The feet, too, can be variable in colour.

◆ ABOVE
In the case of the cinnamon mutation, the grey colour assumes a brownish hue. This is a sex-linked mutation.

COCKATOOS

Cockatoos are among the most distinctive parrots, thanks to their crests, which they will raise when excited or alarmed. They originate from islands off the coasts of Indonesia and New Guinea, and their distribution extends to Australia. The group can be broadly divided into two categories – the black cockatoos and those with predominantly white feathering. The black are rare in aviculture compared with the white.

One of the greatest difficulties is in ensuring compatibility between the members of a pair. It is not uncommon for a pair to live in harmony until the start of the breeding season, when the cock will turn on his mate, seriously attacking or even killing her. Even a proven pair can offer no guarantee. Starting out with odd birds is especially dangerous, particularly if the hen is younger than her mate and nesting for the first time. The safest option is to acquire young birds, having had them sexed by the DNA method, and then wait for them to breed in due course. Having grown up together, the bond between them is likely to be greater than when two adult birds are put together. Once established, pairs of cockatoos may breed successfully for more than 20 years.

◆ OPPOSITE
Strikingly attractive, but expensive and problematic to pair up successfully, the Major Mitchell's or Leadbeater's cockatoo is only suitable for experienced breeders.

◆ LEFT
When resting, cockatoos like this citron-crested keep their crest feathers folded back over the top of the head. The shape of the crest varies between the members of this group.

LESSER SULPHUR-CRESTED COCKATOOS

The lesser sulphur-crested cockatoo (*Cacatua sulphurea*) is commonly kept as a pet and for breeding, and is recognized by its yellow ear patches and crest. Another popular choice is the citron-crested (*C. s. citrinocristata*), with its distinctive orange plumage.

Cockatoos are not an ideal choice for the novice bird-keeper because of their temperament. They will screech for long periods and can be destructive; they need well-built accommodation and no neighbours. Their behaviour may worsen as they grow older, particularly if hand-reared, because they then have no instinctive fear of people, and will bite readily.

BREED BOX	
Length	30 cm (12 in)
Incubation period	28 days
Fledging period	75 days
Clutch size	2 eggs

◆ LEFT
A lesser sulphur-crested cockatoo reveals the beauty of its crest feathering. The greater sulphur-crested is not only significantly larger but also has far less distinct yellow patches on the sides of the head.

◆ ABOVE
The citron-crested subspecies of the lesser sulphur-crested cockatoo can be easily identified by the orange rather than yellow areas of plumage.

UMBRELLA COCKATOOS

The largest of the white cockatoos is the umbrella (*C. alba*), so-called because of the shape of its broad crest. It measures 48 cm (19 in) in length, and originates from the northern and central Moluccan Islands of Indonesia.

BREED BOX	
Length	48 cm (19 in)
Incubation period	28 days
Fledging period	84 days
Clutch size	2 eggs

Sexing is carried out visually: the hen's iris is red-brown, whereas that of the cock is usually black. Young birds can be identified by the grey colour of their eyes. Male and female birds share the incubation of a clutch of two eggs. If both eggs hatch, a size difference will develop as one assumes dominance and takes more of the food. The weaker chick will need to be hand-reared if it is to survive.

◆ RIGHT
The broad crest feathers that help to distinguish the umbrella cockatoo, along with its white plumage, can be clearly seen here.

DUCORP'S COCKATOOS

In recent years, a small number of the attractive Ducorp's cockatoo (*C. ducorpsi*) from the Solomon Islands have become available to bird-keepers. These birds are beginning to breed and are becoming established in overseas collections. They average about 30 cm (12 in) in length, have a relatively short crest, and blue skin around the eyes. Unlike many cockatoos, they can be persuaded to sample greenstuff, fruit and vegetables quite readily, particularly when they are rearing chicks.

BREED BOX

Length	30 cm (12 in)
Incubation period	25 days
Fledging period	62 days
Clutch size	2 eggs

◆ RIGHT
Ducorp's cockatoo has a relatively small crest and a blue area of skin surrounding the eyes.

GALAH COCKATOOS

The galah or roseate cockatoo (*Eolophus roseicapillus*) is one of the easier species to manage, although over-reliance on sunflower seed in the diet can cause problems, giving rise to lipomas (fatty tumours). It can be difficult to persuade cockatoos to alter their dietary preferences, so always offer them a varied diet from the outset. Try a complete diet, which offers a more nutritionally balanced alternative to seed alone.

The pink and grey colour scheme of the galah cockatoo is unique. These birds may mature as early as two years old and are more prolific than the white cockatoos, sometimes laying four or five eggs. Incubation is shared in typical cockatoo fashion. Compatability between members of the pair is far less a problem in the case of these cockatoos, compared to their *Cacatua* cousins. Occasional colour variants have also been recorded, noticeably a white-backed form where grey plumage is replaced by white feathering. As with other cockatoos, galahs are hardy when housed in aviaries, while, temperamentally, they make better pets than other species. No cockatoos are especially talented as talking birds, although they can learn to whistle a passable tune.

BREED BOX

Length	35 cm (14 in)
Incubation period	25 days
Fledging period	49 days
Clutch size	2–5 eggs

◆ RIGHT
The galah cockatoo is one of the more dependable species of cockatoo for breeding, although much depends on the individual temperaments of a pair.

LORIES AND LORIKEETS

These colourful parrots originate from islands off the coast of Indonesia, New Guinea, the Pacific Islands and Australia. Many display areas of bright red in their plumage and their striking coloration is part of the appeal of this group of birds, quite apart from their friendly personalities.

Lories and lorikeets differ from other parrots in their feeding habits. They rely heavily on flowers for the nectar and pollen, which is the mainstay of their diet, although they will also eat fruit and roughage. In the past, keepers were forced to rely on their own recipes, which were not always nutritionally sound, but today, excellent commercial brands are available in powdered form to be mixed with water. Read the instructions carefully and do not mix up more nectar than will be required for one day, as any that is not consumed must be discarded before it sours. It is important to clean out the drinker thoroughly, using a bottle brush and washing up liquid to remove any trace of old residues. Never provide nectar in open containers because the birds will try to bathe in them. For those housed inside, provide a separate container of water for bathing.

Dry lory diets are available, which can be offered separately or sprinkled over fruit. Few breeders use them exclusively in place of a nectar solution, although they do add variety to the diet when used in moderation.

◆ OPPOSITE
Various lories and lorikeets like these Musschenbroek's are small, quiet birds. They are easy to accommodate in aviary surroundings.

◆ LEFT
Active, lively and inquisitive by nature, lories like the black-winged make personable aviary occupants, often becoming very tame with their keepers.

LORIES AND LORIKEETS

Feeding lories is not especially difficult in most cases because their lively, curious natures ensure that they are usually quite willing to sample unfamiliar items in their food dish with little hesitation. This means that you can take advantage of fruits in season, but offer only small quantities at first, increasing the amount gradually, so as to avoid changing the birds' diet suddenly. Especially when first acquired, they can be vulnerable to enterotoxaemia, a bacterial illness which is likely to be rapidly fatal.

The liquid droppings of this group of birds means that they are not popular as pets, being messy in the home, but they do make very lively companions and can master a few words. In aviary surroundings, their accommodation needs to take account of their diet. Easily washable surfaces should feature on the walls of the shelter, while it helps if the floor of the flight is of paving slabs or concrete which can also be washed off easily. Visual sexing is not possible.

GREEN-NAPED LORIKEETS

The green-naped lorikeet (*Trichoglossus haematodus*) is one of the most widely distributed lorikeets, occurring in more than 20 different forms across its wide range, which extends from parts of Asia to southern Australia. Dark green wings, a colourful breast, bluish head feathering and a contrasting green area on the sides of the head is the typical coloration of green-naped lorikeets.

Pairs will usually nest quite readily. It is sensible to line the nest box with a thick layer of wood shavings, in view of the liquid nature of their diet. The incubation period lasts for 27 days, with the chicks fledging at about eight weeks old. This stage can be identified by the fledglings' dark irises and bills.

Feather-plucking of the chicks can be a problem with some pairs; often the problem will be resolved only when the chicks leave the nest. The damaged plumage will regrow but there is a danger that the young birds will behave in the same way towards their own offspring.

Green-naped lorikeets will live happily enough in a colony in a large aviary, where they make an entertaining sight, although they can be noisy. Have the birds sexed first, and space the nest boxes around the flight at the same height to prevent any squabbling. Providing a choice of nest boxes is also important to breeding success.

✦ LEFT
Green-naped
lorikeets have
patches of greenish-
yellow plumage on
the nape of the neck,
and darker edging
to the plumage on
the breast.
Subspecies differ in
their coloration and
markings. None can
be visually sexed.

BREED BOX	
Length	23 cm (9 in)
Incubation period	27 days
Fledging period	56 days
Clutch size	2 eggs

GOLDIE'S LORIKEETS

Goldie's lorikeet (*T. goldie*) originates from New Guinea and averages just 17.5 cm (7 in) long. They tend to be quieter than most lorikeets, and are usually quite hardy once properly acclimatized. Sexing on the basis of their head coloration or streaking on their bodies is unlikely to be reliable. The hen lays two eggs which hatch after about 24 days. The young fledge at around two months of age.

BREED BOX

Length	17.5 cm (7 in)
Incubation period	24 days
Fledging period	60 days
Clutch size	2 eggs

✦ ABOVE
Goldie's lorikeet is a very attractive species. Pairs are generally keen to breed. The calls of these birds are not loud.

MUSSCHENBROEK'S LORIKEETS

Musschenbroek's lorikeet (*Neopsittacus musschenbroekii*), from New Guinea, needs more seed in its diet than other nectar-feeding parrots, although the mixture of dissolved sugars and other ingredients is still important.

✦ RIGHT
Musschenbroek's lorikeet can suffer from tapeworms, and it may be worthwhile to have their droppings screened. Cock birds can be distinguished from hens by the more extensive brown feathering on the head.

BREED BOX

Length	23 cm (9 in)
Incubation period	26 days
Fledging period	65 days
Clutch size	2 eggs

CHATTERING LORIES

The beautiful chattering lory (*Lorius garrulus*), with the striking red plumage, is from the Moluccan Islands of Indonesia. The yellow-backed chattering lory (*L. garrulus flavopalliatus*) is instantly recognizable by the area of yellow plumage across the top of the wings. These are noisy birds, as their name suggests.

Pairs breed reliably over many years. The hen incubates the two eggs for about 26 days, and the chicks leave the nest by about 11 weeks old.

BREED BOX

Length	30 cm (12 in)
Incubation period	26 days
Fledging period	77 days
Clutch size	2 eggs

✦ LEFT
Chattering lories are robust and long-lived. Pairs are usually keen to breed. They can be noisy. Note the absence of yellow plumage across the back in this individual.

CARDINAL LORIES

Another lory with predominantly red plumage, the cardinal lory (*Chalcopsitta cardinalis*) originates from the Solomon Islands and is so named because its colour matches a cardinal's robes. It is a relative newcomer on the avicultural scene.

Pairs nest quite readily. The hen lays two eggs which hatch after 24 days. The young fledge at 10 weeks and they can be identified easily at this time by their brownish bills.

Like other members of this particular genus, such as the yellow-streaked lory (*C. sintillata*), the calls of these birds are relatively loud.

BREED BOX	
Length	30 cm (12 in)
Incubation period	24 days
Fledging period	70 days
Clutch size	2 eggs

✦ RIGHT
Red plumage predominates in the case of the cardinal lory. Visual sexing, as with many lories and lorikeets, is impossible.

BLACK-WINGED LORIES

The black-winged lory (*Eos cyanogenia*) is a member of the *Eos* group of lories, which are well represented in aviculture. The red plumage is broken by areas of black or dark blue. Measuring approximately 28 cm (11 in) in length, the black-winged lory occurs on islands around the Geelvink Bay area of New Guinea. It may have a musky odour, more noticeable if the birds are housed in an indoor flight. This smell is quite normal.

BREED BOX	
Length	28 cm (11 in)
Incubation period	24 days
Fledging period	77 days
Clutch size	2 eggs

✦ LEFT
The black-winged lory is characterized by the large areas of solid black plumage on the wings, although the precise extent of these areas varies between individuals.

STELLA'S LORIKEETS

The main difference between lories and lorikeets is the shape and size of the tail feathers; lorikeets' tails are longer and more tapering than lories' tails. Stella's lorikeet (*Charmosyna papou*), originating from the highlands of central New Guinea, is a striking example. Stella's lorikeets have two distinct colour phases. In the black phase, known as the melanistic form, the red feathering is largely replaced by black; in the red phase, the hen has yellowish markings in the vicinity of the rump. The red areas which are retained in the melanistic cock bird allow the sexes to be distinguished.

Bills should be bright red – pale coloration is usually a sign of liver failure or other chronic illness.

✦ RIGHT
Stella's lorikeet – this one's a male – is one of the most exquisite of all lorikeets. They tend to hop rather than walk along perches. These birds become very tame in aviary surroundings.

BREED BOX	
Length	38 cm (15 in)
Incubation period	26 days
Fledging period	56 days
Clutch size	2 eggs

DUSKY LORIES

The dusky lory (*Pseudeos fuscata*) from New Guinea has distinct colour phases. The markings of these birds are individual, varying from a fiery shade of orange to a relatively dull yellow. It can be possible to distinguish pairs by the colour of the feathers on the rump; the cock bird's are more yellow than the hen's. Pairs usually nest readily and the hen lays two eggs which hatch after 24 days. The young emerge from the nest box 10 weeks later. Like most of the larger lories, the dusky is quite hardy once properly acclimatized, especially when provided with a nest box for roosting. Chicks which have been plucked in the nest will be vulnerable to chills.

BREED BOX	
Length	25 cm (10 in)
Incubation period	24 days
Fledging period	70 days
Clutch size	2–4 eggs

✦ RIGHT
This is an example of the yellow phase of the dusky lory. The coloration in this case is not as intense as in orange phase birds.

SWIFT PARAKEETS

The distinction between lorikeets and parakeets is blurred in the case of the swift parakeet (*Lathamus discolor*), also known as a lorikeet. Its tongue is not so well adapted as lorikeets' with the tiny papillae that can be raised to act as brushes to collect pollen. Seed should feature in the swift parakeet's diet, as well as fruit, greenstuff and livefood such as mealworms.

Visual sexing is difficult, though hens are generally duller in colour than cock birds. It is usually suggested that cocks have slightly larger areas of red plumage with odd red feathers evident, especially on the breast and abdomen, whereas hens are more yellow-green overall, with paler legs. Young swift parakeets are less colourful than adults, with darker irises. A yellow mutation has been recorded in the case of this species, but it is very rare. The typical green plumage is replaced by yellow in this case, with the remainder of the coloration being unaffected. It is possible to house these attractive parakeets on a colony basis in a large aviary, and they can be bred successfully in these surroundings. Introduce the pairs at the same time and provide a choice of nesting sites.

BREED BOX	
Length	25 cm (10 in)
Incubation period	18 days
Fledging period	42 days
Clutch size	4–5 eggs

✦ LEFT
The swift parakeet shares characteristics with both lorikeets and parakeets. It is a southern bird, breeding on the Australian island of Tasmania and migrating back across the Bass Strait, which divides Tasmania from the mainland, for the winter.

PARROTS

Although the number of parrots favoured as household pets on the basis
of their powers of mimicry is relatively small, a much wider range of species is bred
in aviary surroundings. While some are highly destructive by nature and have loud
calls, which means that they may be unsuitable for aviaries in urban areas, there are
actually many others, such as the parrotlets, which can be housed
without great expense in a typical suburban garden aviary. The hanging parrots
can even be accommodated in a planted flight with softbills, while the colour
varieties that have been developed in the case of the peach-faced lovebird,
mean that there is plenty of scope if you are interested in colour-breeding.
Even some of the larger parrots are not especially noisy, as with members
of the *Poicephalus* group, such as the Senegal.

◆ OPPOSITE
Yellow-faced parrotlets are one of the
relatively few South American parrots
which can be sexed by sight. They are also
quiet, making them suitable for housing
in town aviaries.

◆ ABOVE LEFT
Yellow-collared macaw. Like a number of
other parrots, these particular birds have a
beautiful, almost iridescent sheen on their
green plumage, which is seen at its best in
bright sunlight.

HANGING PARROTS

There are 13 different species of hanging parrot, and distribution ranges from south-east Asia across the islands to the south. Apart from those species mentioned here, the remaining species are scarce in aviculture worldwide. Hanging parrots are small birds, about 13 cm (5 in) in length, predominantly green in colour. This allows them to blend in with their background, making them hard for predators to spot. Head markings help to distinguish one species from another.

Hanging parrots are quiet, secretive birds, preferring a well-planted flight where they can conceal themselves among the vegetation. They are not destructive or aggressive and may be kept as part of a mixed collection, including softbills. Their dietary needs are similar to softbills' – a fresh daily supply of a nectar solution and fruit such as diced apple and grapes sprinkled with a soft

food. Some hanging parrots will also eat invertebrates, such as mealworms, and many enjoy bite-size pieces of sponge cake soaked in nectar: offer the cake in a small container which is too small for the bird to bathe in, otherwise it will jump right in and its plumage will become very sticky. It is important to give these small parrots an opportunity to bathe each day. Provide a container of water for this purpose, in addition to fresh drinking water.

As the breeding season approaches, the hen cuts down leaves for nesting material, tucking these in among the feathers of her rump and transporting them back to the nest box. The nest box should be about 15 cm (6 in) square and 20 cm (8 in) in depth internally. The hen lays three eggs and these hatch after 20 days. The young emerge about a month later.

BLUE-CROWNED HANGING PARROTS

The blue-crowned hanging parrot (*Loriculus galgulus*) is probably the most widely kept member of the group. Its natural distribution extends from the Malay Peninsula southwards to Sumatra and neighbouring islands. Cocks are instantly recognizable by the circular blue area on the top of their heads and their scarlet throats. Their rumps are red, with an adjoining area of tawny yellow feathering. Hens

are much duller in comparison. They normally lack the red area seen on the throat of the cock bird, as well as the yellow band across the lower back. The highly characteristic

◆ LEFT
This blue-crowned hanging parrot is a cock bird. Interestingly, hens have occasionally been recorded as having a red throat spot, so do not rely entirely on this feature for sexing purposes.

BREED BOX	
Length	13 cm (5 in)
Incubation period	20 days
Fledging period	33 days
Clutch size	3 eggs

blue spot on the cock's crown is barely visible either. Chicks in this case are duller in plumage than hens. Their foreheads are a grey colour, with a bluish tinge, and the red feathering on the rump is much duller than in the adults. The chicks' legs are significantly paler in colour than those of the parents, and the bill is a pale horn colour, rather than black. On fledging, the young parrots are fed by the cock bird for several weeks until they are fully independent, by which stage, the hen may already have begun to nest again.

VERNAL HANGING PARROTS

The vernal hanging parrot (*L. vernalis*) occurs mainly in Asia, ranging from India to Vietnam, although it is also to be found on the Andaman Islands. Both male and female are the colour of new leaves. Cock birds may be distinguished by their white irises; the hens' irises are brown.

BREED BOX	
Length	13 cm (5 in)
Incubation period	20 days
Fledging period	33 days
Clutch size	3 eggs

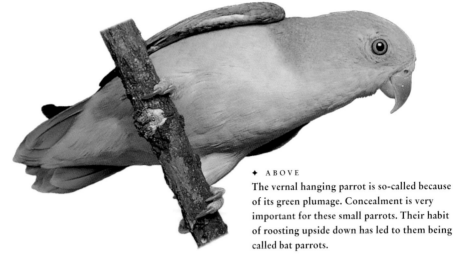

✦ ABOVE
The vernal hanging parrot is so-called because of its green plumage. Concealment is very important for these small parrots. Their habit of roosting upside down has led to them being called bat parrots.

They roost by hanging upside down off a secure perch or the aviary mesh. The roof of the flight must be covered to prevent them from being attacked by passing cats or foxes. It is important to check their claws regularly; overgrown claws hamper the bird's ability to roost.

CELEBES OR RED-CROWNED HANGING PARROTS

The attractive Celebes or red-crowned hanging parrot (*L. stigmatus*) has become more popular in aviculture in recent years. These birds are slightly larger and more active than the vernal, but they roost in a similar way, and their care is identical in all respects. They can be sexed easily.

BREED BOX	
Length	15 cm (6 in)
Incubation period	20 days
Fledging period	33 days
Clutch size	3 eggs

✦ LEFT AND RIGHT
In a pair of Celebes hanging parrots, the cock bird is more colourful than the hen. These birds are not as common in aviculture as previous species mentioned.

LOVEBIRDS

This group of nine different species of small, short-tailed parrots from Africa is one of the most popular among bird-keepers across the world.

In most cases, it is not possible to sex the birds by sight and for many years breeders were forced to rely on the pelvic bone test to distinguish pairs. This method is only reliable during the breeding season, however, when the space between the hen's pelvic bones enlarges to allow for the passage of the eggs. Keeping unsexed birds on a colony basis is fraught with danger because they may fight viciously. Reliable scientific sexing methods have removed the guesswork from identifying pairs, and even though these tests can be costly compared with the price of the birds, they should ensure breeding success.

Lovebirds are generally hardy by nature, particularly when established in their quarters, but the peach-faced is especially susceptible to frostbite. These birds should not be encouraged to remain on perches in the open part of the flight when the temperature is set to drop below freezing. Most pairs will use a nest box for roosting; alternatively, design the shelter so that they can be shut in when the weather is at its worst.

The aggressive nature of lovebirds means that when they are housed in adjacent flights, the adjoining faces must be double-wired so as to prevent the birds from biting their neighbours' toes severely when they are within reach. Check the double-wiring regularly – over time, and after much aggressive biting, the mesh may sag on the frames, making contact between the birds possible. The two layers of mesh can be pushed apart again by inserting wooden notches in-between the opposite strands of mesh, to keep the two faces apart.

Otherwise, feeding and caring for lovebirds is straightforward. They will eat a diet of budgerigar seed, groats, sunflower and safflower seeds, augmented by greenstuff which must be given regularly. Soft food may be eaten when there are chicks in the nest. Lovebirds' bills are quite strong; they can whittle away branches, so be prepared to replace perches. Young hand-reared lovebirds, or those which have just become independent, can develop into friendly pets and can be taught to talk and whistle quite successfully, although they are not as talented in this respect as budgerigars. The average lifespan is 10 to 15 years.

PEACH-FACED LOVEBIRDS

The peach-faced lovebird (*Agapornis roseicollis*) is probably the most widely kept of the group, and is bred in a range of colour varieties. As the name suggests, these parrots have salmon-pink facial plumage, which is offset against a green body and blue rump. They are one of the larger lovebird species at about 15 cm (6 in) in length.

The first colour mutation in the peach-faced was reported in 1954 from Japan. It is a yellow variant which retains its pink face, and is known as the golden cherry. More spectacular is the lutino, an American mutation from the 1970s. It can be identified by its red eyes and white rump.

Pied versions of the peach-faced lovebird occurred in the United States, with a separate strain being developed in South Africa. These birds were originally green with variable areas of yellow feathering. Now the pied characteristic has been combined with blue series peach-faced birds.

◆ RIGHT
The slight green tinge on the wings of this white-faced cobalt reveals that it is not a true blue, but a dark factor form of the pastel blue.

◆ ABOVE
The American golden cherry is in effect the yellow form of the peach-faced, with the United States mutation emerging after this colour was originally reported from Japan. It is the oldest of the peach-faced colours.

◆ LEFT
This normal pied shows roughly equal areas of yellow and green plumage. The precise markings can differ quite widely in the case of pieds.

BREED BOX

Length	15 cm (6 in)
Incubation period	23 days
Fledging period	42 days
Clutch size	4–5 eggs

◆ ABOVE
The peach-faced lovebird cannot be sexed visually, but in spite of this handicap, these lovebirds are now the most widely kept of the entire group.

The first blue variant to be developed appeared in 1963 and was of Dutch origin. Today, this variant is most commonly known as the pastel blue. These birds are not pure blue in colour, but retain a green hue to their plumage. Their facial colour is a very attractive pale salmon pink.

The appearance of a dark factor mutation, matching the dark factor seen in the budgerigar, meant that both green and blue series lovebirds could be bred in light or dark tones. The lighter coloured variants are known as dark green or jade, and cobalt, whereas those with darker coloration are described as olive and mauve. Among other peach-faced mutations which parallel those in the budgerigar are cinnamon and grey.

By combining the primary mutations, a much wider range of colour varieties has been developed, including the appropriately named buttermilk, which is a creamy pale yellow shade. There have also been changes to the facial coloration in more recent times, thanks to the creation of the orange-faced mutation, although this is still quite rare.

Not surprisingly, with such a large number of colours available, there is increasing interest in exhibiting lovebirds. The birds are very often exhibited in pairs and their appearance together can be quite stunning; a well-matched pair is certain to win over an individual if the birds are equal in other respects. Condition is vital, however, and both birds must be in perfect feather.

◆ LEFT
The orange-faced mutation affects only the facial coloration, as its name suggests. Here it is seen in combination with the dark factor jade (or dark green) mutation.

◆ RIGHT
An attractive young pair of pastel blue pieds show the characteristic but variable sea-green and pale lemon markings.

MASKED LOVEBIRDS

The masked lovebird (*A. personata*) has several colour variants, and although there are not as many as the peach-faced, it does have a much longer history.

The blue is the best-known form, in which the usual yellow areas are replaced by white, and the green by blue. There is also a dilute form of the masked, sometimes rather misleadingly called the yellow, in which the colour is paler than normal. When combined with the blue mutation, this gives rise to the so-called white, in which the blue plumage is paler and the black area on the head is much paler than normal.

The masked lovebird is a member of the white eye-ring group of lovebirds, distinguished by the prominent bare area of skin around the eyes. The group is also linked by its nesting behaviour. Nesting materials are carried to the site in the bills, rather than tucked between the feathers like the peach-faced lovebirds.

✦ ABOVE
The masked lovebird is recognizable by the black coloration, extending over its head like a mask, as well as by yellow feathering beneath.

✦ LEFT
The blue mutation of the masked has been bred for over 70 years, making it the oldest of all the known colour varieties in the lovebird group.

BREED BOX	
Length	14 cm (5$^{1}/_{2}$ in)
Incubation period	23 days
Fledging period	42 days
Clutch size	4–5 eggs

FISCHER'S LOVEBIRDS

The widely kept Fischer's lovebird (*A. fischeri*), one of the white eye-ring group, originates from Tanzania. Fischer's construct an untidy, often domed nest in the nest box. Colour mutations exist, but are less common than in the masked. A blue form was bred in South Africa but was not established. Today's Blue Fischer's are descended from a bloodline developed in California in 1979, while in Australia a black-eyed yellow variant has also emerged.

BREED BOX	
Length	14 cm (5¹/₂ in)
Incubation period	23 days
Fledging period	42 days
Clutch size	4–5 eggs

✦ LEFT
The prominent area of white skin around the eyes of Fischer's lovebird marks these birds out as belonging to the white eye-ring group. They cannot be visually sexed.

ABYSSINIAN LOVEBIRDS

The Abyssinian lovebird (*A. taranta*) originates further north than members of the white eye-ring group and, unlike them and the peach-faced, it can be sexed easily – cock birds have a broad area of

✦ BELOW
A pair of Abyssinian lovebirds in which the cock can be distinguished by the red feathering on the head. They are sometimes called black-winged lovebirds because of the colour of their flight feathers.

BREED BOX	
Length	16 cm (6¹/₄ in)
Incubation period	23 days
Fledging period	45 days
Clutch size	3–4 eggs

red plumage extending back up the face from the bill over the eyes. Abyssinians do not construct an elaborate lining in their nest box. The hen will lay on a soft pad of feathers that may have been plucked from her own upper breast. The plumage will soon regrow.

This particular species is also known as the black-winged lovebird, thanks to the colour of its black flight feathers and the underwing coverts.

GREY PARROTS AND ECLECTUS PARROTS

Both these species are widely bred – the grey parrot is very popular as a pet – but neither has close relatives within the parrot family. They were both brought to Europe as early as the 1500s, although it was not until much later that it was realized that the cock and hen eclectus are in fact the same species, such is the striking difference in their appearance.

The grey parrot extends right across Africa, living in the equatorial region south of the Sahara. There are two recognizable forms, the timneh and the red-tailed. The timneh (*Psittacus erithacus timneh*) is found only on the western side of the continent. It can be distinguished from the red-tailed (*P .e. erithacus*) by its smaller size, darker grey coloration, lighter-coloured upper bill and maroon tail feathers. Young birds of either type can be identified by their dark irises; mature birds have whitish irises.

Sexing grey parrots visually is very difficult, although in some cases cock birds may have recognizably darker colouring on their wings.

BREED BOX	
Length	33 cm (13 in)
Incubation period	29 days
Fledging period	80 days
Clutch size	3–4 eggs

For breeding purposes, DNA sexing is recommended, although simply having a true pair offers no guarantee of success. Compatibility is an important consideration, and it is for this reason that a proven pair of grey parrots is likely to command a premium price compared with sexed pairs which have not bred together previously. Should you find that after two years or so, a pair has shown no interest in breeding, it may be

worthwhile swapping the male. Success may then follow quite rapidly, with the hen already well established in her quarters.

A standard quality parrot seed mix can be used as the basis for their diet, but a complete diet is better. Greys are prone to feather-plucking, particularly in the home, and this may be linked to poor diet coupled with lack of bathing facilities. Daily spraying is necessary if the parrot is kept in the house. Greys dislike cold damp weather and in an aviary it is vital they have suitable indoor accommodation when the weather is bad. Only well-acclimatized birds should be expected to overwinter without heating.

♦ LEFT
Grey parrots develop into excellent pets and are unrivalled mimics, but they do have a shy side to their natures.

BREED BOX

Length	35 cm (14 in)
Incubation period	30 days
Fledging period	77 days
Clutch size	2 eggs

◆ BELOW
In the case of eclectus parrots, the cock bird is
predominantly green, while the hen is mainly
red. Young birds show these different colours
as soon as they start to feather up in the nest.

It is important to obtain a grey
parrot soon after weaning if you are
seeking a pet. They are shy birds,
and it is very difficult to win the
confidence of an untamed adult bird.
Greys nest through much of the year
and are bred and hand-reared on a
large scale, so there is usually a ready
choice of chicks available in Europe
and North America.

Eclectus parrots (*Eclectus roratus*)
do not have a fixed breeding
season, but can breed through much
of the year. Hens lay two eggs in a
clutch, with incubation and fledging
details similar to those of the grey
parrot. Pairs will often produce young
of one sex only, for biological reasons
which are as yet unclear. It is vital that
eclectus parrots have a good supply of
greenstuff such as spinach, chickweed
and dandelion as part of their regular
daily diet, along with vegetables such
as corn-on-the-cob and carrot. A
vitamin and mineral supplement is
advisable if the birds are eating seed
rather than a complete food.

POICEPHALUS PARROTS

There are nine different species of poicephalus parrot, all of which are widely distributed across Africa. The colour of the birds is variable, and they range in length from 22–30 cm (9–12 in), although they are all quite stocky and short-tailed in appearance. They need to be housed in reasonably strong aviaries, constructed using 16 gauge mesh. The timber should be protected from the birds' bills, which can cause substantial damage. These parrots make attractive aviary occupants. Adult birds will probably remain shy, but hand-reared chicks can develop into friendly companions. They have a good lifespan; Senegals have been known to live for over 40 years.

SENEGAL PARROTS

The most widely kept member of the poicephalus group is the Senegal parrot (*Poicephalus senegalus*) from west Africa. It has a greyish head and a green breast and wings. The underparts vary in colour from yellowish orange to red. Visual sexing is impossible.

Senegals are not noisy; their calls consist of a series of rasping whistles rather than discordant screeches.

The hen often flares her tail in the vicinity of the nest box as the time for nesting approaches, and she spends time inside the box before actually laying. It is essential to site the nest box in a reasonably dark corner of the aviary, preferably in the shelter, as all poicephalus parrots are reluctant to nest in the open. The hen lays three or four eggs which hatch after 28 days. The young fledge when they are about nine weeks old.

✦ LEFT
This Senegal parrot (*Poicephalus senegalus versteri*) can be distinguished by its deep orange underparts. It also tends to be a darker shade of green than other forms.

BREED BOX

Length	25 cm (10 in)
Incubation period	28 days
Fledging period	63 days
Clutch size	3–4 eggs

MEYER'S PARROTS

Meyer's parrots (*P. meyeri*), found over a wide area of eastern and southern Africa, show even greater variation in appearance than the Senegal. Generally, they are brownish grey on the head and wings, with bluish green underparts. In some but not all cases, there will be a yellow area of plumage on the crown, while all of them display yellow at the bend of the wings, at the top of the legs and on the undertail coverts. It is often assumed that slight differences in plumage provide a means of distinguishing cocks from hens but this is not the case.

Breeding details are the same as for the Senegal. Fledgling Meyer's parrots are predominantly grey with no yellow markings, and their irises are dark.

BREED BOX

Length	23 cm (9 in)
Incubation period	28 days
Fledging period	60 days
Clutch size	3–4 eggs

✦ RIGHT
Meyer's parrot occurs in a number of different colorations, some of which are more colourful than others. These parrots cannot be sexed visually.

RUPPELL'S PARROTS

Ruppell's parrot (*P. rueppellii*), from south-west Africa, is not widely kept. Visual sexing is straightforward; unusually, the cock bird is less colourful than his mate, being silvery brown on the head and underparts, with a distinct shade of grey over the wings. Yellow markings are evident at the highest point on the wings and on the thighs. Hens have a blue abdomen, upper back and rump.

BREED BOX

Length	23 cm (9 in)
Incubation period	28 days
Fledging period	68 days
Clutch size	3–4 eggs

Ruppell's prefer to nest during the northern hemisphere's winter months, when the likelihood of success is significantly reduced unless they are housed in indoor accommodation with extra heating and lighting available. A flight, forming part of a birdroom, is probably the best option, with the nest box indoors. Some pairs of Senegals may show a tendency to breed at this time of year, but this is less common. Ruppell's parrots may take insects when rearing their young, so mealworms should be offered to them at this stage. Other rearing foods, such as egg food, may also be eaten.

✦ LEFT
Ruppell's parrots can also be sexed by sight; the hen is the more colourful.

RED-BELLIED PARROTS

Probably the most colourful and certainly one of the most attractive of the poicephalus parrots is the red-bellied (*P. rufiventris*) from East Africa. Visual sexing is relatively straightforward; the head and wings of both sexes are brown, but the underparts of the hen are lime green and the underparts of the cock bird are brilliant orange. The cock also has green feathering on the legs.

BREED BOX	
Length	23 cm (9 in)
Incubation period	28 days
Fledging period	84 days
Clutch size	3 eggs

Feeding can present problems. Some birds will eat only a mixture of sunflower seed and peanuts, which are frequently a particular favourite of this group of parrots. This leaves them vulnerable to Vitamin A deficiency, and a vitamin and mineral supplement is essential. Offering a selection of fruit and greenstuff will show you what your birds like – pomegranates are often a favourite.

✦ BELOW
Red-belllied parrots can be easily sexed by the colour of their underparts. It is possible to sex young chicks on this basis, as they start to feather up.

JARDINE'S PARROTS

Not all poicephalus parrots are found
in fairly open countryside. The
attractive Jardine's parrot (*P. gulielmi*)
occurs in forested areas of central
Africa. There are three types, varying
mainly in the extent and depth of their
orange plumage. The Masai (*P. g.
massaicus*), from Kenya and Tanzania,
has less orange-red plumage on its
head and is a slightly paler shade of
green than the most widely distributed
central African type (*P. g. gulielmi*),
which extends as far south as Angola.
The northern type (*P. g. fantiensis*),
from Ghana and the Ivory Coast, has
paler orange markings than the
others, and more prominent green
edging to the feathers over the back.
It is important not to pair these
different types haphazardly in order
to maintain the variations.

   Jardine's parrots are among
the larger members of the
poicephalus group, averaging
about 28 cm (11 in) long.
Cocks have reddish-brown eyes
whereas hens' eyes are brown,
but this is not a reliable means
of distinguishing between the
sexes. The skin around the eyes
is especially pronounced. However,
it should not be swollen because this
could indicate an upper respiratory
tract infection, especially if one or
both nostrils appear blocked as well.

✦ LEFT
Another Jardine's
parrot reveals the
difference in types.
This is *Poicephalus
gulielmi massaicus*
from east Africa.

✦ LEFT
This Jardine's parrot (*Poicephalus gulielmi
fantiensis*) comes from Liberia, the Ivory Coast
and Ghana in West Africa. The orange plumage
is prominent on the head in this individual.

BREED BOX	
Length	28 cm (11 in)
Incubation period	27 days
Fledging period	80 days
Clutch size	3–4 eggs

PARROTS

As their name suggests, parrotlets are miniature parrots. There are seven recognized species of these birds, and they are all predominantly green in colour, with short, square tails. Their original distribution extends from Mexico down into South America.

Parrotlets are ideal for back garden aviaries, but these are aggressive birds and must be kept in separate pairs. They will usually nest very well. The nest box should be about 13 cm (5 in) square and 20 cm (8 in) tall, and lined with wood shavings. Despite their small size, parrotlets cannot be bred satisfactorily in flight cages; cock birds are often aggressive in these surroundings, particularly to their own male offspring. They may inflict fatal injuries on the male chicks prior to fledging. Parrotlets are prolific when nesting, usually proving to be double-brooded, and the adult birds will probably be keen to nest a second time after chicks are hatched.

Feeding is straightforward. Parrotlets will readily take a seed mixture comprising mixed millets, plain canary seed, groats, some sunflower, small pine nuts and a little hemp, augmented by greenstuff and fruit. Seeding grasses are a particular favourite. A supplement should be given regularly, and grit and cuttlefish bone or a calcium supplement must be provided. Parrotlets can live for around 20 years or more, and have been known to breed successfully well into their late teens.

CELESTIAL PARROTLETS

The celestial (*Forpus coelestis*), the most widely kept and bred of the parrotlets, originates from parts of Ecuador and Peru, in north-western South America. It is one of the most attractively coloured members of the group and can be easily sexed. The cock bird is silvery-green; the sides of the face are of a bright apple-green and there is blue behind the eyes and on the edges of the wings. The rump feathering is blue. Hens are recognized by a less silvery tone to their plumage and a smaller blue area on the face. These little parrots make good companions if obtained at an early age, and will even learn to say a few words, although they are not talented mimics.

◆ LEFT
The celestial is the most widely kept parrotlet. These birds can be very aggressive, however, in spite of their small size.

BREED BOX

Length	13 cm (5 in)
Incubation period	23 days
Fledging period	28 days
Clutch size	4–9 eggs

YELLOW-FACED PARROTLETS

The yellow-faced parrotlet
(*F. xanthops*) is found in a very
restricted area of Peru. It is closely
related to the celestial but at nearly
15 cm (6 in) in length, slightly larger.
Distinctive facial colouring extending
down to the throat sets it apart from
other species. Sexing the bird is
straightforward: the feathering over
the rump is of a light blue shade in the
hen and a deeper shade of cobalt in
the cock. The yellow-faced has bred
successfully in captivity and so chicks
are often available. Its care does not
present any particular problems.

BREED BOX

Length	15 cm (6 in)
Incubation period	23 days
Fledging period	28 days
Clutch size	4–6 eggs

✦ ABOVE
Yellow-faced
parrotlets are the
most colourful
members of the
Forpus group, as well
as being the largest
in size.

GREEN-RUMPED PARROTLETS

Some colour mutations are available
in parrotlets, particularly the Guiana
or green-rumped (*F. passerinus*).
Unusually, the hen is more colourful
in this species than the cock, with a

yellow area around the bill. Among
the colours which have been reported
in this species are blue, lutino and
cinnamon forms. These birds are
popular with bird-keepers in South
America. At the present time,
however, they are less well-known
than elsewhere. In spite of their small
size, these parrotlets are quite hardy
once acclimatized. Provide the hen
with a nest box for nesting purposes.

BREED BOX

Length	13 cm (5 in)
Incubation period	23 days
Fledging period	28 days
Clutch size	5–6 eggs

✦ RIGHT
In the case of the green-rumped parrotlet, the
hen, with the yellow on the head, is more
colourful than the cock bird.

PIONUS PARROTS

There are seven species of pionus parrot, and they are widely distributed across parts of Central and South America. Although not especially well-known in bird-keeping circles, these parrots are bred regularly in small numbers and are a much better proposition, both as pets and as aviary occupants, than their larger relatives, the Amazons. Pionus parrots (their generic and common name is the same) are quieter by nature than Amazons, and they are less temperamental once they mature. Nevertheless, if you are seeking a pet, it is vital to obtain a hand-reared youngster because adults, unused to human contact, can be very shy, even in aviary surroundings.

DUSKY PARROTS

The coloration of pionus parrots may be unusual and there can be considerable individual variation. The light plays a part; seemingly drab plumage is transformed by sunlight, with shimmering shades appearing that had previously been invisible.

♦ RIGHT
Coloration is a notable feature of pionus parrots. White, brown, pink, blue and red are all apparent in the feathers of this dusky parrot.

An example is the dusky parrot (*Pionus fuscus*). In sunlight, hues of brown, pink, blue, violet and red are all apparent, with flecks of white feathering on the head.

When purchasing pionus parrots, especially adult birds, take time to watch them in their quarters before reaching any decision. Notice if the bird is perching with sleek plumage and is alert. If not, these are signs that something could be wrong, especially if coupled with any indication of weight loss over the breastbone. Also, they can wheeze rather alarmingly when handled, and it can be difficult to determine whether this is just because they are distressed by being caught, or whether they are suffering from the chronic fungal disease, aspergillosis, of which wheezing is a symptom.

Pionus parrots will benefit from a secluded aviary, and interference should be kept to a minimum when a pair do decide to breed; otherwise, these parrots may neglect or even attack their chicks. Hens lay three or four eggs which hatch after 26 days or so. The young birds leave the nest for the first time when they are approaching 10 weeks of age.

BREED BOX	
Length	24 cm (9¹/₂ in)
Incubation period	26 days
Fledging period	70 days
Clutch size	3–4 eggs

BLUE-HEADED PARROTS

The blue-headed parrot (*P. menstruus*) has the greatest range of the group, extending from Costa Rica as far south as Bolivia. It is also the most commonly encountered of the pionus parrots in bird-keeping circles. It is unmistakable, thanks to the rich deep-blue plumage covering the entire head. The ear coverts are black. The blue

becomes reddish where it merges with the green coloration that predominates over the rest of the body. These parrots are about 28 cm (11 in) in length; they cannot be sexed visually.

✦ ABOVE
This is a blue-headed parrot. The pinkish colour on the throat is variable in extent. The upper bill is unusually coloured – black with red areas on the sides.

BREED BOX

Length	28 cm (11 in)
Incubation period	26 days
Fledging period	70 days
Clutch size	3–5 eggs

BRONZE-WINGED PARROTS

✦ RIGHT
Like other pionus parrots, which are active by nature, the bronze-winged will benefit from having a spacious flight. Only in flight will the stunning sky-blue plumage under the wings be revealed.

The bronze-winged parrot (*P. chalcopterus*) has dark blue underparts, and isolated pinkish feathers under the throat, often extending on to the head. The bill is a pale shade of yellow. As these parrots come into breeding condition, so the pink skin around their eyes darkens in colour. This area is yellow in young birds, which also have brownish feathering on their underparts.

BREED BOX

Length	28 cm (11 in)
Incubation period	26 days
Fledging period	70 days
Clutch size	3–4 eggs

AMAZON PARROTS

Amazons are probably the best-known group of New World parrots, having been kept as pets in Europe for over 500 years. The advent of reliable sexing methods has been partly responsible for triggering greater interest in breeding these birds, and pairs can nest reliably for many years. They also rank among the longest-living of all parrots, with an average life expectancy equivalent to our own.

Keeping an Amazon is not something to be undertaken lightly, however, because they can be very demanding birds. First and foremost, they are noisy and given to regular periods of screeching at sunrise and sunset. This is normal behaviour but is not guaranteed to endear them to neighbours who do not share your enthusiasm for these parrots.

Young Amazons can develop into excellent mimics, both of speech and sounds, although they are probably not as talented in this respect as the grey parrot. Amazons have bolder, brasher, more confident natures, however, and this is why they often do well in talking bird competitions, where they delight in running through their repertoire in front of an appreciative judging audience. There is considerable debate amongst *aficionados* about which species of Amazon has the potential to be the best mimic, but this probably depends more on the teacher than the bird.

Diet is critical to Amazons' well-being. Many species are prone to weight gain unless their diet is carefully controlled. They need a regular daily supply of roughage, vegetables and fruit, as well as seed, if they are to remain in good health, particularly as they are prone to vitamin A deficiency. Hand-reared birds often take to a complete diet, avoiding concerns over vitamin and mineral deficiencies, but it is more difficult to wean adult birds off a seed mix comprising sunflower seed and peanuts. Supplementation will be essential in this case.

Aside from becoming more vocal and destructive as the time for breeding approaches, cock Amazons may become aggressive, and if so they will not hesitate to attack you if you venture too close to the nesting site. This is a particular problem encountered with hand-reared birds because they have little if any instinctive fear of people. Careful siting of the nest box can avoid possible conflicts at this stage, allowing you to attend safely to the birds' daily requirements.

Most pairs breed in the spring. Hens lay three or four eggs in May in northern temperate areas. Incubation lasts 26–29 days. The young leave the nest seven to nine weeks later. Soaked seed is valuable as a rearing food. It will be several years before the young birds nest for the first time.

BLUE-FRONTED AMAZON PARROTS

The blue-fronted Amazon (*Amazona aestiva*), from south-eastern South America, is often kept as a pet. Young birds are recognizable by their duller coloration and dark irises. The species is one of the longest-living, and records show that individual birds have lived for almost 100 years. There is no way of sexing these birds by differences in coloration – DNA sexing will be required. Pairs should be allowed to settle in their quarters before being expected to breed. This can take a year or two, but after this they are likely to breed annually.

✦ RIGHT

In common with other Amazons, blue-fronts show variable coloration on their heads, allowing individuals to be recognized without difficulty. Some have more blue feathering above the cere than others.

BREED BOX

Length	38 cm (15 in)
Incubation period	27 days
Fledging period	60 days
Clutch size	3–5 eggs

ORANGE-WINGED
AMAZON PARROTS

The orange-winged Amazon (*A. amazonica*), from north-eastern South America, is slightly smaller than the blue-fronted, averaging about 33 cm (13 in) overall. It may have some blue plumage on the head, mixed with yellow, but can be distinguished by the colour of its upper bill, which is mainly horn-coloured rather than black. The orange, rather than red, coloration on the wings and tail are further points of distinction, which separate it from the blue-fronted Amazon.

BREED BOX

Length	33 cm (13 in)
Incubation period	26 days
Fledging period	60 days
Clutch size	3–4 eggs

◆ RIGHT
Orange-winged Amazons are so-called because of the areas of orange plumage in their wings, which can be clearly seen when these parrots are in flight.

YELLOW-FRONTED
AMAZON PARROTS

The yellow-fronted Amazon (*A. ochrocephala*) occurs in nine different forms throughout its wide range. These include the double yellow-head (*A. o. oratrix*), which is the variety most in demand. It is also the largest, averaging 38 cm (15 in). The head of the adult birds is entirely yellow; youngsters have yellow plumage just on the forehead and crown. Red plumage is visible on the shoulders.

In the case of the yellow-naped Amazon (*A. o. auropalliata*), which is also found in Central America, the yellow plumage is restricted to the nape of the neck, and young birds show virtually no trace of yellow on their heads.

More limited distribution of yellow plumage is a feature of the yellow-fronted Amazon itself, found in northern South America. Its bill is horn-coloured at the sides. The entire bill of the Panamanian yellow-front (*A. o. panamensis*) is a pale horn shade. This bird is approximately 30 cm (12 in) long, and is the smallest of the group.

BREED BOX

Length	38 cm (15 in)
Incubation period	26 days
Fledging period	60 days
Clutch size	3–5 eggs

◆ RIGHT
There are nine different forms of the yellow-fronted Amazon. They differ in size and in the distribution of the yellow plumage on the head.

MEALY AMAZON PARROTS

The mealy Amazon (*A. farinosa*) spans both Central and South America, the more colourful variety being found to the north of its range. The top of the head of the blue-crowned mealy (*A. f. guatemalae*) is blue, becoming greyer over the nape extending down to the mantle. Its range extends from Mexico to Honduras, and it has become better known to bird-keepers in recent years.

The mealy is the largest of the mainland species, slightly larger than the double yellow-headed Amazon. Confusion can arise between them because some mealy Amazons from South America have a yellow area on their heads, but this does not usually extend up from the cere, as it does in the yellow-fronted Amazon.

BREED BOX

Length	38 cm (15 in)
Incubation period	26 days
Fledging period	60 days
Clutch size	3–4 eggs

As with the majority of Amazons, visual sexing is not possible, and pairs can only be recognized with any certainty by DNA sexing. A stout aviary will be needed to house these noisy birds. Unless you have no close neighbours, the mealy Amazon is not likely to be a good choice of pet because of its loud calls. As with other Amazons, the mealy is at risk from a deficiency of Vitamin A if fed mainly on seed. Fruit and greenstuff should therefore figure in the diet, along with a vitamin and mineral supplement if the parrot is not being fed on a complete food.

✦ RIGHT
The mealy Amazon has a voice to match its size, often proving to be the noisiest member of a raucous group.

WHITE-FRONTED AMAZON PARROTS

The white-fronted (*A. albifrons*), the smallest of the Amazons measuring about 25 cm (10 in) in length, is widely distributed through Central America, from Mexico southwards to Costa Rica. It is the only one of the Amazons that can be sexed on the basis of its coloration. The leading edge of the wings has red plumage in cock birds, green in hens. These Amazons may be easier to manage than their larger relatives, but they can still be noisy and they need a robust aviary with a ready supply of perches, because these will be whittled away quite frequently by the birds' powerful bills. Young white-fronted Amazons can be recognized quite easily because the area of white plumage on the head is reduced in extent and has a yellowish tinge. The red feathering around the eye is also reduced in extent. It is possible to sex these parrots by the time they fledge, thanks to the red plumage present on the wings of the males.

BREED BOX

Length	25 cm (10 in)
Incubation period	26 days
Fledging period	60 days
Clutch size	3–4 eggs

✦ LEFT
The white-fronted Amazon is instantly recognizable by the white area above the cere and the adjoining area of red plumage, which forms a narrow band around the eye. These parrots are sometimes called spectacled Amazons.

PRIMROSE-CHEEKED AMAZON PARROTS

The primrose-cheeked or red-lored Amazon (*A. autumnalis autumnalis*), from Central America, is one of the most colourful and attractive Amazons. Its black eyelashes – which are actually modified feathers – are especially evident against the white skin surrounding the eyes. Other, less colourful varieties of this species, such as Salvin's Amazon (*A. a. salvini*), occur in South America but are rarely seen in collections. Young birds in all cases have dark irises when they first leave the nest.

✦ RIGHT
In spite of its name, the primrose-cheeked Amazon manages to combine red, yellow and lilac markings on its head. It is a species which has grown in popularity over recent years.

BREED BOX

Length	33 cm (13 in)
Incubation period	26 days
Fledging period	60 days
Clutch size	3–4 eggs

MACAWS

The macaws are one of the most distinctive groups of New World parrots, thanks to the seemingly bare areas on the face which are in fact covered in patterns of tiny feathers. These thinly covered areas of skin can reflect the bird's mood, becoming redder when the bird is excited or angry.

No other group shows such a variation in size as the macaws. They range from approximately 91 cm (36 in) long down to the diminutive red-shouldered macaw (*Ara nobilis*) which is just 30 cm (12 in) in length. All macaws have a similar body shape, with long tails. The largest macaws are also the most colourful. There are no distinctive differences in plumage between the sexes, although hens can be recognized by their smaller heads.

Macaws in general are long-lived birds – they can live for well over half a century – and it may take five years or more for youngsters of the multi-coloured species to reach maturity. Youngsters can become very tame and will learn to talk, although none of the macaws is especially talented in this respect, but their powerful bills, loud

voices, and for the larger ones, their size, mean that they are difficult to accommodate satisfactorily in the home environment. The dwarf macaws are easier to cater for, although they too can be noisy and are destructive by nature. In contrast to their larger relatives, they are predominantly green in colour.

It is usually not difficult to convert macaws to a complete diet compared with some other parrots. Read the instructions on the package carefully; some are only recommended for use when birds are breeding. Otherwise, walnuts, hazel and Brazil nuts should figure prominently in the diets of the larger multi-coloured macaws. Mixed nuts are obtainable from specialist seed merchants.

Macaws should be housed in individual pairs for breeding; only the red-shouldered macaw can be bred successfully on a colony basis. Stout nest boxes are essential for all macaws, in view of their destructive natures. Large reinforced barrels, mounted on secure platforms, are good for the larger species.

RED AND GOLD (SCARLET) MACAW

The red and gold macaw (*Ara macao*) has the largest distribution of any parrot in the Americas, from Mexico southwards right down to parts of eastern Peru, Bolivia and parts of Brazil. Unfortunately, however, these birds have now been declared an endangered species under the international CITES convention, largely as a result of loss of habitat in the northern end of its range. In practical terms this means that,

depending on where you live, you may need to obtain official permission before you can advertise chicks that you breed for sale, or adult birds. Advice on the current situation should be obtained from the government department concerned with wildlife matters, which acts as the CITES management authority.

These particular macaws are easy to distinguish from the closely-related green-winged, not just by the golden yellow feathering over their wings, but also by their red plumage, which is scarlet rather than crimson. As a result, they are also known as scarlet macaws. It is virtually impossible to sex the birds by sight, although the heads of cock birds will often appear more bold. Young birds can be recognized by their dark irises and shorter tail feathers. The care of

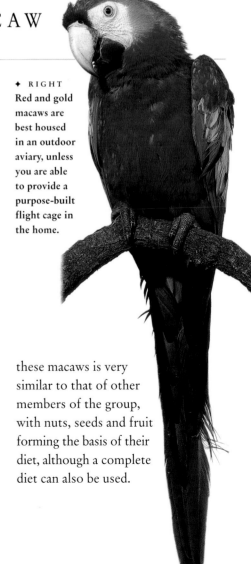

◆ RIGHT
Red and gold macaws are best housed in an outdoor aviary, unless you are able to provide a purpose-built flight cage in the home.

these macaws is very similar to that of other members of the group, with nuts, seeds and fruit forming the basis of their diet, although a complete diet can also be used.

BREED BOX

Length	85 cm (34 in)
Incubation period	28 days
Fledging period	90 days
Clutch size	2–3 eggs

BLUE AND GOLD MACAWS

The striking blue and gold macaw (*A. ararauna*), one of the most widely kept macaws, is found over a huge area, from Panama down across much of South America. It has deep sky-blue plumage, extending from the vicinity of the crown over the entire back and wings. There is a small area of greenish plumage above the bill, and a small area of black adjoining the whitish facial skin. The tiny feather tracts on the face are unique to the individual

BREED BOX	
Length	82.5 cm (33 in)
Incubation period	28 days
Fledging period	90 days
Clutch size	2–3 eggs

bird and can be used to prove identity if a bird escapes or is stolen. Microchipping is a safer option, however, because there is a register to confirm the bird's identity.

An interesting mutation of this species is the blue, in which the gold is replaced by white feathering. One such bird was exhibited in France and another in the UK some years ago. In 1999, two young blue and white macaws were displayed at the UK's National Exhibition of Cage & Aviary Birds and hopes are high that this mutation can be successfully established. At present, there are no other colour variants.

GREEN-WINGED MACAWS

The green-winged (*A. chloroptera*) is another of the multi-coloured macaws, with a massive range from Panama to

BREED BOX	
Length	89 cm (35 in)
Incubation period	28 days
Fledging period	90 days
Clutch size	2–3 eggs

northern parts of Argentina. Crimson-red feathering predominates, with an area of green and blue plumage across the wings. The lower back and rump are also blue. Young birds can be identified by their dark irises and shorter tails, and by the maroon rather than crimson feathers in the prominent feather tracts extending across the face. Although gentle by nature in most cases, housing these birds in the home presents difficulties, especially as they have powerful calls.

◆ ABOVE
Like others of its kind, the green-winged macaw needs plenty of strong perches to exercise its powerful bill. Perches have to be replaced regularly as they are whittled away.

YELLOW-COLLARED MACAWS

The yellow-collared macaw
(*A. auricollis*), well established in
aviculture, is found in Latin America,
in parts of Brazil, Paraguay, Bolivia
and Argentina. It is one of the more
colourful dwarf macaws, with a
relatively loud call. As with other
macaws, the cock and hen form a
strong bond.

BREED BOX	
Length	40 cm (16 in)
Incubation period	26 days
Fledging period	70 days
Clutch size	2–3 eggs

✦ ABOVE RIGHT
The neck feathering of the yellow-
collared macaw enables it to be easily
identified. Some birds may have an
orange tinge to the yellow feathering.

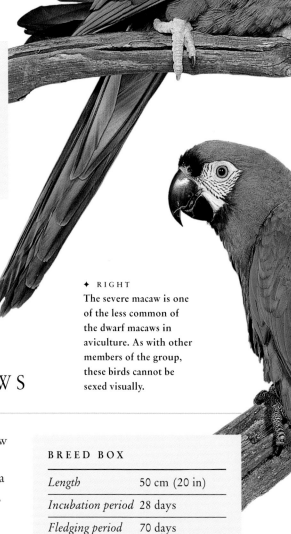

✦ RIGHT
The severe macaw is one
of the less common of
the dwarf macaws in
aviculture. As with other
members of the group,
these birds cannot be
sexed visually.

SEVERE MACAWS

The severe or chestnut-fronted macaw
(*A. severa*), less colourful than its
relatives, ranges from parts of Panama
to Bolivia and Brazil. A dwarf macaw,
it is slightly larger than the yellow-
collared. A broad band of chestnut
coloured plumage, just above the cere,
gives the bird its alternative name.
The remainder of the plumage is
predominantly green, with blue on the
head, wings and tail. Red patches are
evident on the edge of the wings, in
the vicinity of the shoulders. This
feature is seen in a number of macaws.

BREED BOX	
Length	50 cm (20 in)
Incubation period	28 days
Fledging period	70 days
Clutch size	2–3 eggs

The birds often use this as a threat,
by opening their wings to reveal the
colour and intimidate a rival. They
may also use it in their mating display.

RED-BELLIED MACAWS

The red-bellied macaw (*A. manilata*) originates from northern South America. It is instantly recognizable by the maroon feathering on its lower underparts, and the bare area of pale yellowish skin on the sides of the face. While most macaws are hardy once acclimatized and easy to look after, the red-bellied has gained a reputation for

being more problematic. They have a tendency to become obese very easily, which shortens their lifespan, and therefore, unless feeding a complete diet, fruit, vegetables and greenstuff should figure prominently. Offer them mixed nuts in preference to a standard parrot seed mix containing sunflower and peanuts. They will also require secluded aviary surroundings to give them a sense of security. Should the birds appear very nervous, screen the sides of the flight for added privacy until they are settled.

BREED BOX

Length	48 cm (19 in)
Incubation period	27 days
Fledging period	77 days
Clutch size	2–4 eggs

✦ RIGHT
The red-bellied macaw can be vocal, like other members of this group, and the calls of these dwarf macaws can be quite loud.

RED-SHOULDERED MACAWS

The red-shouldered or Hahn's macaw (*A. nobilis*), the smallest member of the group, is predominantly green in colour, with red markings on the undersides of the wings in the vicinity of the shoulders. They closely resemble their larger relatives and, being of a manageable size, make excellent pets. Red-shouldered

macaws are more prolific than their larger relatives. Hens lay clutches of four eggs whereas bigger species may produce two or three. The incubation periods are similar, 24–26 days, but young red-shouldered macaws leave the nest at just eight weeks of age while multi-coloured macaws are likely to remain there for a further month. Just like their larger relatives, however, these so-called "mini macaws" can display their mood by blushing when excited or alarmed: the facial skin becomes redder as a result of increased blood flow.

BREED BOX

Length	30 cm (12 in)
Incubation period	25 days
Fledging period	54 days
Clutch size	3–4 eggs

✦ ABOVE
The red on the wing that gives the red-shouldered macaw its name is clearly visible in this individual.

DOVES AND PIGEONS

There are no clearly defined features that separate pigeons from doves, except that pigeons are usually larger in terms of their overall size. In fact, these names are sometimes used interchangeably in the case of some species. A number of pigeons and doves are highly coloured, with hues to rival those of parrots, but the majority will not become tame, and especially when transferred to new accommodation, they may fly around wildly and are at risk of injuring themselves. Planted aviaries are generally favoured for housing purposes, especially for the more nervous or ground-dwelling species, with the likelihood of breeding success also being increased in these surroundings. The cover helps to provide a hen with retreats where she can escape the ardour of the cock bird, as he may become very aggressive towards her during courtship. Despite their image as birds of peace, doves and pigeons can be surprisingly aggressive on occasions, and generally, pairs need to be housed individually rather than as a group. They can be kept quite satisfactorily in the company of other birds, however, although it is important to match the size of the birds carefully, as large pigeons will prove very disruptive if kept in a flight in the company of small finches.

♦ OPPOSITE
The Luzon bleeding heart is one of the doves that inhabits areas of tropical forest, and it will need similar cover in its aviary. Otherwise these birds have a tendency to become very nervous.

♦ LEFT
Names can be deceptive with this group of birds in describing their habits. As an example, the stocky little bare-eyed ground dove will actually spend less time on the ground than perched on a tree branch.

DIAMOND DOVES

Pigeons and doves may be kept as part of a mixed collection alongside finches and softbills, but they are nervous and so not suitable as household pets, with the exception of the diamond dove (*Geopelia cuneata*), which originates from Australia. These small doves, averaging about 17.5 cm (7 in) long, are quite steady by nature and can be housed in a large flight cage in the home. They may even breed in these surroundings. However, they are more usually kept in an aviary where the pairs will nest readily, laying several clutches in one season.

The diamond dove is greyish in colour, with delicate white spots over the wings. The wings are of a browner shade than the body. There is a prominent area of red skin around the eyes, which becomes more pronounced in the cock bird at the start of the breeding season.

The young are much duller than adult birds, with mottled wing markings, and the bare skin around the eyes is indistinct. It may be possible to recognize young cock birds before they moult if they start to display in the characteristic manner to hens. Courtship often takes place on the ground, with the cock bird bowing to the hen and fanning his tail feathers to her.

Pairs should be provided with a canary nest pan to support their nest, which will be constructed using pieces of moss, small twigs, feathers and other material collected around the aviary. Although these doves breed for much of the year, it is preferable to restrict breeding activity to the summer period, when success is more likely. The hen

◆ LEFT
The red periorbital skin surrounding the eye becomes more pronounced in cock birds at the start of the breeding period, as shown by this individual.

◆ ABOVE
This is the usual grey form of the diamond dove. These birds spend a lot of time on the floor of their quarters searching for seeds.

◆ LEFT
A family of diamond doves, comprising a blue cock bird, a dilute hen and their two young chicks which have recently left the nest. Young birds are much duller in colour than adults at this stage. They are also vulnerable to chilling during prolonged spells of wet weather.

BREED BOX

Length	17.5 cm (7 in)
Incubation period	13 days
Fledging period	13 days
Clutch size	2 eggs

✦ ABOVE
The zebra dove is so-called because of the distinctive black and white striped patterning on its chest and underparts. These are not particularly lively birds.

✦ BELOW
Red coloration in the case of these doves is of an auburn shade.

✦ BELOW
The cream form of the diamond dove displays a warmer, slightly yellowish shade compared with the silver.

lays two white eggs, which hatch after 13 days. The chicks develop rapidly and fledge after a similar period of time, often leaving the nest before they are fully able to fly. This need not be a cause for concern, provided that the young doves can retreat under cover, because the cock bird in particular will continue to look after them and they will soon be perching.

Diamond doves are best accommodated as individual pairs rather than in small groups. Fighting may break out between cock birds, and breeding results are likely to be less satisfactory.

There are a growing number of colour varieties. The first was the silver; other colours include cream, fawn, chestnut-red and greyish-blue varieties. Pieds have also been developed, and wing markings with bar patterns.

Diamond doves are easy to feed. A mixture of millets is an ideal diet, augmented with other small seeds. They also eat greenstuff such as chopped chickweed. Soft food should be provided during the breeding and moulting periods.

The zebra dove (*G. striata*), slightly larger and not as widely kept as the diamond dove, occurs over a huge area from India eastwards across Asia, and down to Australia. They vary somewhat in appearance as a result of this range but, as a general guide, hens are always duller than cock birds. They require similar care.

AUSTRALIAN PIGEONS

These large birds are often to be found on the floor of the aviary, seeking out spilt seeds and other foods. During warm sunny weather, they will often sunbathe in typical pigeon fashion. This can be quite alarming at first sight, since the bird will lie at an abnormal angle, with one or both of its wings outstretched, suggesting that it may have had a fit or suffered a blow to the head. Most Australian pigeons are actually very hardy and generally long-lived, however, with pairs frequently nesting readily once they are established in their quarters.

GREEN-WINGED PIGEONS

The green-winged pigeon (*Chalcophaps indica*), also known as the emerald dove, is very colourful. Approximately 25 cm (10 in) long, its pinkish body is offset by the rich emerald-green plumage of the wings. Hens may be identified by the grey rather than whitish feathering on their foreheads.

BREED BOX

Length	25 cm (10 in)
Incubation period	13 days
Fledging period	14 days
Clutch size	2 eggs

Like many birds that originate from forested areas, the emerald dove is nervous and should be accommodated in a planted flight where there is plenty of ground cover. This will also increase the possibility of breeding success. A varied diet, including seeds, invertebrates, berries and diced fruit, along with a softbill food or pellets, keeps these doves in good condition. They can be housed in the company of non-aggressive softbills and are unlikely to interfere with them in any way because they spend much of their time on the aviary floor. Emerald doves are not hardy, even once acclimatized, and their outside flight must be well protected from the elements, with good drainage to prevent any flooding of the aviary floor.

Wicker nest baskets or a plywood platform, concealed in among the vegetation, may encourage a pair to breed. Either of these provides support for the nest, which is often a loose jumble of twigs and other material. Hens lay two eggs and incubation and rearing take about 14 days each. Remove the chicks about a week later because the adult pair may want to nest again.

◆ LEFT
This is a green-winged pigeon or emerald dove. Outside Australia, it is the Asiatic forms which are most commonly seen in aviculture. Cock birds have white or grey head markings, not evident in the Australian form.

AUSTRALIAN CRESTED PIGEONS

The Australian crested pigeon (*Ocyphaps lophotes*) is a very striking bird, not just because of its upright crest, but also on account of the kaleidoscope of colours which is the result of the iridescent plumage in the wings and tail. These pigeons are reasonably placid by nature but, nevertheless, they are better suited to an aviary where the other occupants

BREED BOX

Length	33 cm (13 in)
Incubation period	15 days
Fledging period	21 days
Clutch size	2 eggs

✦ LEFT
The Australian crested pigeon may be hard to sex, but as in the case of most pigeons and doves, established pairs will breed readily.

are of a similar size, approximately 33 cm (13 in) long, rather than being housed in the company of small birds.

Visual sexing is very difficult, although hens may be smaller than cock birds. The hen lays two eggs and the pair share incubation duties, in typical pigeon and dove style, with the cock sitting for much of the day. The young will acquire adult plumage at around six months old. Young cocks can then be recognized by their display, when the wing colours will be clearly apparent. Young birds may be nervous when first introduced to new accommodation, but they soon settle, and are quite hardy.

COMMON BRONZE WING PIGEONS

Common bronze wing pigeons (*Phaps chalcoptera*) are more nervous than Australian crysteds, but are very similar in their requirements. Hens are paler in colour than the cock birds, with greyish rather than white plumage on the head. They also lack the red coloration seen on the breast of cock birds. A pigeon seed mix, plus greenstuff and livefood, will keep

BREED BOX

Length	35 cm (14 in)
Incubation period	16 days
Fledging period	21 days
Clutch size	2 eggs

✦ RIGHT
A male common bronze-wing pigeon, showing the characteristic iridescence over the wings. Compatability can sometimes be a problem with these birds; cocks can be very aggressive at the start of the breeding period.

them in good health. Grit and cuttlefish bone should also be provided. Cocks can sometimes be aggressive towards their intended mates at the start of the breeding period, and it may be necessary to separate them briefly, taking the cock bird away from the aviary and reintroducing him later in the season.

ASIATIC PIGEONS AND DOVES

A range of different species originates from Asia. It includes the various collared doves, recognizable by a black neck band, which are amongst the easiest to manage and require little more than a mixture of seed, through to the fruit pigeons and doves, widespread across the islands of south-east Asia, which need to be offered a softbill type of diet. Careful handling is necessary to avoid damaging the birds' feathers.

RED TURTLE DOVES

The attractive red turtle dove (*Streptopelia tranquebarica*) is one of the collared doves. The sexes can be easily identified because only the cock birds display the typical reddish coloration; hens are brown. These turtle doves thrive on a diet of mixed seeds and greenstuff, and can be bred successfully in mixed collections, even in the company of cockatiels. A nesting platform is important to provide support for the nest; if left to the birds to construct, the nest may collapse, particularly if other birds attempt to steal pieces of material from it, as is highly likely.

BREED BOX	
Length	23 cm (9 in)
Incubation period	13 days
Fledging period	14 days
Clutch size	2 eggs

Hens lay two eggs and incubation lasts about 13 days. The chicks grow readily and leave the nest after two weeks. In some cases, one of the chicks may be neglected, its sibling taking more of the food. Supplementary feeding at this stage, when they are feathering up, is then essential. Pairs are likely to nest several times in rapid succession, so the young should be removed as soon as they are feeding independently and transferred to another flight.

✦ LEFT
The red turtle dove – a cock bird is shown here – is also sometimes called the red collared dove. Their relatively small size and the ease of identifying pairs means that this species is a popular choice with many bird-keepers.

BLEEDING HEART DOVES

This small group of birds is under threat in many parts of their home-land, the Philippines, as a result of forest clearance. However, reasonable numbers are bred in captivity, especially the Luzon (*Gallicolumba luzonica*). As the name suggests, these birds have red plumage on their chests.

Bleeding heart doves must have a well-planted enclosure, affording them plenty of seclusion, with heated winter-time accommodation in temperate areas. A varied diet, including livefood such as mealworms, suits them well. They spend much of their time foraging on the ground, and are likely to choose a nesting site in this area. The pair will take turns to sit, over the course of a fortnight, and the young may leave the nest at 10 days old. At this stage, they are dull brown in colour, and it will take at least six weeks for the red area on the chest to become apparent.

Remove the young when they become independent.

BREED BOX	
Length	25 cm (10 in)
Incubation period	14 days
Fledging period	10 days
Clutch size	2 eggs

PIED IMPERIAL PIGEONS

Not all pigeons are adaptable in their feeding habits. The imperial pigeons, and their smaller cousins, the fruit doves, both require a softbill-type diet. They must be provided with a selection of chopped and diced fruit, sprinkled with softbill food or mynah pellets. The pied imperial (*Ducula bicolor*) is a striking example of the group, with a large gape which enables it to swallow whole fruits such as grapes without difficulty. DNA or surgical sexing is necessary to distinguish pairs. A nesting platform should be provided. The birds use twigs, and anything else they can find as a basis for the nest. When the young pigeon first leaves the nest it will not be able to fly properly. As it starts out, it will fly around its quarters in a wild fashion, and can very easily injure itself. Take care not to frighten young birds at this early stage, to avoid provoking panic and the risk of serious injury.

✦ RIGHT
The pied imperial pigeon differs significantly in terms of its dietary needs from most pigeons and doves. It must be treated like a softbill rather than a seed-eater.

BREED BOX	
Length	45 cm (18 in)
Incubation period	28 days
Fledging period	30 days
Clutch size	1 egg

AFRICAN PIGEONS AND DOVES

Few of these species are well-known in bird-keeping circles, but their care presents no great problem. A number of species require heated winter accommodation, however, such as the Cape dove, which is often kept as part of a mixed collection alongside waxbills. Planted enclosures are recommended for wood doves in particular, greatly increasing the likelihood of breeding success with these birds.

LAUGHING DOVES

The genus *Streptopelia*, to which the turtle dove belongs, is found in Africa as well as Asia. The laughing dove (*S. senegalensis*) extends across both continents but is widely distributed across most of Africa. The plumage of the laughing dove varies within the range, but as a guide, the hens have a greyer tone on the upperparts than the cock birds. These doves grow to 25 cm (10 in) in length, and can become tame if housed in aviary surroundings.

Laughing doves require a diet of mixed seeds, including millets and canary seed. In common with other seed-eating doves and pigeons, they eat seeds whole, rather than dehusking them as finches and parrots do. Nevertheless, the doves are messy feeders, scattering seeds in search of favoured items; offer the seed mix in a food container with a broad rim to prevent unnecessary wastage.

Laughing doves are named because of their calls, although these are not loud and are unlikely to be a nuisance in terms of disturbance.

BREED BOX

Length	25 cm (10 in)
Incubation period	13 days
Fledging period	14 days
Clutch size	2 eggs

The birds should be provided with a nesting basket in the aviary during the breeding season. The hen will often peck at cuttlefish in her quarters before laying a clutch of two eggs. The young grow rapidly and will fledge at two weeks.

◆ BELOW
The laughing dove is a robust, popular and free-breeding species with a vast natural distribution. The African form is also known as the Senegal dove.

CAPE DOVES

The Cape or black-masked dove (*Oena capensis*) is a very elegant bird, reminiscent of a butterfly in flight. Only the cock bird has the characteristic black marking extending from the head down on to the chest. They are easy birds to feed, on a mixture of small cereal seeds plus some chopped greenstuff, and sometimes a small amount of livefood, but it is often difficult to persuade pairs to nest. Cape doves appreciate warm conditions, and tend to breed better in temperate areas when summers are hot. Patience is needed because, unlike many pigeons and doves, a pair may take two years or more to settle down in new

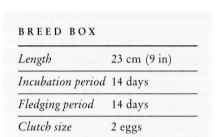

✦ ABOVE

This pair of Cape doves shows the clear sexual dimorphism that exists in this species, thanks to the black plumage of the cock bird.

BREED BOX

Length	23 cm (9 in)
Incubation period	14 days
Fledging period	14 days
Clutch size	2 eggs

quarters before attempting to nest. They will construct their nest on a canary nest pan. The chicks hatch after a fortnight, and fledge after a similar period. Cape doves are not hardy and should be brought inside for the winter, or provided with additional heat and lighting, which makes them ideal companions for waxbills. They may even prefer to breed in these conditions, so nesting facilities should be provided indoors.

WOOD DOVES

Wood doves are more of a challenge to breed than some other doves, requiring time to settle in new surroundings before attempting to nest. The blue-spotted wood dove (*Turtur afer*) is one of three species, all of which have iridescent spots on their wings. The red bill and the

✦ RIGHT

The blue-spotted wood dove uses the iridescence on its wings for display. As their name suggests, these doves benefit from being housed in a well-planted flight, which offers them a sense of security.

BREED BOX

Length	20 cm (8 in)
Incubation period	13 days
Fledging period	13 days
Clutch size	2 eggs

blue spots enable it to be distinguished from its near relatives. These wing spots form part of the cock bird's display, although they are present in the hen as well, which makes sexing difficult. While it is possible to overwinter these small doves outside in mild areas, they cannot be considered entirely hardy in temperate latitudes.

NEW WORLD PIGEONS AND DOVES

None of the doves originating from the New World are especially colourful, particularly those which are well-known in aviculture. Most have predominantly brown feathering, although it is often possible to recognize pairs without difficulty, since cocks are a brighter shade than hens. The pygmy doves are best-known, and pairs often breed well, but cocks can be aggressive towards hens in the early breeding season.

MOURNING DOVES

The mourning dove (*Zenaida macroura*) extends over a wide area of North America and the Caribbean. It averages about 30 cm (12 in) in length. Cock birds are more brightly coloured than hens and show greater iridescence on the plumage of the neck. These doves are easy to keep. Pairs breed readily but cock birds can be very aggressive

✦ LEFT
The call of the mourning dove explains how they acquired their common name.

BREED BOX	
Length	30 cm (12 in)
Incubation period	14 days
Fledging period	14 days
Clutch size	2 eggs

towards their intended mate, persecuting her relentlessly and pecking at the back of her neck. It is advisable to separate them at this stage because the hen could be seriously injured or even killed by her partner. The situation usually arises because the cock is more advanced in terms of breeding condition than the hen, who does not respond to him. Try reintroducing the cock bird at a later stage; things may then proceed without problems.

House them in a planted aviary – do not expect them to nest in the open – and provide several nesting sites, giving the birds an opportunity to select a site where they feel secure. This can help to avoid conflict, especially with a pair that have not nested before. Several clutches of chicks may be reared in rapid succession, with incubation and fledging lasting approximately two weeks each. As with other doves, these birds can live for 10 years or more in aviary surroundings.

GOLD-BILLED GROUND DOVES

A number of ground doves are popular in avicultural circles, although contrary to their name, those from South America rarely spend much time on the ground. One of the best-known species is the gold-billed ground dove (*Columbina cruziana*), which is also known as a pygmy dove because of its small size. These birds average about 17.5 cm (7 in) in length, and originate from north-western South America. Cocks can be easily distinguished from hens by their more

✦ RIGHT
This is a male gold-billed ground dove. Pairs make attractive aviary occupants and often nest readily; cock birds are less aggressive towards their mates than is usually the case with similar species.

colourful bills and greyer heads. Hens are also duller in overall colour. A canary nest pan makes an ideal nesting receptacle for them, and these doves can be bred in the company of

finches and small softbills, but they should be kept apart from their own kind because they will prove to be aggressive. Gold-billed ground doves can live for over 10 years.

BREED BOX

Length	17.5 cm (7 in)
Incubation period	14 days
Fledging period	14 days
Clutch size	2 eggs

BARE-EYED GROUND DOVES

While virtually all pigeons and doves nest in the open, the bare-eyed ground dove (*Metropelia ceciliae*), which originates from the Andean region of South America, is unique in requiring

a nest box for breeding. They also roost in the box. These doves are quite hardy once acclimatized. Breeding behaviour is otherwise the same as that of other ground doves from the region. Chicks should be removed as soon as they become independent because the adult birds are likely to continue with a second nest.

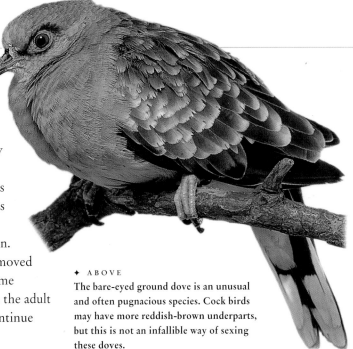

✦ ABOVE
The bare-eyed ground dove is an unusual and often pugnacious species. Cock birds may have more reddish-brown underparts, but this is not an infallible way of sexing these doves.

BREED BOX

Length	15 cm (6 in)
Incubation period	14 days
Fledging period	14 days
Clutch size	2 eggs

ACKNOWLEDGEMENTS

The author and publishers would like to thank the following for their help and cooperation in making this book:
Ghalib Al-Nasser; Dennis Avon; Paul and June Bailey; Fred Barnicoat; Henk Branje; E. F. Cannon; Harry Carr; Irene Christie; Stuart Christophers; Dave Coles; John Daniels; Alain and Janine Delille; Philip Dobinson; Alan Donnelly; Joseph Forshaw; Ken Griggs; Steve Hailey; Barry Hammond; John and Sharon Harris; Harold and Mary Haslam; William Horsfield; Jos Hubers; Graeme Hyde; Colin Jackson; Alan Jones; Ernst Kruger; Peter and Connie Landry; Kees Lansen; Cyril Laubscher; Errol Laubscher; E. R. Lemon; George and Jill Lewsey; Leon Malan; Chris Mason; Stanley Maughan; Jan Muller; Doug Nudd; Arthur O'Bray; Ron Oxley; Roderick Parrish; Nathan Reynolds; Danny Roels; Max Sanderson; Francesca Sherfield; Harry Stephan; Stan Sindel; Rebecca Taylor; Tony Tilford; George Urquhart; Peggy Winser; Michael Woods.

PICTURE CREDITS

t=top; b=bottom; c=centre; l=left; r=right

Dennis Avon 1; 2; 3; 34cr; 35br; 39cl; 39c; 39bl; 39bc; 39br; 41t; 41cl; 41c; 41cr; 41bl; 41bc; 41br; 43cl; 43c; 43cr; 43bl; 43bc; 43br; 44br; 49; 70t; 72cl; 72bc; 72br; 84bl; 84bc; 84br; 93bl; 93br; 105tl; 105tc; 105tr; 107tr; 109tc; 109tr; 114tl; 114tr; 114bl; 114br; 126; 128; 129t; 129b; 130tr; 130b; 131t; 131b; 132t; 132b; 134t; 135t; 135b; 136t; 136b; 137b; 138t; 139t; 139c; 139b; 140; 142t; 143c; 143br; 146t; 146b; 147t; 147c; 147b; 148tl; 148tr; 148b; 149t; 149c; 149b; 150tl; 150c; 150b; 151t; 151bl; 151br; 152; 154; 155t; 155b; 156; 157t; 158t; 158b; 159b; 162; 163t; 163b; 164t; 164b; 166t; 168t; 168b; 169b; 171b; 173; 174c; 175b; 178tr; 178bl; 179t; 179b; 180tl; 180bl; 180br; 181tl; 181tr; 181br; 183br; 184cl; 184br; 185bl; 186t; 187t; 188t; 188b; 189t; 189cl; 190tl; 191t; 191b; 192b; 193t; 193b; 195b; 196t; 196b; 197cl; 200bc; 201tr; 201cr; 201br; 204t; 204c; 208; 209t; 209c; 209b; 210t; 210c; 210b; 211t; 211b; 212; 214; 215t; 215b; 217tr; 217bl; 218t; 218b; 219b; 221t; 221b; 223t; 224; 225t; 225b; 227t; 227b; 230; 231t; 236t; 237b; 240t; 240b; 241br; 245b; 248; 249b.

Cyril Laubscher 5; 4; 7b; 8–9; 10; 11; 12; 13tr; 13b; 14t; 14b; 15t; 15b; 16; 17; 22; 23t; 23bc; 23br; 25t; 25b; 26; 27; 30t; 30b; 31t; 31b; 32t; 32b; 33b; 35bl; 36; 40t; 40b; 42; 44t; 45t; 46c; 47t; 47bl; 48t; 50t; 50bl; 51t; 51br; 52; 53; 59; 60; 62c; 62bl; 62bc; 63t; 63b; 64c; 68; 69; 70b; 71tl; 71tr; 71b; 73tl; 73tr; 73br; 74t; 74b; 75t; 75bl; 76t; 76b; 77t; 77b; 78; 80t; 80c; 80bl; 80br; 81bc; 81br; 82t; 82cl; 82cr; 82bl; 82br; 83tc; 83tr; 83bl; 83br; 84t; 85tc; 85tr; 85bl; 85br; 86; 87tl; 87tc; 87b; 88; 89t; 89b; 90; 91; 92b; 93tl; 93tc; 93cl; 93cr; 93tr; 94t; 94bl; 94br; 95tl; 95tr; 95b; 96t; 96b; 97t; 97b; 98; 99; 100t; 100b; 101t; 101b; 102; 103; 104b; 105c; 105b; 106t; 106c; 106bl; 106br; 107tl; 107b; 108t; 108c; 108b; 109c; 109br; 110t; 110b; 111t; 111b; 112t; 112bl; 112br; 113t; 113c; 113bl; 113br; 115t; 115bl; 115bc; 115br; 116tc; 116tr; 116bc; 116br; 117t; 117bl; 117br; 118t; 118b; 119t; 119b; 120t; 120b; 121b; 121tl; 121tr; 121bl; 121br; 124–5; 130tl; 133t; 133c; 133b; 134b; 137t; 138b; 143t; 144; 153; 157t; 160; 161; 165t; 165b; 166b; 167; 169t; 170b; 171t; 172t; 172b; 174br; 175t; 176; 182t; 182bl; 182br; 183t; 183bl; 184t; 184c; 185t; 185br; 186bl; 186br; 187b; 189b; 190tr; 190bc; 190br; 192t; 194t; 194b; 197t; 197b; 198; 199; 200bl; 201tl; 202; 203; 204b; 205t; 205b; 206; 216bl; 216br; 217tl; 217br; 219t; 220; 222; 223b; 226; 228; 229t; 229b; 231b; 232; 233t; 233b; 234; 235r; 236b; 237t; 238; 240c; 241t; 241c; 242; 243t; 243b; 244; 245t; 247t; 247b; 249t; 250; 251; 252; 255; 256.

Tony Tilford 141; 142b; 143bl; 159t; 170t; 180tr; 195t; 235l; 246.

STOCKISTS AND SUPPLIERS

UNITED KINGDOM

Birkett Fencing
Rowah
Frizington
Cumbria CA26 3XS
Tel: (01946) 861420

Ernest Charles
Copplestone
Crediton
Devon EX17 2YZ
Tel: (01363) 84842

Grange Aviaries & Pet Centre
Woodhouse Lane
Botley
Southhampton SO30 2EZ
Tel: (01489) 781260

Oaklands Park Farm Aviaries
Patridge Lane
Nr Newdigate
Surrey RH5 5BU
Tel: (01293) 871 408

Livefoods Direct
Houghton Road
North Anston Trading Estate
Sheffield S25 4JJ
Tel: (1909) 518888

Safari Select
Warren Farm
Sundridge
Kent TN14 6EE
Tel: (01959) 562193

Southern Aviaries
Tinkers Lane
Hadlow Down
Uckfield
East Sussex TN22 4EU
Tel: (01825) 830283

UNITED STATES
*Contact the following web pages for mail
order suppliers of bird cages, bird foods, bird
toys, bird breeder suppliers, bird treats and
other bird products:*
www.birdsnways.com
www.creativebird.com
www.hornbecks.com
www.pets.com
www.wildwingsorganic.com

AUSTRALIA
Australian Bird Co. & Breeding Farm
578 Springvale Road
Springvale South
VIC 3172
Tel: (03) 9548 2422

Bird Man
1964 Wanneroo Road
Weerabup
WA 6031
Tel: (06) 9407 5090

Pet City
224 Wishart Road
Mt Gravatt
QLD 4122
Tel: (04) 3349 2086

Pets Paradise
Shop 35, Gilchrist Drive
Campbelltown
NSW 2560
Tel: (02) 46325 2855

Oxford Pet Supplies
350 Oxford Street
Bondi Junction
NSW 2022
Tel: (02) 9389 9294

FURTHER READING

*Although some of the books listed below may
be out of print, they can often be obtained
from public libraries, or from secondhand
bookstores specializing in aviculture titles.*

Alderton, D. (1988) *A Birdkeeper's Guide
to Budgies*, Tetra Press

Alderton, D. (1988) *A Birdkeeper's Guide
to Finches*, Tetra Press

Alderton, D. (1989) *A Birdkeeper's Guide
to Parakeets*, Tetra Press

Alderton, D. (1989) *A Birdkeeper's Guide
to Parrots & Macaws*, Tetra Press

Alderton, D. (1989) *A Birdkeeper's Guide
to Cockatiels*, Tetra Press

Alderton, D. (1990) *A Birdkeeper's Guide
to Breeding Birds*, Tetra Press

Alderton, D. (1990) *A Birdkeeper's Guide
to Cockatoos*, Tetra Press

Alderton, D. (1991) *The Atlas of Parrots*,
T. F. H. Publications

Alderton, D. (1992) *You & Your Pet Bird*,
Dorling Kindersley

Alderton, D. (1995) *The Handbook of
Cage and Aviary Birds*, Blandford Press

Alderton, D. (1998) *The Complete Guide
to Bird Care*, Howell Book House

Alderton, D. (2000) *The Complete Book
of Finches and Softbills: Their Care and
Breeding*, T. F. H. Publications

Bielfeld, H. (1988) *Canaries and Related
Birds*, T. F. H. Publications

Bracegirdle, J. (1981) *The Border Fancy
Canary*, Saiga Publishing

Cole, B. H. (1985) *Avian Medicine and
Surgery*, Blackwell Scientific Publications

Cooke, D. & F. (1987) *Keeping Cockatiels
– A Complete Guide*, Blandford Press

Cross, J. S. (1978) *The Gloster Fancy
Canary*, Saiga Publishing

Dodwell, G. T. (1982) *The Lizard Canary
and Other Rare Breeds*, Triplegate

Goodwin, D. (1982) *Estrildid Finches of
the World*, British Museum
(Natural History)

Harper, D. (1986) *Pet Birds for Home and
Garden*, Salamander Books

Hayward, J. (1979) *Lovebirds and Their
Colour Mutations*, Blandford Press

Howman, K. C. R. (1979) *Pheasants –
Their Breeding and Management*,
K & R Books

Howson, E. (1980) *The Yorkshire Canary*,
Saiga Publishing

Immelmann, K. (1982) *Australian Finches*,
Angus and Robertson

Low, R. (1977) *Lories and Lorikeets*,
Paul Elek

Low, R. (1986) *Parrots – Their Care and
Breeding*, Blandford Press

Low, R. (1992) *Parrots in Aviculture –
A Photo Reference Guide*, Blandford Press

Mobbs, A. (1985) *Gouldian Finches*,
Nimrod

Restall, R. L. (1975) *Finches and Other
Seed-eating Birds*, Faber and Faber

Robbins, G. E. S. (1984) *Quail – Their
Breeding and Management*,
World Pheasant Association

Smith, G. A. (1979) *Encyclopedia
of Cockatiels*, T. F. H. Publications

Trollope, J. (1983) *The Care and Breeding
of Seed-eating Birds*, Blandford Press

Vince, C. (1980) *Keeping Softbilled Birds*,
Stanley Paul

Walker, G. B. R. & Avon, Dennis (1987)
Coloured, Type & Song Canaries,
Blandford Press

INDEX